# Subscribe Now!

## Building Arts Audiences through Dynamic Subscription Promotion

### BY DANNY NEWMAN

*Theatre Communications Group, Inc.*
*New York*

Design by Winston G. Potter
Illustrations by Deborah Sims

Produced for Theatre Communications Group by the Publishing Center for
Cultural Resources, New York City. Manufactured in the United States of America.

LC 77-081452
ISBN 0-930452-00-3/cloth
ISBN 0-930452-01-1/paper

*To the late Sherman Marks, a greatly gifted man,*
*through whom the wonder and excitement*
*of theatre were first revealed to me*

*About TCG*

*Theatre Communications Group is the national service organization for the nonprofit professional theatre, established in 1961 to provide a national forum and communications network for the profession and to respond to the needs of its constituents for centralized services. TCG offers a variety of artistic, administrative and informational programs and services aimed specifically at assisting noncommercial professional theatre organizations, professional theatre training institutions and individual theatre artists, administrators and technicians. Theatre Communications Group is supported by the William H. Donner Foundation, Exxon Corporation, Ford Foundation, Andrew W. Mellon Foundation, National Endowment for the Arts and New York State Council on the Arts.*

# Contents

# *Foreword*

I have been associated in my career with two foundations which have had real impact upon the performing arts. One was the Ford Foundation. The other was a one-man foundation in the person of Danny Newman. No third foundation to this date has put as much financial stability into theatres, symphonies, operas and dance companies.

Danny did not use money. He used brains, enthusiasm, and the know-how that had once sold 13,000 subscriptions to a not yet launched theatre company in Chicago. When I asked him to attend a meeting of Theatre Communications Group (TCG) in Washington, I knew that something important would happen. I did not know that the subscriptions of individual theatres would be raised by 200% to 400% within two years. Nor did I know how quickly Danny Newman would escalate the scale of his activities. A half-time consultant on the staff of TCG, he was soon under pressure from the other performing arts organizations, who up to then had thought he belonged entirely to the Lyric Opera of Chicago. At the same time the commercial theatre, with which Danny had had extensive experience, raised its bids.

The talk Danny and I then had confirmed everything I had suspected. This salesman, missionary and technician was at bottom a philanthropist and was moved at my recognition of the fact. He would not surrender his great love, the Chicago Lyric, nor would he move his office from there. But he would give up everything else. TCG continued to support his work for nonprofit theatre. Now he would take on symphony, opera and dance as a consultant to the Ford Foundation. At one time, I guess, I had as steady a travel schedule as anyone working in the arts. It was nothing compared to what Danny now took on.

When he first slipped over the border into Canada, it was on that country's invitation. For a while we disbelieved that he would or could take on the whole country. As was our rule, we asked each organization to consult Mr. Newman's desire and convenience. After a while the Canada Council came into the act. Since the Ford Foundation did not give direct support to Canadian performing arts groups, I had less of a day-to-day impression of Danny's range in that country. So I was caught short when a lady at a Central Opera

Service meeting in New York asked me to describe our grants to Canadian opera companies. I said we had none. She was very patient with me when, after the panel discussion, she came up to remind me of how our Mr. Newman had changed their whole scene. (When Danny added the United Kingdom and Australia, he was ''on vacation'' and the Ford Foundation was not implicated.)

It is hard even to touch upon Danny Newman's performance without succumbing to the impression of his gargantuan energy and health. But Danny Newman is as complex as his approach to audience building is simple (in his *own* understanding, that is). Energy and health, yes. Confidence and compulsiveness. But humility, too—in the presence of the true artist, or in the company of any person equally dedicated to a cause. And sensitivity, perhaps known only to a few. Finally, of course, above and beneath all is the moral universe in which Newman finds his being: There is hope for everyone.

Danny Newman, like many others of rare or special abilities, has simply been too busy accomplishing his all-consuming tasks to raise up successors. Peter Zeisler and Theatre Communications Group are to be congratulated for provoking Danny into writing this book.

*W. McNeil Lowry*

*Mr. Lowry, while Vice President of the Ford Foundation's Division of Humanities and the Arts, engaged Mr. Newman as a consultant to performing arts organizations.*

# *Preface*

The information and insights contained in this handbook have been gathered not only in my own projects where I have been in charge of promotion—but in the observation of the functioning of the myriad professional performing arts companies with which I have been, and am, currently consulting.

I shall always be indebted to the Ford Foundation's W. McNeil Lowry, through whose vision I have been afforded a unique opportunity for involvement to date in the affairs of more than 200 performing arts institutions, and to Marcia Thompson for her warm and wise, day-to-day guidance in that connection. During my army training, I hated my tough sergeant but, after undergoing infantry combat, I blessed him. This illustrates my feeling toward Theatre Communications Group's director, Peter Zeisler, upon whose implacable insistence I began to write and have finally completed this manual. I acknowledge, too, the special efforts of my editor, TCG's Lindy Zesch, and her associate, Arli Epton, in bringing this book to publication.

I am most grateful to the former Canada Council directors, Peter Dwyer and André Fortier, to their successor Charles Lussier and to Council officials, Timothy Porteous, Hugh Davidson, David Peacock and Monique Michaud, for having opened an entire nation's performing arts plant to my brand of DSP (Dynamic Subscription Promotion). I appreciate, too, that it was Tom Hendry and the Canadian Theatre Centre, who gave early impetus to my activities in so many north-of-the-border places.

I am thankful to two of the ladies in my life—my beloved colleague Carol Fox, who has long suffered my frequent absences from Lyric Opera of Chicago so that I could carry on my work in so many places, and my dear wife Dina, for her understanding forbearance during my "Danny Appleseed" performing arts odyssey of so many years.

I have attempted here to speak about the audience development-by-subscription requirements of the full range of nonprofit professional performing arts entities—theatres, symphony orchestras, ballet companies, opera companies and festivals, too—in the knowledge that, although each field has its special characteristics and problems, the basic promotional approaches which work for one, *work for all*. Thus, when I write in terms of theatre, I assume that the reader who may be with a musical arts or dance company will make the necessary transpositions for himself, and vice versa. Some already experienced promotional practitioners in these fields may feel that I am preaching to the already converted or teaching to the already knowledgeable. However, one of my major considerations in selecting these materials has been to be of maximum assistance to the many younger people who are, after only academic training, now entering the professional performing arts in ever-increasing numbers.

Many readers of this book may be surprised that so much of it is concerned with arguments in behalf of the subscription concept's merits and benefits, to the extent that the nuts and bolts of subscription promotion itself seem to be accorded secondary importance. If this is indeed so, it is because I am convinced that when professional performing arts organizations fail to fully utilize this powerful audience developmental instrument, it is often because their leaders are victims of certain myths and misconceptions about it. I have found that the prerequisite to getting effective subscription campaigns going is to vigorously challenge and, hopefully, change these attitudes. Only if I succeed on that initial level can we then, together, get on with the job and begin to implement those methods of promotion which I recommend—or somebody else's methods—with the only criterion being, "Do they bring us the results we need?"

I do allow for the possibility that some of my recommendations may not be applicable under all circumstances to every performing arts entity. However, I know of many cases in which organizations have much benefited by the implementation of only one or two of the numerous planks in this promotional platform, and I have noted that some, who have at first thought their cloth didn't fit the pattern, later found that it did. While subscription has previously been employed mainly by performing arts institutions of a more traditional variety, the same techniques can apply to less traditional performing arts organizations and nonperforming arts as well (including galleries, museums, public TV and radio). For further discussion, please see the chapter on alternative formats for subscription.

The reader will, no doubt, take note of the fact that a number of my points are stated, restated and stated once again throughout this book, in a number of different contexts. The reason is that I believe (as you will discover in the chapter on duplications in direct mail) that repetition is a successful convincer, and that most problems are widespread and not unique or limited to one institution, one art form, one locality or even to one country.

As to the methods which I suggest, I wish to say that I have by no means attempted to describe *all* the possibilities—just a number of the most useful ones, knowing that they will work for those who employ them with zeal and on a scale large enough to match not only immediate subscription sales requirements, but aspirations for future expansion of committed audiences, too. These methods are, I feel, rather ordinary and perhaps obvious ways in which to accomplish the job, and I don't think they're all that special. I'm fairly certain that anybody really wanting to promote subscription sales for his project badly enough would arrive at some of the same methods or similar ones. *The prerequisite is the understanding of how tremendously important subscription itself can be in the life of the given performing arts company* (even to the point of increasing grants and contributions as discussed in the chapter on subscription and fund-raising). For, only with that realization comes the will to do the job that needs to be done. It is when I have successfully led people of our field in that direction, helping them heighten their perception of what subscription can mean to their organization, that I feel I have done my best work.

I would like to point out that the methods I have outlined permit all sorts of adaptations, and I would hope that they will also stimulate the readers of this book to generate many additional promotional activities, some of which might well turn out to be very effective in selling subscriptions, in which case, I ask my readers to let me know about them. I can be reached through Theatre Communications Group, 355 Lexington Avenue, New York, N.Y. 10017.

## 1

# *My Unabashed Enthusiasm for Subscription*

I am and have been an unabashed enthusiast for the concept of subscription to the performing arts since I first entered the theatrical world when I was 14 years old. For it was then that I sold my first subscription—to the Mummers of Chicago, a civic theatre group—by going from house to house, apartment to apartment, ringing doorbells and convincing those who dwelled therein to sign up for my season. Perhaps they bought the subscription because they were touched by the zeal of a spindly lad who seemed obsessed with his mission. For I was the child prodigy press agent of the company and, as such, I saw my role in quite romantic terms.

I thought of myself as the brave knight fighting the battle for the lady fair, with the artists I represented in the latter category. Poor, dear, helpless artists—they could create their wonderful art, but they were impractical and certainly incapable of buttonholing people or grabbing them by their lapels, while shouting at them, "I'm great, see, great! Y'gotta come to see me perform tonight!" And would we ask this of the artists? No, but the press agent could do it, the manager could, the board people could. And it was our obligation to do so, the way I looked at it. After all, wasn't that "paying our dues"? On what other basis could we justify our continued association with the project? If the artists *couldn't* do these things and we *didn't* do them, why were we hanging around?

In the mid-1930's, as an emergent press agent, I was constantly troubled by the early demise of legitimate plays I "handled," despite my newspaper-space-grabbing talents. Why did the patient die so many times on the Saturday night after opening? Why didn't the single-ticket buyers buy? I became fascinated with the brilliant subscription ideology of the visionaries who founded the Theatre Guild, which had come onto the scene a decade earlier with a Eugene O'Neill, a John Galsworthy, a George Bernard Shaw up their sleeves. They had intelligently concluded that they would, in short order, be "murdered mallards" if, with their plans for a better repertoire in the commercial New York theatrical climate of the 1920's, they were to submit themselves to the vagaries of the box office, to the tender mercies of single-ticket buyers. So they organized a subscription audience in New York, and began an historic, successful revolution in the aspirations and achievements of its legitimate stage. Then they toured their superior plays to the superior audiences which they organized to receive them in many other American cities.

During that same era, Columbia Concerts, through its Community Concerts Division, was bringing professional classical music to hundreds, and then thousands, of communities in an allied field of the arts. It is interesting that these two organizations, the Theatre Guild and Columbia Concerts, were both commercial entities. Their stunning demonstration of the efficacy and power of subscription in building new audiences, the creation of new employment opportunities for artists, the generating of activity where there had been a void, seemed to make little impression on the nonprofit sector which, in the main, continued to operate on a basically nonsubscription economy, through the 1920's, '30's, '40's and '50's.

The main exceptions were the symphony orchestras, which were the oldest subscription practitioners of our arts society; but they had not, except in a very few instances, attempted to increase the size of their subscription audiences so as to bring about more performances and longer seasons. Not until pressures from the musicians for longer seasons and fuller employment forced the hand of orchestra managers, did it become important to boards and managements to create additional series and seek additional subscribers.

It is what I have called the "congealed" series-ticket audiences of the old, established symphony orchestras (and they are almost always the oldest, most established of the arts organizations in a given community) that have sometimes given a bad reputation to subscription. I will explain. An orchestra was founded in 1883 in a medium-size city, with 2,000 subscribers. By 1933, a half-century later, it had held its own and still had 2,000 subscribed seats (1,000 husbands and wives). By 1973, it had 1,912, a net loss of 88 subscribers after 90 years of promotional inertia. However, since its hall seats 3,000 and single-ticket sales practically never happen, there remain about 1,000 unsold seats for the average concert. And, the actual attendance is nowhere near the 2,000 that the records show, since at least half of the 1,912 season-ticket holders are the third-generation heirs of the original 1883 subscriber complement. Their seats have been handed down to them by inheritance. They send in their checks for renewal annually, in the family tradition, but they (the grandchildren) just don't go to the concerts. The grandparents liked music and were devout followers, but the grandchildren have no such tradition. To compound the problem for this orchestra, these subscribers simply ignore all pleadings to get them to send in their tickets so that they can at least be given to impecunious students. Thus, we have the demoralizing embarrassment of whole sections of the best seats empty at concert after concert.

Needless to say, this orchestra has enjoyed no expansion and is still playing a series of 11 individual concert performances per season, just as it did in 1883. What I have just described is certainly grim and depressing. This utter stagnation is unfairly blamed on subscription by some unthinking people. There is nothing wrong with subscription, but there was a lot wrong with the orchestra's promotional philosophy, which had neglected subscription's tremendous potential. They did nothing to increase its audience for 90 years, remaining content to have and to hold their orchestra, even if hardly anybody came to hear it. Perhaps snobbism came to be synonymous with their kind of subscription, for I sometimes suspected that the audience was purposely being kept small and select. Had big audience development drives been entered into, others besides the old-line, blue-blooded patrons might have started attending concerts.

Prominently displayed in public places, in parks and squares and in plazas, in so many towns and cities throughout the United States, are impressive equestrian statues of long gone Civil War military leaders—the General Jubilation T. Cornpone Memorials of Al Capp's comic cartoons. These statues have been there since before any of us was born. We pass them every day of our lives, but we don't really see them any more, and if a visitor were to ask us the name of the memoralized bronze horseman up there, we'd probably have difficulty recalling it. And what is the fate of such statues? Pigeons roost on them. Well, that was the situation of so many symphony orchestras in American communities. They are the oldest of our performing arts organizations. Often, they've been in their communities for generations (I recently met with the board of one which had been established for 116 years). Ninety-nine and nine-tenths of the population would pass them by daily and never attend their concerts. The community, at best, was only subliminally aware of their existence. One had the feeling that there were heavy, moldering drapes on the great windows of their concert halls, deeply impregnated with the dust of long ago, and one felt the urge to tear them down, to wash the glass, to let in the promotional light—to shoo away the roosting pigeons and start great subscription drives that would fill those halls to overflowing with new audiences!

And that is just what has happened in the many subscription-oriented organizations with which I have been meeting and working. Some of them were, not many years ago, in that grim and depressing category, but they have since seen the light, have campaigned hard for good results, and are now benefiting in many ways.

I am very often told by staff executives that it is their artistic leaders' lack of charisma and poor judgment in programming that are the causes of the public's apathy in the face of subscription offers. However, in many such instances, upon close inspection, it turns out that the fault really lies with the complaining administrators, whose failure in promotional initiatives is a far greater factor in creating the problems they decried than were the alleged deficiencies of their artistic leaders. At a certain symphony orchestra that comes to mind, the music director, a most distinguished conductor, was being blamed for the organization's inability to replace what I would consider to be the normal annual attrition of its subscribership. Each season, the subscription audience was shrinking, as an insufficient number of new people were entering the committed audience bloodstream. When the administrators were convinced to make what was, for them, an unprecedented major promotional effort, there was an immediate, dramatic response from the public and, overnight, new sales increased more than 500% over the previous season. The orchestra entered into a new era of sellout seasons. The music director was the same man as before. The programming was of the same character. The difference was unquestionably the changed attitude toward the promotion of subscription on the part of the management, and the actions that resulted.

In the many years that have passed since I began proselytizing for Dynamic Subscription Promotion and working in close association with hundreds of performing arts projects, I have had cause to reflect all too often upon the parasitism that plagues our field, which by its authentic glamour draws "dilettantish" types, inevitably and inexorably, as moths to the flame—often pleasant persons who have little or nothing to contribute to these arts, although they want to be around them with all their hearts and souls. But they simply haven't the will to undertake the "dirty work," the mundane, very unglamorous and difficult tasks the performance of which is so desperately needed by so many organizations. Such unworthy practitioners are not beyond redemption, however. I have seen cases where these indolent "administrationis personae" have come to life and given up long discussions about art in cafes and endless hours of lolling at rehearsals. (Who needs them at rehearsals when they should be out beating the bushes to get an audience for the actors, singers, dancers or instrumentalists, come performance time?) They have found pride in giving an honest 15-hour day's work for their pay, satisfaction in bringing audiences to the artists they represent and revenues to the projects that have depended upon them. To be fair, many of these people had not understood or appreciated how important their roles could be, and once they did, their attitudes underwent great changes for the better.

Theatrical publicists come in all sizes and shapes, of course, and are varied in the range and level of their abilities and modes of operation. However, one attribute which I believe is all-important for those in our profession is a genuine, affirmative, even loving feeling for the art and for artists. Only in that spirit of involvement can we truly represent the interests of both. Albert Camus said it beautifully: "...the only people who can help the artist are those who love him." That brings to mind a sour, older colleague of my theatrical "advance agent" days, who was fond of belligerently proclaiming, "Actors? I hate 'em. They put paint on their faces, don't they?" I wonder how he would have felt about Camus' sentiments.

I have occasionally found an organization's own administrative employees talking down its productions or programs outside the confines of the offices, thus gratuitously assuming the role of quasi-critics, and using what they claim are the deficiencies of the artistic product as justification for their failure to better promote its interests. Whether you call this crutch seeking, copping out or just plain treason, it isn't right and is not going to help either the renewal or sale of new subscriptions.

Certainly we want the highest level of artistic excellence at all times for our various operatic, dramatic, balletic and symphonic projects. But, if there should come a time when this quality is not achieved, I would no more run all around town talking about it than I would if my child had failed to pass his school examinations. Certainly, if there should be a pattern of recurring failure on the part of the artistic department, the board of directors should deal with the situation. However, managers, publicists, box office employees and office personnel are not critics-at-large, and they should be both sensitive and circumspect in any statements they make outside the organization's immediate family circle. Particularly unethical and destructive are employees, anxious to demonstrate their own superior and sophisticated taste to friends they may have in the communications media, who find themselves slipping into negative statements about the very cause they represent. As an attitude for all of us who work in support of the art and artists, I recommend wholeheartedly the classic press agent's stance, "If it's my show, it's great. If they're my artists, they're the greatest!"

While not every resident professional theatre which has sprung into being through the 1960's and '70's is now operating on the level of the British National Theatre or the Comédie-Française, remember that, nursed through their difficult periods, young, fragile artistic institutions can become rooted and successful, providing the possibilities of employment and artistic development to large numbers of creative people in all the fields. Think of how many actors and actresses, directors, designers, choreographers, dancers, singers, conductors and instrumentalists have found not only careers through subscription-supported arts institutions, but have been able to hammer out the kinks in their talent on the anvil of the audiences which subscription has brought them. Thus, we now have a constant enrichment in terms of professionalism in the performing arts picture, made possible by permanent institutions which would almost certainly have collapsed in their early stages, had not the people to whom they were dear fought for their interests at every step, and had they not built subscriberships large enough to achieve their stability, viability and longevity. Only in such a context can the arts flourish.

I am often impressed by some of the promotional methods which I find in operation upon my initial visits to performing arts groups, and I advise that these sound activities be continued. If there are efforts in progress by which subscriptions are being sold, I consider them sacred, and I would bite off my tongue before I suggested changing them. But I try to get the *scale* of these activities considerably increased and to introduce additional components which may have been omitted entirely, often for no reason except their having been overlooked despite their use by so many other organizations in the same field. In many cases, no more encouragement is needed than the pointing out of what is happening in those other places. I always seek to instill confidence in those who will most likely have to do the job. I try to induce their belief in the enormous importance of successful subscription campaigning to their projects and to their own careers. I want them to allocate the proper value to the wonderful contribution which non-artists who are associated with artistic causes can make. For only when they—the promoters—succeed, can the artists attain the conditions in which to flourish.

The idea of subscription seems to rouse the hackles of many people and to evoke all sorts of unfounded arguments as to why this method of arranging attendance of the performing arts will not be accepted in this or that community. I think a perfect example was the oft-repeated assurance I was given about the futility of attempting to introduce subscription attendance at the theatre in predominantly French-speaking Montreal. I was told that despite the stunning successes of our subscription campaigns in English-speaking communities throughout Canada, the Francophone playgoer was simply too individualistic, too nonconformist, too selective in his tastes, to submit to the advance planning and the discipline which organized attendance imposes on subscribers. In every way, I was discouraged from beginning such efforts in New France. Once, when I participated in an arts seminar in Quebec City, a charming functionary in the employ of the province's cultural ministry explained to me in great detail the reasons the French-speaking theatre buff would *never* submit to the regimentation of subscription. Then, one day the visionary artistic leader of French Canada's leading theatre company, the Théâtre du Nouveau Monde, Jean-Louis Roux, and his administrator, Lucien Allen, informed me that they were ready to try; from a standing start (not one subscriber), we immediately sold 8,300 subscriptions, achieving percentage results from brochure distributions which were higher than we were obtaining in the same period in the English-speaking sectors of the country or in the U.S. (As I write this, I believe that TNM has over 14,500 subscribers.) The subscription fever spread to the English-speaking minority's theatre companies there and the two leading ones, the Centaur and the Bronfman, now have about 19,000 subscribers between them. And the Montreal Symphony, which did have a subscribership, has now increased it by over 150%. So, I have learned to take with the proverbial grain of salt the protestations which I so often hear along the lines of, "You see, Mr. Newman, our town is different. . . ."

A retarding factor in the audience development of some companies is the infinite capacity of their artistic directors and their managerial personnel for self-deception and their resulting indulgence in fatuous generalities which tell anything but the truth to themselves and others, whenever the issue of "people paucity out in the house" comes up for discussion. In that connection, I relate the following:

I had just returned to the hotel after my first meeting with the board leaders and staff of a small but fairly well-known nonprofit performing arts enterprise which was surviving only because of its heavy subsidy from a funding agency that apparently never looked at its attendance figures. For I had that day been surprised to learn that, despite the very limited number of performances given in a very small auditorium, they had been regularly playing to 45% unsold seats. I turned on the TV set hoping to catch the late newscast and, suddenly, there appeared on the screen the face of the artistic director of this project which I had been sent to assist. He was being interviewed. Because there had recently been a remarkable and considerably publicized audience-building success by another arts organization in a nearby community, the interviewer asked our man if his group were taking similar steps to enlarge its following. To my astonishment, he replied, "No," and went on to say, "We have found that we have only to make the art available to the people and they will come." And right at my elbow, in my briefcase, were the copies of the box office reports which absolutely belied what I was hearing. What he was saying was something we all wish were the case, but we know that it isn't. His statement was a cliché that I have heard uttered time and again by otherwise intelligent artistic directors and arts administrators, but it bears little or no resemblance to the reality with which we live. We must accomplish intensive and effective therapy in dealing with these escapist individuals. Perhaps this book will help.

Speaking of negative points of view about subscription brings to mind some advice to new producers, from the dilettante founder of a now (understandably) defunct drama organization, which appeared in a published article some years ago and which a friend has only recently called to my attention. The printed advice was, "Don't sell *any* subscriptions in advance. This will save you from the temptation to use subscription money for financing your theatre." These "words of wisdom," if heeded, would certainly multiply the fiscal problems faced by performing arts organizations during their planning and rehearsal periods, when no ticket income is being generated. The article goes on to assure us that "... responsive audiences are not composed of people who are obliged to commit themselves to a certain date months in advance." Having for years been attending performances at a number of heavily subscribed theatres where excited, involved audiences "responded" to the performances with all of the animation that this former producer could desire, I would challenge her ill-founded generalization. Just why she thinks a hit-happy single-ticket buyer, on those rare occasions when he actually does show up, should be a more responsive audience member than a dedicated goer who takes his going seriously enough to plan ahead (to subscribe), I am unable to fathom. I have been the press agent of an overwhelmingly subscribed major opera company for many years, and I submit that the subscriber hysteria which reigns when one of our tenors hits that glorious high-C would compare favorably with the response of the ancient Roman arena's "single-ticket buyers" to a gladitorial triumph. In winding up her sage counsel to new producers, our savant flatly delivers her manifesto on the civil rights of the single-ticket buyers, saying, "You *must* allow the audience the privilege of purchasing tickets at its own comfort and convenience." Even if I agreed with this autocratic decree (which I don't), I would still have to ask, "At what price?" For, if we were foolish enough to follow this recommendation, the price would be the wholesale closing down of performing arts companies all over the North American continent.

A well-thumbed copy of the Theatre Communications Group *Theatre Directory* is always at hand in my center desk drawer and another one goes with me on my considerable travels, in the front section of my briefcase. I use it constantly, for the addresses and phone numbers of what has now come to be an enormous listing of nonprofit professional theatres of various kinds and sizes throughout the country, to so many of which I am assigned as TCG's audience-building consultant. There would have been no need for such a directory 15 years ago, since there were so few such theatre companies. Why, in the past dozen or more years, has there been such a prodigious growth in this field? Were there no talented, aspiring theatre people in all of these communities before? Certainly there were. But these talents and aspirations were cut short, time and again, by the simple inability of the artists and their backers to find an audience on the hit-or-miss basis of individual ticket sales for individual plays. I believe the record will show that it was the coming into its own of the subscription dynamic in the resident professional theatre picture and its constantly more successful implementation that has, more than any other single factor, made this new era possible. Having personally been at the epicenter of this movement through the years, I cannot help but burst with enthusiasm for the proved potential in subscription for all in our field who are willing to give it truly major consideration in their institutional lives.

One of the most exciting qualities of such subscription promotion is its potential for dramatic, affirmative, overnight changes in the position of an arts entity. Whether or not this happens is, in so many cases, in our hands. It's up to us. If we attack dynamically enough and massively enough, we can win a vast new audience at once, eliminating unnecessarily wasted years. And while this handbook has been prepared mainly for use by North American performing arts groups, the principle of this shortcut approach to audience development success is being carried out in other places (and other art forms) as well. Recently, the Scottish Opera, via one charter subscription campaign was able to double the number of performances in its Glasgow season, selling most of it out on series tickets before the first curtain went up. (A certain number of individual tickets were retained for public sale because the board leadership felt this to be an obligation in the light of various levels of governmental subsidy which provide their main financial support. Need I point out that such a high level of subsidy, while generally provided in other countries, is not the case in the U.S.) And, a few years back, the Old Tote Theatre in Sydney, Australia—in one fell swoop—was able to break out of its 3,000-subscriber mold, and surpass the 11,000 mark, with all of the obvious benefits pertaining to such instant progress. By the second year of its effort, it was able to report that its subscribership exceeded 20,000.

I now know, too, that related fields, such as public TV and art museums, have immediately benefited when they have, inspired by the performing arts' example and experience, come out of the promotional closet, so to speak, to wage aggressive campaigns. They, too, have thereby reached new levels of subscribership or membership. One television station located in a major city has been able to increase an already substantial subscribership (they call their annual contributors ''subscribers'') by 450%—by abandoning its former low-key approach in favor of unashamed Dynamic Subscription Promotion. The project director of an art gallery has just written me that, by introducing the successful subscription-selling techniques employed by several performing arts groups in that community, the gallery has achieved a membership gain of 35% in a matter of a few months. And, now that she has seen the results, she predicts an overall gain of 250% within less than a year and a half.

I continue to be so enthusiastic about subscription because I have seen its constantly recurring miracle in the cases of hundreds of professional arts projects which have, through it, reached new, high levels of audience development. Though they have admittedly gained these greatly enlarged audiences by the ''artificial'' stimulation of their successful promotional efforts, once those audiences have jammed their performances or participated in their programs all season long, their new positions of strength are not artificial. They are real. The people who are now part of their much larger audiences are real. When they renew for the next season and the ones that follow, that's real, too.

I have derived much satisfaction in observing the extremes of subscriber loyalty, not the least manifestation of which was a bitterly contested divorce suit (there may be others which I don't know about), in a midwestern city, in which the lawyers contended, not for the custody of their clients' children, but for the custody of their clients' cherished subscription seat locations!

# 2

# The Slothful, Fickle Single-Ticket Buyer vs. The Saintly Season Subscriber

When entering into a subscription-selling campaign, one should consider well the alternative, which is dependence upon the whims and vagaries of the nonsubscribing single-ticket buyer. Clearly, that way lies madness. Certainly there are a few unusual situations in the nonprofit performing arts where single tickets have been or are being sold in sufficient quantities to fill houses, but they are the exceptions to the rule. In the overwhelming number of cases, theatres, symphony orchestras, dance companies and opera companies simply could not exist without the backing of subscribed goers who comprise the largest part of their audiences. In fact, a great many of these organizations would never even have come into existence without the spur of the subscription dynamic.

It has been argued that those audience members known as ''single-ticket buyers'' aren't really all bad. For do they not belong to that tiny portion of the population that does go occasionally (on Saturday nights only, of course)? And doesn't that make them a lot better than the philistine hordes who never go at all?

Well, perhaps they are better, but they do not compare with the committed men and women who buy the series and then renew for the next season. To really do justice to that paragon of all audience members—the season or series subscriber—we would have to contrast him, in all his shining virtue, with the slothful, fickle single-ticket buyer, whose very designation is a misnomer, considering how rarely he buys tickets, while prating his rationale, ''I'll call my shots.'' The single-ticket buyer doesn't buy (most of the time) for reasons which seem very reasonable to him, but which are entirely unreasonable to those who have the responsibility for the company which seeks to produce the art at a certain standard of excellence and then to perform it for an audience large enough to fit the scale of the project—that is, the size of the house and the length of season which the economy and artistic aspirations demand.

The single-ticket buyer doesn't buy when it's too hot or too cold outside. He stays home if it snows, if it rains, if there's ice on the roads, sleet in the air, or if any of those unfavorable weather conditions so much as threatens. He is so perverse that he doesn't even come if it is a beautiful day, claiming that he must be outdoors, in communion with Nature when it smiles on Man. He doesn't make it to the performance if he feels tired, or if out-of-town visitors appear, or if he isn't "in the mood." If we happen to be producing a serious work at the moment, he'll say he hankers for light entertainment. He is deflected by reading what he interprets to be a negative review in the press. And even if the notices are unanimously splendid, he conveniently remembers one of six years ago that was bad. Should the town's toughest critic suddenly pen a panegyric about the work, he has the answer, too: "That critic is and always has been an idiot, and if *he* likes it, *I'm* sure to hate it!"

Then, once in a blue moon, he cracks and appears at the box office. Why? It's his 25th wedding anniversary and he's promised the Li'l Woman that he's going to take her to the theatre. The last time he made this supreme sacrifice was for their 15th anniversary, but he'll do anything, anything to make her happy. This he confides to the box office manager, who informs him that the fifth row, center seats he's requested are, of course, in the hands of subscribers. He is at once surprised and annoyed, because he cannot obtain choice locations at the last minute (we'd be in pretty bad shape if we still had 'em in the rack). After much argumentation, he finally accepts the best available tickets and enters the house with an it-had-better-be-damn-good attitude. Yes, he is the very model of a contemporary single-ticket buyer and must be counted, I suppose, as one cut above those who never buy tickets.

Every time the single-ticket buyer doesn't buy, he strikes us a cruel blow, both financially and morally. His empty seat mocks our artists and screams its reproach to our promotional effort for its failure to entice him. Ironically, the real victim is the recalcitrant ticket purchaser himself. If he could but understand that, by not coming, he has not permitted us to so inform him, to so inspire him, to so entertain him, that he would surely have become a subscriber to the next season, thereby improving the quality of his life. He might even have become a better man. And that's my idea of a better man—*a subscriber!*

The subscriber is our ideal. In an act of faith, at the magic moment of writing the check, he commits himself in advance of the season's beginning (often many months in advance, and we then also enjoy the interest on his money which we have put into banks or into short-term securities). Perhaps because he has made this initial judgment in our favor, he believes in us from that point on. He arrives at our auditorium with a positive attitude. He wants us to succeed, and he's thrilled when we do. If we occasionally let him down, he takes his punishment in good spirit and, in most cases, doesn't hold it against us at renewal time. By attending all of our productions, season after season, he develops discernment and perspective as a member of the audience. His repertoire-acceptance threshold constantly rises. His awareness of everything connected with the art form heightens. He begins to develop and articulate his own opinions about performance values. Now, should a critic, in his estimation, attack us unfairly, he may write a denunciatory letter to the editor. He also begins to write *us* letters—16-page ones—advising us on casting and repertoire selection.

He is now "knowledgeable" in our art. He is involved—hooked—and we love it, for he has become the fine audience member that we require. He has become a wonderful instrument for our artists to play upon. He remains our greatest booster. He loves to see sold-out houses. He delights in regaling the single-ticket buyers-come-lately with his sagacity and foresight in having subscribed years ago, thereby obtaining his own choice seats, which are renewable each season. He is a very important man to us. He underwrites our right to experiment. And once he comes to understand our economic dilemmas, he will often send us contribution checks. He provides the base for our expansion. It seems that he is the man for whom we have built our company. He is our hero. And because he renews annually, he is our "man for all seasons"!

I have taken much pleasure in recent years in the fact that an increasing number of performing arts organizations are in the happy position of being entirely sold-out before their seasons even begin, on the strength of their own spectacularly successful subscription-selling efforts. And I have noted with mixed irritation and amusement the stream of angry letters to the editor appearing in the newspapers in such cases, after the frustrated single-ticket buyers, long accustomed to leisurely picking the raisins out of our cake, have arrived at the box office, only to find that the cupboard was bare. Their ranks are swelled by those who never showed up before, but who have responded like Pavlov's dogs to the stimulus of the "sold-out" dynamic. That is, word is out that you can't get in, and this brings them to the window in a desperate mood. For just because one can't get in, they *must* get in. "It's sold-out, isn't it? This must be a sensational show! Maybe somebody has taken ill and has turned back a ticket for resale? What, you mean we really can't get a ticket? Well, then, I'm going to write letters of protest to the newspapers." So, in high dudgeon, they complain, "Music is now for the favored few," or, "The average citizen has now been effectively excluded from concerts," and they belligerently ask, "What are they running down there at the Rep, a private club?"

For the single-ticket buyers who came only to our biggest hits and would have let us die when we were hungry for their attention and their patronage, I find it hard to feel much sympathy. To those who never came at all and now wish to jump on our rolling bandwagon, one part of me cries out, "Where were you all those years when our tickets were a drug on the market? Why do you pose now as disenfranchised music lovers, theatre buffs and dance devotees, when bowling and bingo are your true enthusiasms? Admit that you don't give a plugged nickel for our arts, and that the only reason you've come down is because, 'Look Ma, We're a Hot Ticket!' " But I'm not going to say those things to them. In the interest of art, I will restrain myself and im-mediately plan to make room for them by squeezing in a few extra perform-ances for this season and an additional series for next season, by which time they will have presumably learned their lesson, will subscribe, and thus will start to attend regularly. The healthy process of their becoming part of the kind of audience we want and we need will have begun; their conversion from slothful, fickle single-ticket buyers to saintly subscribers will have taken place.

To be fair, I think that I should admit that there *are* some unusual single-ticket buyers who do attend with some level of consistency, and it is from their thin ranks that we make some conversions to the higher status of subscription. However, to give you an idea of how bad off we would be if we depended upon them, an analysis of the mail-order records of goers to a major theatre company's productions reveals that only 10% of these single-ticket buyers attend three or more of their plays per season. Nothing that I have written in the preceding paragraphs of this chapter is meant to be unduly critical of those nonsubscribers who really cannot enroll for such valid reasons as living too far away to attend regularly, or inability to pay the price of a multiple offering. But the other single-ticket buyers, steeped in their obstinacy, are not forgiven!

# 3

# Judges, Yes!
# Executioners, No!
# Subscription and the Critics

For the commercial theatrical producer, running the gauntlet of the critics' opening night is one of the most harrowing hazards imaginable. If they pan his show, it usually means that it will be shuttered by Saturday night. The corporate entity which had been organized for the limited purpose of raising the money and producing that one play, lapses. And that is the end of the affair. The routed entrepreneur and his backers sadly come to the same conclusion that the renowned caricaturist-humorist Al Hirschfeld did, when he titled one of his books, *Show Business Is No Business*.

However, a new nonprofit professional theatre aims to establish itself permanently, not to produce one play but a succession of them, for an entire season and for a succession of seasons, and to represent a point of view in the art of the drama. For such a producing organization, the critics' naysay following the opening night of the first play of the first season can be even more catastrophic than in the case of the commercial producer stated above. For not only does the play close on Saturday night, but so does the institution, with all its fine plans and lofty artistic aspirations cut off in its earliest beginnings. Such was all too often the situation in the early era of American resident professional theatres. It is hard now to believe, considering the recent proliferation of these organizations, that less than 15 years ago there were hardly more than a half-dozen such resident companies in the country. The growth of this movement had long been retarded by the nonexistence of large subscription audiences, ready and waiting to attend entire first seasons—something which would have enabled a new theatre company to roll with the initial critical punches and to keep on its feet until it could overcome its problems of limited artistic resources and undercapitalization.

Were the critics of newspapers in so many American cities outside of New York unduly harsh to these new companies? No, they simply had different standards. For all through the 1940's, 1950's and into the 1960's, when the chicken of subscription began to beget the eggs of the burgeoning resident theatre movement, practically the only professional stage plays that came to many of these cities were the touring ones from New York—the hits—the hardy survivors of the mass of productions which had been presented the previous season to Broadway audiences. This phenomenon held true except for certain eastern ''tryout towns.''

Let us take the Broadway season of 1950-51 for example. There were 64 plays produced, of which 15 might be considered hits. The New York critics had suffered through all 64 to get to the 15 nuggets. And of these, only the sturdiest were selected to face the vagaries of touring. Thus, the "road" critics in most of the United Booking Office cities saw their theatre through a special prism. They judged only from the 15 hits of New York, and often still had reservations about some of them. So, the *best* of the New York theatre was their *ordinary* fare. True, sometimes the original stars, after a long run in New York, didn't make the tour, and there were times when the replacements were not of the same calibre. But even allowing for such instances, there was no doubt that the "road" saw the best of what had played in New York and almost entirely avoided the chaff.

Now, let us say that in one of these many good-size American cities an aspiring, indigenous producing organization tried to lift its head. Assuming that it had somehow managed to squeeze through its first season, either without a subscription audience or with a very small one, its struggle for survival was especially bitter, because the expectations of the press and of the public which they influenced were very high. The city had long been isolated from the realities of a major producing center, where theatregoers would most likely have seen many poor productions in a row before coming upon a good one. So, if the new resident company presented five plays, of which two were hits (more than *double* the New York producers' average of one hit out of every five-and-a-half plays produced), there was still the feeling that it lacked talent or professional judgment and obviously couldn't "cut the mustard." In some cases, these charges were undoubtedly true, but oftentimes, they were really unjust. Then, too, there were some converse instances where patroniz- ing critics were "too kind," which didn't help the company either.

But the word of the critics was a life-and-death matter for grass-roots theatre companies in the days before the dynamic of large-scale subscription became the means of holding out until a new balance in expectations evolved and a new understanding developed of the difference between glittery, pre-packaged road productions and seasons of dramatic work produced by professional theatre institutions in residence in the community.

Nowadays, the continued presence of the heavily subscribed resident theatres in many cities has brought about this necessary orientation and has contributed to a broader outlook on the part of many critics. While critical disapproval of any individual production in a given season is certainly grounds for concern, it has receded more and more as a decisive factor in the possibility for these companies to survive. And if the subscription is large enough in relation to the theatre's capacity, it might have little effect even on the attendance of that particular play. The real critical power has now passed to the subscribers, who vote thumbs up or down at renewal time each year, not on the basis of one show, but on the basis of their reaction to the entire season.

Unquestionably, in those situations where successful subscription has circumscribed critical power, some critics continue to harbor vestigial, fond memories of the time when their authority was absolute, and they would be less than human if at times they did not resent what appears to be a diminution of their role. However, I believe that what has happened is essentially healthy, in that for the first time the critics are performing their function without those strained, self-conscious old postures of: "I'm a holy terror. I can make you or I can break you," or at the other extreme: "I must withhold any sharp criticism, because if this project folds, its blood will be on my hands." Once the audience base has been secured by a strong subscription capable of replacing its annual attrition and maintaining growth beyond that point, arts enterprises and their critics can develop a more mature relationship based on mutual respect and the understanding that each has a job to do. Then, theatre-folk can feel satisfied that, while the critics remain their judges, they can no longer be their executioners.

In another connection in this book, I state that "some of my best friends are board members." Well, I will say, too, that some of my best friends are critics. And in justice to them, I will admit that I have yet to meet an artist who is not resentful of press criticism. Oh, some will bear it with more dignity than others, and you hear much about *constructive* rather than *destructive* criticism. But I assure you that artists do not like *any* negative critiques of their work. Whatever they may say in interviews after being panned by the press, artists feel themselves victimized by what appears at that moment to them to be the inherent parasitism of the critical function, and they rail inwardly at the helplessness of their own position as sitting ducks for the critics' slings and arrows.

Once I saved the life of a music critic by frustrating an irate tenor's plan to murder him. The journalist, young and brash, had not only given the singer a bad review, but a personally insulting one. Just one year later the same critic praised the tenor highly when he interpreted a role in another opera. The tenor immediately pasted the "rave" on his dressing room mirror and told everybody, "He's really a very perceptive critic!" The successful introduction of subscription may temper the effects of the critics' tyranny on the fate of many performing arts organizations, but it has changed neither the artists' sensitivities to the critics' barbs, nor their pleasure in the critics' approbation.

Because subscription has allowed us to build and sustain performing arts institutions which perform seasons of plays, operas, and works of the symphonic and dance repertoires, critics can now look at the development of a whole body of work, rather than individual productions. That means they can now see us in a different light. It is our responsibility to help them understand our various goals and artistic philosophies. We must demonstrate that ongoing institutions have the ability, and perhaps the obligation, to experiment instead of presenting only the tried-and-true. Just as subscribers have begun to judge our work on a seasonal basis, so have critics. At the same time, critics are more likely to be impressed by a full house than by empty seats, for, being human, they find a deserted auditorium just as demoralizing as does any other audience member. And if it's adventure the critics want, we can only afford to give it to them if we are assured that faithful subscribers will be waiting in their seats to experience the new and the unknown. Once managements are relieved of the necessity to expend their energies in the frantic, improvised hunt for single-ticket buyers from performance to performance, they can give their full attention to achieving the high quality of art which not only the critics, but the ever-rising expectations of their subscribers, demand.

# 4

# The Folly of "Let's Have Subscription but Not Too Much of It,"

### and Why 15,000 Subscribers in the Hand Are Better than 75,000 Single-Ticket Buyers in the Bush

Often I have heard performing arts management people say, "Of course, we want subscription, but we don't want too much of it—40% or 50% or 60% would be just fine, with the remainder of the tickets available for single sale at the box office."

They couldn't be more wrong for a wide range of reasons. First of all, what guarantees do they have that those single tickets *will* sell at the window? For, the moment that they are no longer part of a subscription offering, those tickets will or will not be sold on the basis of the specific attraction's individual strength. What will happen then to the attractions which fail to get good reviews? What will happen to the experimental, the esoteric and works of limited appeal, to the productions without big-name performers? What will happen on the below-zero nights? The *only* time when *all* of the attractions of a season or a series are salable is *before* the season begins, when they are in the form of a subscription offering—before the critics have had their whack at the individual attractions, before the whim buyer has the opportunity to make his negative decision, before the bad weather hits, before any of the manifold reasons that stop people from going down to a box office begin to work to our detriment. How will you ever raise the repertoire-acceptance threshold of an audience which will, by our common experience, only buy individual attractions that they are certain in advance they are going to like? Ask the people who work in opera company box offices about the difference in single-ticket demand between a performance of *Carmen* and a performance of a new opera by an unknown American composer or, for that matter, a known one.

When you could have sold many more subscriptions than you have, and you have by choice left, say, 30% or 40% of the seats to be sold individually, you are vitiating one of the most important of the countless benefits of subscription—a special and precious economic benefit. For with so many tickets still to sell, you must enter into an advertising campaign for each and every attraction and performance of your season, something that is very costly, is uneconomical and, worst of all, in many cases will simply not result in making the sales. Therefore, such post-subscription campaign promotional efforts and expenditures will be largely wasted. Some time ago I analyzed the ticket sales record of a symphony orchestra which had performed 24 concerts, had 50% on subscription and had spent a considerable amount of money to promote single-ticket sales for each of those events. Since six of the concerts were very strong in programming and guest soloist values (in my opinion, they would have sold out without advertising expenditures), the single tickets for *those* events were sold. For the other 18 events—all fine ones but not of blockbuster character—the advertising monies and efforts expended were in vain. That season ended with $300,000 worth of tickets unsold. For the season that followed, all the money that the year before had been reserved for the fruitless promotion of single-ticket sales was put into a major subscription drive. The result was 80% sold on subscription and the season ended with only $100,000 worth of tickets unsold, a gain of $200,000 and of thousands of new regularly attending audience members. And I am told that for its forthcoming season, this organization intends to close the gap further by another big subscription push.

This economic moral brings us back to our leitmotif, "If you don't sell it on subscription, you probably won't sell it at all, and the only time the tickets to your concerts, plays, operas and dance recitals are *all* salable is before the season begins, in their pristine form—that is, their season- or series-ticket packaging."

Like rich people who forget what it was like when they were poor, sometimes managements and boards of organizations enjoying the fruits of heavy subscription in relation to capacity, begin to chafe under the annual need to run careful and thorough renewal drives, to make the continuing expenditures of money and effort necessary to replace the inevitable attrition and to insure that any expansions entered into are carried off successfully. Let us say that a well-subscribed theatre company with a 750-seat house is lucky or brilliant enough for three out of its seven productions in a given season to receive fine receptions from both public and press, thus stampeding 150 single-ticket buyers per night to the box office. Since there are an average of

650 subscribers at each performance, too, this means that about 50 people are turned away for each performance of those three shows. The company's officials become intoxicated with this success and forget that the real reason for the ticket shortage is that there are so few single (nonsubscribed) tickets available because of the large subscription. Or, if they do remember the subscription, they do so in terms of, "Why have we been selling all those seats at a discount, when we might have sold them at the full price?" Now, with a new season in the offing, and feeling that they command a seller's market, they make a routine renewal offer without the in-depth process of follow-up which they had employed in past years. They eliminate the pattern of large-scale mailings and intensive staff and volunteer efforts which had brought them success. To fully capitalize on what they now feel is their big single-ticket drawing power, they announce additional performances for the run of each play. Well, the untended subscriber garden yields a crop of only 60% renewal against the previous season's 80%, and new sales, without the mailings and the other promotional components, come in at a record low. The first three plays of the new season are badly received, there are no sellouts, many performances are poorly attended. Since the larger attrition was not replaced by new subscribers, and the single-ticket buyers have disappeared back into those cracks from which they emerge only for hits, the company is now in deep trouble. For, the subscribers who did renew now see all those unsold seats around them and begin to question their own wisdom in having signed up for the entire season. Since seats now seem to be readily available, why not withhold their renewal the next time around and buy tickets only for the plays which turn out to be hits? Hits without the guaranteed audience of the large subscribership, by the way, will be harder than ever to achieve. Thus, all that had been worked for so hard begins to unravel because of bad judgment on the part of the people in charge.

As I write this, I have a certain organization in mind which recently sustained great damage along the lines I have just described—a trip down the drain that was unnecessary. The management became so overconfident as a result of being sold-out for several consecutive seasons (possible only because of a great many subscriptions and very few single tickets available) that it imprudently ran a too-little-too-late series-ticket drive. The disastrous effects of the inept campaign were compounded when the number of performances was increased 50% and three "bombs" were produced in a row, murdered by the press and abjured by the single-ticket buyers. The rout was total, and the theatre company's very existence has been in question ever since. If it folds, it will undoubtedly be said that the public failed to support it, and that would not be the truth. In fact, the company already *had* achieved the public's support when it had embraced the subscription concept entirely. When it irresponsibly put itself at the mercy of the unsentimental single-ticket buyers, it simply pulled the plug out of the lifeboat's floor while in mid-ocean with the sharks all 'round.

In poring over the box office accounting reports of 185 concert programs presented by a cross section of American symphony orchestras in a recent season, one discovers that only 12 of them sold all of the single (nonsubscribed) tickets which were available. I say "available" because most of these concerts, before offering single tickets, already had basic subscription audiences of varying sizes. Most of those 12 sellouts came about because such superstars of classical music as Artur Rubinstein and Van Cliburn were the guest stars, or because of the strong audience appeal of "pops" events, including one which had Arthur Fiedler as the attraction. The other 173 times, the available single seats went unsold—often largely unsold—and one realizes how much *more* abysmal the record would be were it not for the subscriber attendance, which reduced the number of single tickets that had to be sold. And what is sobering indeed is the count of the "deadwood" (unsold tickets) for concerts which featured really distinguished—though perhaps not blockbuster—guest soloists, who are so well known that it would be unkind to mention their names here. However, I will just give a half-dozen sets of shocking vital statistics, as follows: Out of 1,100 single seats available, *227* were sold; out of 1,871, *346* were sold; out of 1,200, *250* were sold; out of 1,393, *271* were sold; out of 2,129, *418* were sold; and out of 640, *40* were sold. Obviously, these orchestras are not among the rapidly growing number of musical organizations which have, through dynamic promotional efforts, achieved a high ratio of subscribership in relation to their respective capacities.

In light of such oft-recurring debacles as these sales figures reveal, it is all the more amazing that there are still people in performing arts fields who keep mindlessly repeating their obviously unsound advice, "Let's not sell too many subscriptions." Even people who ought to know better have told me that it is really far more desirable to have a limited number of subscribers and to put the real push behind developing the single-ticket, or nonsubscriber market. This idea has even been formalized; learned papers have no doubt been written on this point by academicians who (as his detractors used to say about the late President Roosevelt) "never met a payroll." Often, their arguments are accompanied by what seems to me the preposterous insistence that we owe some kind of duty to the "general public" (the single-ticket buyers) to always have tickets available for them, whenever they decide to come. How this indifferent general public responds to such generous (and bankrupting for our organizations) consideration can be seen in the figures just given. When did these single-ticket buyers show up? When Arthur Fiedler, Artur Rubinstein and Van Cliburn were the guest soloists. What were our orchestras supposed to do for an audience all the other times? Fortunately, they did have subscribers—but not enough, in too many instances.

I submit that professional performing arts institutions, in a society where government subsidy is a new and still minor element in their economies, owe very little to the general public. They owe a great deal to their specific public, their subscribers, who are more and more becoming their contributors, too. If I were a symphony orchestra manager, told to put the brakes on my subscription sale in order to hold seats for this alleged general public audience, I would reply, "What general public? I know about subscribers, but I don't know about any other kind of ticket buyers except when we have blockbusters—and brother, *they're* few and far between."

On some occasions I have been told by people who run performing arts projects that they believe a large subscription audience would lead to artistic stagnation, and to becoming part of the "establishment." In such cases, I have often found that their organizations are in fact already artistically stagnant without what they consider the "handicap" of large subscription, being forced by the tyranny of the single-ticket buyer into a very limited repertoire framework. Any attempt by their artistic directors to produce more innovative work is met by the apathy, indifference and absence of the non-subscribing public. If such nonsubscription-oriented projects bravely persist in presenting catholic and provocative programming, they all too often find themselves out of existence. A classic example is a theatre, which although it is located in a large city, years ago used to restrict the number of subscriptions sold, so that the bulk of the seats would be available for the adventurous single-ticket buyers. Night after night, brilliant performances of such fine, serious, but little-known plays as Ionesco's *Exit the King* and de Ghelderode's *Pantagleize* were greeted most enthusiastically by the subscribers, but all the millions comprising the rest of the city's metropolitan population produced a pitiful number of those adventurous single-ticket buyers. Many more purchasers of individual tickets turned out for another of the plays the company produced that season, but that one—George Kelly's *The Show-Off*—provided them with light entertainment and Helen Hayes in a central role, and did not require the same spirit of adventure on the audiences' part. Persisting in its limited subscription policy ("Our main public will be the single-ticket buyer."), the theatre was forced to fold its tent after several badly attended seasons, despite unquestioned artistic distinction. A leading critic berated the area's theatregoers for their indifference, not knowing that a great many of them would have gladly subscribed and gone regularly if the company had not purposely limited the scale of its season-ticket promotion.

I recall, too, that one of the dividends the company had confidently expected from its policy was that the single-ticket buyers would pay the full price per ticket, where subscribers received a modest discount. Since there were so few single-ticket buyers, this financial benefit was a delusion.

Subscription at resident professional theatres seems to have caused no problem of artistic stagnation at all, as a perusal of their repertoires would indicate. Just how stagnant and establishmentarian can they be when recent seasons have included plays written by John Guare, Samuel Beckett, Douglas Turner Ward, Tom Stoppard, David Storey, Israel Horovitz, Sam Shepard, Lanford Wilson, Peter Weiss, Ed Bullins, Jack Gelber, David Mamet, Athol Fugard, Edward Bond, Preston Jones, Joanna Glass, David Rabe, Robert Patrick, and so on, "ad avant-gardum"? How could the American Place Theatre have possibly found an audience for its original plays, often by totally unknown playwrights, were it not for its thousands of "members" (that is, subscribers)?

Many theatre companies produce original plays on both their main stages and their second stages. Their subscribers do not think in terms of hits and flops, as single-ticket buyers do, but retain impressions of entire seasons. They tend to say, after the play series has run its course, "We've had a good season." And the facts show that they demonstrate their opinion by renewing their subscriptions in considerable numbers. They have, in theatre after theatre, enabled us to overcome the tyranny of the single-ticket buyer, who would force his own narrow range of repertoire acceptance upon all of us. They are worthy audiences for worthwhile theatre companies. They are committed. They are subscribers.

Now, what is the point? Well, if you have a theatre of 500 seats, and you perform each of, shall we say, the five plays of your season 30 times, you have

75,000 individual seats to sell for that season. If you *could* sell them individually, you could, theoretically, reach 75,000 different people with your art. You would, thus, be *reaching* and influencing, on behalf of theatre, this much greater audience. If, on the other hand, you sell them all on a subscription basis, you will reach only 15,000 people who will be going to all of the plays. I submit that the mythical 75,000 individual single-ticket buyers going to one play would each be given a superficial, "once over lightly" treatment, incapable of providing the variety and depth of theatregoing experience that becomes possible when people attend a series of plays. If any considerable number of the 75,000 were to betray the premise of my theory and attend several or more of our plays, there would no longer be room for all of them to get in. However, this is all an exercise in futile hypothesizing, for it is all wrong for the simple reason that, except in the rarest of circumstances, you cannot get the 75,000 people to buy tickets to all of the plays, because many plays do not attract sufficient individual sales. Only when the theatregoer takes the subscription offering in its entirety do the "weak sister" plays get an audience equal to the stronger plays.

The resident professional theatres that we are speaking of produce classics, standard contemporary works, avant-garde plays and original plays, many of which simply have little drawing potential at the box office, even from that tiny fraction of the population that goes to live theatre at all. A major factor in the present existence of some 245 nonprofit professional theatres on the North American continent, when there were hardly more than half a dozen 15 years ago, is the successful introduction of subscription. Now theatres have found an audience for all the plays they produce. If they depended for the bulk of their audience upon individual ticket buyers, they either could not exist or could exist only at starvation level.

Some of these theatres and other kinds of performing arts groups at one time were attempting to function with mainly single-ticket selling orientation and only began to enjoy major growth and development when they struck out for—and achieved—big subscription in relation to their capacities. Others have come into existence riding the subscription wave and have thus eliminated unnecessary years of hardship or what would probably have been quick extinction. With the single-ticket buyer a minor element in most of their economies, their survival rate is high.

In the mid-1960's, among the theatres to which I was assigned by Theatre Communications Group, were two which had a number of things in common.

They had both existed for some years. Both operated in industrial cities which had population areas of approximately two million. Both had a very small amount of subscription in relation to their capacities and to the number of performances they presented.

I met with both for the first time within the same year. Although neither committed itself fully to the recommendations made, both gave a similar output of effort, achieving similar results—not sensational ones, but good, considering their limited investment in energy and money. Theatre A went from its tiny base of 1,900 subscribers to 3,200 subscribers and Theatre B rose from its larger but nonetheless small base of 3,200 to 4,600. When it came time to make plans for the next season's campaign, the management of Theatre A admitted that it had, in the recent effort, done much too little, and said that it stood ready to greatly increase the scope and scale, including the expenditure of whatever monies were required for the job. Obviously, they were saying, "Before, we weren't really certain about the direction that we ought to take, but now we *know*." From that point on, Theatre A did everything right and has long had over 20,000 season subscribers and a magnificent new playhouse. It now operates in a completely different league from its old hand-to-mouth days of dependence upon the single-ticket buyer.

On the other hand, when I met with the administrators of Theatre B following the first push, expecting that they would be anxious to promote in a bigger and better way, now that they had tasted blood as a result of even a quite limited effort, I was very disappointed to hear the decision maker say that his organization could not be expected to "work like that every year," and that, "We couldn't possibly afford the cost of all that printing and postage."

Looking at it now, from the perspective of the decade that has passed since this judgment was arrived at, we can all the more clearly see how faulty it was, not just for the season that followed, but for all the years that have passed since then, in which that theatre has remained at the same low subscription level, with all of the resultant disabilities. Here was a lack of capacity to understand the difference between an inadequate, routine expenditure of promotional funds and organizational effort (based on, "How much can we afford to do in relation to our present box office income?") and a truly ambitious program of audience building which requires an extended period of investment of both funds and work force. Thus, Theatre A prospers on many levels, while Theatre B remains very much mired in the marginal situation I found there some 10 years ago.

I once read in a certain "artsy-craftsy" publication the preposterous claim that Dynamic Subscription Promotion may indeed be capable of creating an instant, large, regularly attending audience for a brand new performing arts company, or for an ongoing one which previously had only a small subscribed following, but that these sensational gains were destined always to be short-lived—a sort of ephemeral, flash-in-the-pan bedazzlement. The author contended that these large subscriberships would have no staying power; that almost immediately after all the excitement which these initial successes achieved, the new audiences would begin to wither away; and that, in short order, the subscriberships would be back at bedrock. These rash assertions not only denied the validity of all that I was working for, but I felt that the writer denigrated the artistic worthiness of all of the groups I was assisting, assuming as he did that people could be talked into coming to their performances *once,* but would then reject them forever after. He based his claim on *one* aberrant situation (which to this day remains a unique case), in which the magnificent results of an excellent initial subscription campaign had dissipated in several successive seasons, to the point that eventually over 75% of that subscribership disappeared. Many different theories have been advanced for this catastrophe. Suffice it to say that this organization, which at first reacted in disillusion with the subscription concept (thus further contributing to its decline), has since made great strides in rebuilding its committed audience and has already regained over 50% of its losses. Soon, I believe, its subscription will surpass its previous highest peak.

Some years have passed since that article was written, during which time I have continued to keep meticulous records of the respective annual achievements of scores of professional performing arts projects, and they show an overall picture of solid, continued growth. Certainly, there appears, here and there, an occasional step backward; but then two steps are taken forward in the seasons that follow. Thus, we see a clear pattern of subscriptions sold in rising crescendo over the years, following the initial breakthrough. Often they arrive at a plateau so high that only new, larger auditoriums will permit further increases in season-ticket sales.

Dynamic Subscription Promotion has enjoyed a practically unbroken string of striking successes since it began to be embraced by performing arts organizations in the early and mid-1960's, when tiny subscriberships were the rule. One of the then handful of resident professional theatres, for instance, had attained a subscriber list of only 1,200 after 15 years of operation. Such organizations, in an amazingly short time, once they began to deal with the problem effectively, found themselves performing to audiences hundreds of percent greater. Subscriberships up to 10,000 became common, and I could list many North American performing arts entities which have done much better than that—in some cases, a great deal better. I think that the weight of the evidence is overwhelmingly on the side of Dynamic Subscription Promotion and that the writer of that dead wrong article in the arts journal to which I have referred has clearly been proved a false prophet.

# 5

# Artillery and Infantry:
## We Need 'Em Both

For many more years than present-day practitioners of the passionate art of theatrical press agentry have been around, the question has been asked, "Why was the advance sale so poor despite the terrific publicity campaign that we carried out for this attraction?" This slip between the cup of our propagandizing the public and the lip of their buying the tickets is a constant factor. In effect, what the public says back to us so often is, "Oh, we know about it. In fact we might say that you have magnificently informed us about your forthcoming presentation. Yes, we know about it, but we don't intend to go to it!" We who are charged with the responsibility of bringing the audience under all circumstances, cannot cop out with the argument that the attraction, for whatever the reason, has no box office drawing power. In the specific case of producing companies which are concerned not with individual attractions but with entire seasons of them, the need to assure an overwhelmingly subscribed attendance is all the greater. And for subscription, we have only the advance sale to look to, for the moment the curtain rises on the new season, subscription selling effectively ends.

Listening to the stream of consciousness of a symphony orchestra manager with too many empty seats, we might hear the following: "Did we not get big space in the newspapers for many weeks before the season's opening? Did we not 'break' the fine arts section of the papers with repertoire listings, interviews with artists, board leaders and managers? Were we not ingenious enough to land our material on the pages of the cooking, fashion, sports and financial sections, too? And did we not get many free public service spots on the radio and TV? Didn't we prevail on the mayor to declare the week before the season began 'Symphony Week,' which we celebrated with a parade down Main Street with our orchestra playing a rousing march on a beautifully decorated float, which flew a banner reading 'Subscribe Now'? Does our press agent not have a bulging scrapbook, testifying to his triumphs?" To deal with the orchestral official's puzzlement, I will make a military analogy, juxtaposing the roles of artillery and infantry in classic, prenuclear military strategy:

When a general wanted to successfully attack a strongly held enemy position at the top of a hill, he first ordered the artillery to pound 'em with shells mercilessly. When he was satisfied that the enemy's equipment was smashed, and that their soldiers were stunned and dazed by the ferocity of the barrage, he stopped the artillery, sent his infantry up the hill (they got up there in relative safety); then, the riflemen took the position and occupied the terrain. In subscription terms, they made the sale.

Now, many of us in performing arts organizations have traditionally done a more or less good job in conventional publicity campaigning. We have put on powerful artillery bombardments, but after all those shells have been expended and exploded, no infantry ever appears on the scene to go in and mop up! So, we have magnificently informed the public and interested them, we softened 'em up but we failed to *follow up*.

Often I groan inwardly when administrators relate, with great enthusiasm, the number of bumper stickers attached to guild members' cars, the cases of matchbooks with advertising printed on them which have been distributed, the billboards, the bus cards, etc.—all with no process of practical follow-up in their plans.

Thus we must develop a range of *infantry* tactics. One is the creation and large-scale distribution of brochures which so effectively state our case that we have a good chance of the reader filling out, tearing off and sending in the order form with an accompanying check. Other tactics are coffee and cocktail parties, parlor meetings, patio parties (call them by any name you wish), organized for the purpose of making direct sales of subscriptions to the people who attend them. Still others are: the solicitation and use of private mailing lists ("Xmas Card" lists), with carefully prepared letters coming from the list owner and return envelopes enclosed; telephone solicitation of selective lists; bloc sales of subscriptions to industry, service clubs and private individuals to subsidize subscriptions for students and senior citizens who are unable to pay their own way; on-campus solicitations of students who are able to pay their own way; conversion of single-ticket buyers (nonsubscribers) of past seasons to subscribership; careful and forceful restoration of subscribers who have dropped out in recent years to subscribership; recruitment of present subscribers in the campaign in an effort to sign up their friends and relatives;

special solicitations of professionals in the community such as doctors, lawyers, dentists, schoolteachers, university faculty members, architects and accountants; enlistment of philanthropic, religious and fraternal organizations to sell subscriptions to their own members and friends in return for a commission from us; door-to-door direct sales of subscriptions.

All of the infantry components mentioned above are practical methods for building subscription audiences, and are in use in the United States and Canada. Ideally, the well-balanced campaign would contain a full range of components, each assigned its sales goal, with the combination of those goals successfully achieved bringing us to the overall subscription goal we have set for ourselves. The hammering out of each component's success is a campaign in itself, requiring that it be manned by both staff professionals and volunteers, according to the stituations of various organizations.

One of the most important things in approaching such efforts is to start out with the assumption that there will be no single-ticket (nonsubscription) sales; that those tickets we don't sell on subscription we just won't sell at all. And in so many cases, it turns out to be just about like that. Once we put ourselves in that state of mind, we are more likely to make a solid plan for our campaign, and then to begin to work at it on time—and "on time" means six to eight months ahead of season's beginning. Then, we must allot sufficient promotional funds and manpower to accomplish what we are setting out to do. And we must make all of our efforts on a scale proportionate to the capacity of the theatre or auditorium we are seeking to fill for the number of performances scheduled.

Many of the most successful campaigns for subscription sales have begun with a simple, one-page listing of all of the components which those organizations planned to put into operation. To arrive at that starting point, it was not found necessary to spend months interviewing the citizenries of the areas involved, as to their repertoire preferences, pricing, etc. with all of the conclusions exhaustively analyzed and finally presented to the management and board in handsome morocco-bound volumes. The experiences of many similar organizations have long been widely known and the sharing of such information is now the norm. And, it turns out, the basic approaches which evoke subscription sales in one place are most often valid in other places—not only in American communities, but in Canadian ones and across the seas. This is not to say that some elements of our campaigns should not be tailor-made according to certain local factors. However, when it comes to the

reactions of the potential subscribers to the stimuli we seek to engender, and
to the methods we employ, there has been a pattern of amazing similarity from
place to place. So, I will now suggest a listing of some basic campaign
components—and their goals—for a mythical resident theatre located in a
city of two million population, which has 8,000 current subscribers and a
capacity of 15,000 seats for the run of each play:

## SAMPLE CAMPAIGN OUTLINE
Total Subscriptions Available: 15,000

| Component | | Goal |
|---|---|---|
| Renewal | Re-enrollment of 70% of current list of 8,000 subscribers. | 5,600 |
| Conversion of Single-Ticket Buyers | Sale of 2 subscriptions each to 5% of list of 2,500 single-ticket buyers. | 250 |
| Restoration of Dropouts | Sale of 2 subscriptions each to 10% of list of 1,250 dropouts. | 250 |
| Current Subscriber Participation | Recruitment of 200 current subscribers to sell 2 pairs of subscriptions each. | 800 |
| Parties | Sale of 4 pairs of subscriptions at each of 50 coffee parties. | 400 |
| Bloc Sales | Sale of 5 pairs of subscriptions each to 50 corporations. | 500 |
| Sale on Commission | Recruitment of outside philanthropic, civic, religious and fraternal organizations to sell subscriptions on commission. | 1,000 |
| Xmas Card List | Recruitment of 50 board members, guild members or subscribers to write 100 personal letters each to friends, with anticipated return of 7% ordering 2 subscriptions each. | 700 |
| Telephone Campaign | Sale of 2 subscriptions each to 4% of 7,000 people called by phone. | 560 |
| Student Discounts | On-campus sale of specially priced subscriptions to students who can afford to buy them. | 500 |
| Senior Citizen Discounts | Sale of specially priced subscriptions to senior citizens who can afford to buy them. | 500 |
| Scholarships | Sale of 5 subscriptions each to 50 individuals, corporations or service clubs, sponsoring scholarship subscriptions for students. | 250 |

## SAMPLE CAMPAIGN OUTLINE (con't.)
Total Subscriptions Available: 15,000

| Component | | Goal |
|---|---|---|
| Donated Subscriptions | Sale of 5 subscriptions each to 50 donors, earmarked as contributions for senior citizens. | 250 |
| Special Letter to Subscribers | Letter to renewing and new subscribers asking them to find additional subscribers among their family and friends. | 275 |
| Direct Mail Phase I | Sale of 2 subscriptions each to $\frac{1}{3}$ of 1% of 350,000-name brochure mailing list during the spring and early summer. | 2,330 |
| Direct Mail Phase II | Sale of 2 subscriptions each to $\frac{1}{3}$ of 1% of second 350,000-name brochure mailing list during the late summer and early fall. | 2,330 |
| | Total Campaign Goal: | 16,495 |

Now, you will note that there is an overkill of 1,495 subscriptions, since 15,000 is the presumed capacity, thus permitting us to come in under the goal on one or more of the campaign components and still come out with our overall goal of a sellout. For this campaign, I have not listed many other possible components, such as radio and television promotion; newspaper advertising; special committees to bring in subscribers in the various professions; door-to-door direct selling; inserts of brochures into the full circulations of newspapers and other publications, and so on. There is much more detail concerning all of these components in later chapters of this book. Obviously, the ability of each organization to implement each of these components—and any others that it chooses to add into its respective promotional mix —is the x-factor here. Dance organizations might find an additional component in the parents of children in their ballet schools, while symphony orchestras might find that the families of their musicians would be helpful. But I have seen, time and again, very successful subscription drives begin at just such a starting point as putting down on one piece of paper such a "battle plan" as the simple outline I have just given. In no instance, has the outline been realized perfectly, and the original plan has most often undergone considerable changes and adaptations before the end of the campaign. But, it is a good way to make a beginning.

The enthusiasm and high resolve with which we begin must be sustained for the full campaign. Many such efforts entered into with gusto have a way of petering out, not only because it is hard to do all of the things that are required, but because the organization's leadership irresponsibly reassures itself with the thought that its attractions are very fine ones and might all be hits, so the single-ticket buyers will come through. It is certainly possible that an event here or there will actually sell out through its naked, commercial box office drawing power. For a theatre company, that could be a Neil Simon comedy; for a dance company, *The Nutcracker*; for a symphony orchestra, an Isaac Stern solo appearance; for an opera company, *La Bohème*. But do they *really* think the single-ticket buyers are going to turn out in sufficient numbers to fill the seats for new or avant-garde plays by unknown dramatists, the regular balletic repertoire, or the concert with a less-than-blockbuster soloist? Certainly, all of us who have suffered the apathy of single-ticket buyers know the answer to that rhetorical question.

And, in case anybody is under the illusion that the advance use of recent, great press reviews about the show or the artist will result in automatic box office sellouts, they should be told that it doesn't work that way a good deal of the time. When I was a young press agent, I was once engaged by a concert impresario to publicize a distinquished pianist's appearance in a large recital hall. The event was not part of the management's subscription series, but was on its own as a single event. I built the publicity and advertising campaign around a "dream notice" which the artist had received from one of the major New York music critics. It said that the pianist possessed "the heart of Rubinstein and the hands of Horowitz." How could I miss? Well, I did. The concert never took place. So few advance mail orders were received that the impresario canceled it, and I was forced to issue a release stating that the artist was "indisposed." (What would publicists do without indisposition?)

Whether we are organizing a new performing arts entity, or we are girding ourselves to produce a new season at an already existing institution, we will be faced with two main areas of concern. The first is to produce our art up to the standard of excellence to which we aspire. The second is to produce the audience that will appreciate the art and will fill the theatre or auditorium in which we perform, for the number of performances which we present, and even for the larger number of performances which we *ought* to be presenting. Experience indicates that successfully producing high quality art does not automatically bring full houses. This conclusion is difficult to accept for most

Americans because we have been raised to believe, "If you build a better mousetrap, the world will beat a path to your door." I would venture to say that this might be true in the mousetrap business but is not necessarily true in the performing arts! In fact, performing arts history is strewn with the wrecks of artistically meritorious groups which foundered for lack of finding their audiences, or to put it more correctly, because they expected their audiences to find them, without the pump-priming processes which are integral to the development of committed audiences.

While we might not approve of it, it may be understandable that a dilettante takes selfish pleasure in being a part of a very small in-group audience or that an artistic director mistakenly equates the empty seats in his theatre with the superiority of his art; however, I have never found it understandable or forgivable when a manager or a publicist adopts this attitude. For they are the very officials who are directly charged with promoting their project's success in building audiences and bringing in revenue.

In one case I recall, a dance company's board of directors, inert through years of stagnation, very belatedly decided to begin subscription for the first time. The manager bitterly opposed the move on the grounds that the real devotees, the single-ticket buyers, ought to be able to obtain the best seats in the house, whenever they decided to come (which wasn't very often). For this completely invalid reason, he would have unnecessarily continued the impoverishment of the company, risked its demise, continued to present very poorly attended performances, denied his artists the opportunity of appearing in a greater number of performances, and stifled the flow of financial contributions. As it turned out, had he not resigned in protest of the board's decision to go ahead, he would have prevented the development of almost as many new audience members in one season as that organization had attracted in the generation of its previous, hand-to-mouth existence. The move to subscription and its successful promotion brought about an immediate 67% increase in attendance over the season before, a 75% rise in box office income and a 50% increase in the number of performances, all of which inspired a vast rise in contributions and subsidies.

In another situation of a fine but struggling opera company, a top official annually faced unsold tickets worth a fortune. Just as if there were some special merit in this defeat, he fought like a lion to keep that status quo, and the word subscription was anathema. When, over his head, the decision was made to launch a subscription drive, he responded by boycotting all meetings connected with it. The drive proved to be an overwhelming success; in fact, that company today has one of the largest subscription audiences in the U.S. and has undergone enormous growth and development, artistically and institutionally. The wrong-headed official who once scraped along on a pittance has long since been converted to a rabid enthusiast for subscription.

Contrasted with some of these obstructive attitudes, there are other cases where the professional administrators involved have immediately welcomed the introduction of major promotional efforts and have given great impetus to them. For instance, the general manager of a ballet company seized upon the major subscription drive concept as the great opportunity it was and converted his entire organization into an "infantry regiment" for this special purpose. He held weekend retreats with staff and board members solely to prepare them psychologically for the battle. He expanded upon the recommended components with considerable intelligence and then led his forces into continuous combat, which eventually resulted in subscription gains of over 3,000%. They kicked off from a base of only 300 subscriptions and worked up to 10,000. In the process, they achieved many long dreamed-of benefits for their company, the most important of which was the establishment of a substantial audience in its own home city, an achievement which had eluded them for many years, despite national and international recognition on tour. I much admire the aggressive spirit of this general manager who has shown real generalship in deploying his infantry.

Whether it is artillery or infantry that we are employing or deploying, or the combination of both, which I believe is necessary for the best results in subscription sales, we must have the ammunition with which to fight the battle. In this connection, I wish to remind boards and managements that we must provide the financial resources which are necessary for the promotional arm to succeed. And it is here that we often find a double standard in operation—one standard for artistic appropriations and another for promotional ones. It is not just that I have always thought this budgetary dichotomy to be inequitable, for that would be beside the point. What is most wrong about it is that it leads to poor results in an area which is of such great importance; that is, the building of audiences.

What do I mean by the double standard? Virtually everything we do in producing our arts is speculative. We have no guarantee of how things are going to come out. We sometimes invest fortunes in the stage settings and costumes for an opera, a ballet or a drama, only to see it all go down the drain on opening night, rejected by the press, at best tolerated by our kindly subscribers and totally shunned by the hit-happy single-ticket buyers.

Let us say, for example, that the music director of a certain symphony orchestra has devoted weeks of intensive, expensive (in musician services) rehearsals to a new work by a hitherto unknown, contemporary Rhodesian composer in whom he believes. Because the score is composed in a devilishly difficult atonal musical idiom, rehearsals go into considerable overtime. Because the music director regards the forthcoming premiere as one of the great events in the orchestra's history, critics have been invited from all over the country, their air fares, hotel bills and meals all paid for by the orchestra. The composer and his family have been flown in from their home in Salisbury for the great event and housed in a fine suite of the leading hotel. The work turns out to be a dud that strains the loyalty of subscribers, and bores the critics. It has, of course, been shunned in advance by the single-ticket buyers, who just don't go to new works by unknown composers. Our board and staff accept the situation with grace (*"C'est la guerre."*) and we go on quixotically to our next speculation.

Or, perhaps the costume designer of a certain play demands the most expensive silks and satins—and real sables for the leading lady's coat—while the decor's designer decrees costly reproductions of the just-the-right-period furniture which must be handmade for the boudoir scene in the second act. The lighting designer goes overboard with new installations of computerized electronic devices to achieve his multimedia effects for the stunning finale of the show. Costs for the physical production go way over the budget. Our loyal board rises to the occasion and signs personal notes at the bank to cover the overage. After all, art cannot be denied!

But should the publicity man ask for an additional promotional appropriation because a poorly received previous season has driven the subscription renewal percentage down, requiring that many new subscribers be found to replace the attrition, he had better be prepared for a hard and perhaps an unsuccessful fight. He is told that all seven plays in repertory might well be hits during the coming season; that we will replace the missing subscribers with greater single-ticket sales and avoid the cost of a new subscription campaign (forgetting that we will instead have to spend much more on wasteful day-to-day advertising all season). And then, the publicist will be asked, "Besides, what guarantee can you give us that you will sell all those additional subscriptions?"

There you have the double standard in operation. From the promotion department they want guarantees. The promotional appropriations are challenged, scrutinized, compromised, denigrated and denied, while the artistic appropriations go unchallenged. Considering that performances find their completion only in the audiences that experience them—and that bringing in these audiences requires incessant pump priming—I think we should seek to establish a new era of the single standard.

The strategy of that single standard—that is, the equal importance of art and audience—must be agreed upon in the war plans, and the troops and ammunition (promotional resources) must be obtained before we can fight the real battle to gain our objective (an audience to attend the art). Otherwise, the whole war will be lost before it is even fought.

**6**

---

## *Getting Off on the Wrong Foot*

Performing arts organizations are often begun by artists who knock on many doors (or their friends do this for them) until they finally convince a prime mover in the power structure of the community that there is a great need for, say, a classical ballet company in that city. The influential lady or gentleman then turns to the would-be founder and says, "In order for me to proceed further, now that I am sold on your wonderful idea of starting this dance company, I have to know what all this is going to cost. Bring me a budget outlining the amounts required to get this project into operation. Of course, it had better not be too costly a proposition, or I might not be able to find the support for it."

So the artist and his friends begin to prepare the budget. They have to provide for all the requirements from scratch, as they have none of the things yet that a ballet company needs, except the aspiration and ambition of the founder. They estimate what it will cost to rent, remodel and equip that big, old vaudeville house which, though somewhat ramshackle, is salvageable. It will require redecorating, rewiring, replumbing, reseating, new stage and lighting installations, an entirely new stage floor and remodeling of the dressing room space. The offices upstairs must be furnished, and typewriters, adding machines, desks and chairs must be provided for the administrative staff. Since the company has not previously existed, it has no stores of scenery and costumes, and these must be constructed for the initial season's repertoire. Most of the artistic personnel must be brought from other places at initial transportation cost. Pre-season rehearsal payroll for artists and other personnel must be figured in, too. When they have all of these and other expenses listed, they total them and inform their sponsor of the sum required. Presumably, they have put in the cost of all of the things they will need. But they have left out (They invariably do!) the cost of getting something which does not yet exist in that community—an audience for the art of classical ballet. Perhaps one of those involved in the budgeting did think of the problem but mentally swept it under the rug, because he didn't want to add to the expense items which were mounting alarmingly, as they thought of one item after another that had to be included. The lack of an established audience for dance did not seem to bother them all that much. After all, the people might just show up by themselves. Besides, they may have reasoned, if we start to put in such "fringe" items as an advance promotional campaign for subscription, that might push total costs so high that it would frighten off our Mr. Power-Structure. So, let's just worry about getting open; our choreographer is very talented, and our dancers are marvelous. Word-of-mouth will be our promoter, and we can't get better advertising than word-of-mouth, can we? And, if we build that better mousetrap, the world will beat a path to our door, won't it?

They have misgivings, late in the game, about the lack of subscription, and so they do come out with a series offer of four programs to be presented for three performances each, on Friday evenings, Saturday evenings and Sunday afternoons. The promotional effort begins with an impractical, though attractive, ad in the Sunday newspaper only three weeks before the curtain is to rise on the premiere, not only of the first dance program, but of what is expected to be a permanent company. The artwork, typographical design and copy for the ad have been donated by a leading local advertising agency. The ad is very institutional, very high class, makes no vulgar statements like "Subscribe Now!" nor does it contain any obvious selling points. An outdoor advertising company has contributed the use of ten billboards and the only charge is $500 per board for painting them. The copy on the boards, prepared by the civic-spirited agency, reads in big, bold letters:

### Ballet Is a Bore, Tickets Are Expensive,
### Parking Is Impossible,
### You Must Pay Baby-Sitters, Too

And then, in tiny letters below:

But It's All Worth It Because The Cylinder City Ballet Company Is Great.

(No comment.) There is no mailing campaign at all because the chairman of the board's wife does not believe that anybody buys anything by mail, despite the success of the vast mail-order industry. There have been no volunteer efforts to sell subscriptions to the series because the same lady does not believe that people should be solicited to buy the entire series. It is her contention that it is unfair to ask the public to take programs they are not specifically interested in along with the ones they wish to attend. She even wants choice seats set aside for the use of these picky people when, and if, they decide to attend individual dance programs. Under these handicaps, they get to their opening night (Friday), hoping that an audience will show up, and maybe it does because a posh medical research organization and its high-powered benefit committee has sold the tickets. But there are two more performances of the program, the next night and the Sunday matinee, and there are three more programs of three performances each, scheduled within the next several months. Only 300 subscriptions have been sold and the house seats 1,500. An average of 300 single-ticket patrons materialize for each of those nine performances, leaving 900 unsold seats for each. The 600 people who come (and see the acres of empty seats around them) leave with the feeling that they somehow have made a mistake, even though the programs are reasonably good.

Thus, the new project is off to an unnecessarily poor start. It may, as a result, collapse before the first season is out. Or, it may agonize along for a while as such enterprises often do, before collapsing. Or, it may continue to operate in an unsatisfying, substandard way for some years like many other such groups. If only they had given prior consideration to lack of an audience as a major problem. If only they had put the cost of solving it into the reckoning of the capital investment necessary to begin operation.

A reason contributing to such lame beginnings of nonprofit performing arts organizations as I have described in the foregoing paragraphs is that their originators sometimes proceed as if they were doing something unique, as if there were no existing criteria or guidelines in the field, which of course, is not so. While it is never too late to implement subscription techniques, it is the incipient and developing organizations that now have the advantage of being able to benefit most from whatever wisdom is compiled in this handbook. For, these emerging institutions have the opportunity to plan according to the experiences, successes and failures of those who have gone before. The body of accumulated experience is by now considerable, and the sharing of information is widespread. The founders of a new project can learn much that will be of value to them through visits to already established, successfully functioning professional producing organizations. Then, too, in each of the various performing arts areas, there are central bodies such as Theatre Communications Group, American Symphony Orchestra League, Opera America, the Association of American Dance Companies (and similar service groups in Canada), all of which could be of assistance in getting new arts undertakings off on the *right* foot.

# 7

# "We've Already Got 'Em All!" (Or, Are There More Where They Came From?)

Some years ago, I found myself involved in the creation of a charter subscription audience for an incipient resident professional theatre in a certain good-size American city. As part of what seemed to be a performing arts boom, a new opera company had just been announced there, too. In carrying out my work in this connection, I made several trips there during that year. On one of those occasions, I received a telephone call from the board president of the local symphony orchestra, a distinguished corporation lawyer, inviting me to a luncheon meeting with his music director and him at a private club. Over the excellent salmon and Pouilly-Fuissé, they told me that they felt "invaded." They believed that parvenu forces in the arts life of the community, aided and abetted by "carpetbagger influence," had entered what had until then been a private cultural preserve. They feared that, after they and their predecessors had worked faithfully and with dedication for 60 years in that vineyard to build up a series subscribership of 2,812, they were now threatened by a repertory theatre soon to open its doors. As if that were not bad enough news, word had leaked out that there was now an opera company on the drawing boards which was seeking the malign carpetbagger's help. "Don't you see, Mr. Newman, we'll all be fighting over the same bone. There are just so many people in this area who appreciate the finer things and we have already found them—all 2,812 of them!"

In fact, of course, there were many more potential members of this aristocracy of good taste in the woodwork; that new theatre and that new opera company found more than 12,000 of them within the year that followed the luncheon, and they have since found an additional 23,000, for a total of 35,000 between them. That symphony orchestra management waited for some years to take the suggestion then given—that they get the names of the theatre and opera subscribers (which would be theirs for the asking) and go after 'em. They have recently moved to do so, with the result that they have now more than tripled the number of their series-ticket holders. They now think of me as a respectable consultant, rather than a carpetbagger.

In the meantime, another theatre company has also taken root in the community, following the promotional prescriptions which have succeeded for the other groups and benefiting from their conditioning of the public. This new company has already found 5,000 subscribers; thus, where there had been only 2,812 subscribers for a single organization, there are now 54,000 subscribers for four healthy performing arts institutions in that city, and I certainly do not think the maximum has yet been reached.

The orchestra's board president and its music director were sincere when they spoke of there being "just so many" people who could be dragooned into enjoying and attending the "finer things" and that these special people were limited to the number which had already been uncovered. They believed just that. They were stating what I have heard innumerable times from other board officials, artistic leaders, managers and publicists of performing arts all over this continent and, for that matter, as far away as Australia. They were speaking of those who, by their education and their general cultural connections, *ought* to have been subscribers. What had not been taken into account was that the arts organizations had not done all that could have been done to find more. Far from it. Upon scrutiny, in case after case, it was learned that their promotional efforts had usually been very circumscribed, almost as if, in trying to write a composition, they were using only one or two of the alphabet's letters. The most common weakness lies in the ridiculously small scale of their efforts, which bears no relationship to their needs, to the size of their halls, to the number of performances they give or ought to be giving.

All of this leads to one of the most oft-repeated questions I hear, and that is, "Just how large is the potential audience for theatres, opera companies, dance companies, symphony orchestras? What is the percentage of regular attendance that we can reasonably expect to develop in our community, given its population?" Well, there have been different surveys made which give us varying figures on how many people attend the performing arts. Meaning no disrespect to the specialists who make such surveys, I contend that this question is difficult, if not absolutely impossible to answer. An enormous oversimplification would be involved, considering the stronger and weaker pulls of the different arts, the number of arts organizations in the community, prices of subscription and number of events on various series, the region of the country and the extent of the arts-attendance tradition, and, of course, the scope and quality of the promotional effort. Nevertheless, I do keep in mind as my own loose rule of thumb, that about 2% of the population is the average potential subscribership. In some places, particularly the smaller ones in population, we have certainly exceeded that figure. And when the community is *very* small, the percentages are sometimes amazingly high. For instance, the Canadian town of Camrose (Alberta), not exactly a metropolitan center, can pridefully point to its 900 concert-series subscribers in a population of only 3,000—a 30% figure—while such remote places as Bella Coola (British Columbia) and Yellowknife (Northwest Territories) boast similarly heavy subscribership in relation to their thinly populated towns. Of course, they do include some of the farm-folk in their peripheries who, along with the town dwellers, have been zealously proselytized by the implacable representatives of Overture Concerts, the pioneer organizing force for performing arts subscription in the far-flung communities of the Canadian Northwest.

In the medium-size and large cities, we are unquestionably doing a great deal better than used to be the case, invariably in direct ratio to the promotional input involved. If Chicago, with a metropolitan population of over seven million, has 21,000 opera subscribers, that equals about .3%. At Edmonton's Citadel Theatre (Alberta), where they have 15,000 subscribers in a 500,000 population area, they have reached 3%. The New York City Opera's peak figure of 37,000 in a population area of 9.9 million was .4%. Of course, if we combine all the subscriberships of all the performing arts organizations in a given community, we can come up with a considerably larger percentage estimate, though the figure would be slightly misleading, since there are duplications among these subscriberships.

We can see that, if we just reached 2% in some situations, it would make us successful beyond our wildest dreams, and we would have to build many new theatre buildings and concert halls in which to house all those people newly come to the arts. We must also not forget that these tiny percentages represent a tremendous boom in sales, compared with what they used to be, when promotion was generally much less aggressive and on a much smaller scale. For a very great number of organizations, just reaching 2% would mean three-, four- and five-fold increases in their present subscriberships, as well as setting off additional waves of single-ticket demand (from the fallout of intensive subscription campaigning). It might also result in major increases in length of seasons and a new proliferation of similar producing entities.

Only when we realistically assay our situation, in light of how few people of the overall population we have a fighting chance to bring into our theatres and concert halls, are we likely to face up to the need for direct subscription-selling action. Far too many board and staff people tend to sublimate this need by substituting still another market survey or new program to improve community relations—a lot of motion, giving the impression of doing audience development work. But in terms of tangible results, they add up to little or nothing and are actually what old-time press agents call "eyewash." Anything but get down to practical tasks.

By the way, I do not mean to imply that all surveys and studies in the field of performing arts attendance and marketing are useless. I will say that, unfortunately, most such studies with which I have had experience did not help at all or duplicated information we already had. Perhaps the fault lies with insufficient planning and lack of expertise in executing such studies. However, replies to queries are notorious for their unreliability. We have found that people who fill out these questionnaries almost invariably elevate their own cultural images, and their response at the point of sale may be far different from their questionnaire. Based on surveys, a certain magazine had supposedly reached a circulation in the millions, but actually possessed a much smaller readership. Very few theatre patrons claim to attend plays for any other reason than their devotion to the principle that "the play's the thing"; yet when "name" actors appear in a given theatre company's productions, they consistently generate a greater ticket demand than exists for the same theatre's very fine presentations without celebrated guest artists.

Even if the answers to survey questionnaires do make sense when aligned with reality, they are most often common knowledge based on experience in the field. I have only recently read an expensively published arts-attendance survey, which brought forth a succession of such "startling" points as: "90% of all audience members say that they prefer evening performances to daytime performances," and, "Those who attend four times or more in a year are in general, wealthier, more highly educated and older than those who attend infrequently (once a year)." In raised letters, it goes on to hammer home the point that "At all kinds of performances, the education factor remained important: the most frequent attenders had considerably more education than those who attended infrequently." Certainly, such conclusions rank with the one arrived at by a university sociological survey, part of an investigation into nutritional deficiencies among various segments of the population, which "discovered" that families with many children and low incomes suffered a higher rate of undernourishment than did those with few children and high incomes. Similarly, a survey recently completed in an eastern city found that, the lower the income of the people queried, the more their complaints about theatre being too expensive. The same study, zeroing in on people who don't go to the arts, informs us that 76.5% of them hate to visit the downtown area at night. So, now that we know this, what should we do—tear down all of the symphony halls, playhouses and other auditoriums in the country which happen to be located in the central city? If we did, and then miraculously obtained sufficient financial support to build new ones in the suburbs, do we have any good reason to believe that this would bring the masses—including that 76.5%—to our performances? The surveyors also reveal that the largest number of these people who don't attend the arts prefer popular music to the classical kind. Now, really! Not only readers of *Variety*, but the whole world knows that rock attractions often sell out stadiums of 30,000-and-more capacity, while symphony orchestras very often cannot sell out their 3,000-and-less seats. What are they (the surveyors) telling us that we don't already know? And how is all this going to help us promote our attendance? It seems to me that this kind of nonsense is a plain waste of money and energy. Worse than that, it unnecessarily diverts us from dealing with our real audience-building problems.

What is one to make of the recent survey which reveals that 41% of Americans now attend live theatre (on an average of 4.6 times) each year. Perhaps the poll was taken from 7:30 to 8:00 on a Saturday night, at 43rd, 44th, 45th and 46th streets, west of Broadway, in New York City. If the pollster really believes in the reliability of his figures, he should lose no time in investing his savings in the construction of a network of new theatre buildings throughout the land. And if his percentages have any relation to reality, I'll eat my Borsalino in Macy's window at high noon.

We do not need to cajole a well-meaning local philanthropist into giving us a grant of $48,000 to conduct a survey so that we can end up with the impressively bound results which will prove, beyond the shadow of a doubt, that suburbanites and farmers for 50 miles around prefer a 7:30 starting time to an 8:30 one on weekday evenings, or that most prospective opera goers would rather attend Verdi's *Aida* than a new work by a Lower Slobbovian avant-garde electronic composer. (That same $48,000, spent on a massive brochure mailing, would probably have sold from 5,000 to 10,000 new subscriptions!) Now, I admit to being personally prejudiced, having once lost a small fortune because of a survey during the years when I owned a motion picture house. When the patrons of my Astor Theatre (located at Clark and Madison streets in Chicago, the intersection to which Hecht and MacArthur dedicated their play, *The Front Page*) were surveyed as to whether they preferred single features to double features, they replied to the man that they wanted single features. Whereupon, I changed my policy to conform with their choice, and they all went right across the street to my alert competitor, who had immediately switched from single features to double features. It took me three years to build my business back up to its previous level. Although 30 years have now passed since that experience, I still turn pale when the word "survey" comes up.

I am also foursquare for improving community relations. But I wouldn't depend on these activities to bring in so many subscriptions per day, every day during the many months of our campaigns. And I am against diverting monies and energies that could be much more effectively used in direct-selling work. I am against a theatre company with a record of 40% unsold seats last season, spending a small fortune to publish a magnificent institutional yearbook—certain to please the artistic director, his friends and the board members, and to win an award at the next state graphic arts convention—while refusing to do a major subscription-ticket mailing compaign which it desperately needs, on grounds that there is no money to pay for such promotion.

A charge often hurled at subscription-oriented theatres is that their audiences consist, in considerable numbers, of the despised members of the middle class. In truth, we have not subjected our subscribers to a hand inspection, as was done at the time of the Russian revolution, when those who could not show work-worn, proletarian hands were taken out and summarily shot. We plead guilty to having sold subscriptions to all persons who would buy one, without any class discrimination on our part. Undoubtedly, the discounts we have often proffered have made our offerings all the more accessible to the blue-collar man, if he chose us instead of—or took us along with—other more popular entertainments. In actuality, we do have manual workers among our subscribers, and we would like to have more of them. It is not subscription that keeps them away from us. They don't buy single tickets either, it seems. The reasons we don't have them in larger numbers are complex sociological ones—and not solely economic.

In most performing arts projects, the artistic directors and the managers are all in favor of increasing the variety of backgrounds represented in their audiences. Some years ago, a company which provided excellent stage productions to lower income and disadvantaged people, giving them free admission, complained to me that the potential "customers" stayed away in droves. While it might seem logical that plays which are clearly antiestablishment should draw huge crowds of the unestablished and the disestablished, it just hasn't worked out that way. In fact, the main audiences for these works remain the much maligned, obviously masochistic middle class theatregoers, who are often the favorite targets of angry young dramatists. But if traditional promotion techniques and large-scale subscription-selling efforts have failed to produce an audience which is a true cross-section reflection of society, it is this guaranteed box office income which allows us to explore other less traditional ways of reaching out for new audiences. Healthy subscribership has been partially responsible for a number of innovative audience development programs in cities throughout the U.S. For without the security of our subscribers, we could not afford to turn our energies to such outreach projects.

Examples of other ways to reach audiences are varied. In Seattle, a ticket van distributes free tickets in low income neighborhoods to performances of the Seattle Repertory Theatre. In the five boroughs of New York, the New York Shakespeare Festival takes productions right into neighborhoods in a mobile theatre, and its Shakespeare-in-the-Park series at the outdoor Delacorte Theatre offers free performances throughout the summer. Many performing arts companies regularly give special performances at union meetings, in factory cafeterias, in prisons, hospitals, nursing homes, senior citizens' centers, etc. And, of course, there are the "public service" offers and bloc sales of scholarship subscriptions—campaign components discussed elsewhere in this book, which are designed specifically to reach new and lower income audiences by providing free or specially discounted subscriptions. We should certainly continue to explore innovative ways to communicate with more elements of society and to diversify our audiences.

I think that it is an affirmative thing when an opera company gives a special performance for high school students and when a theatre company visits the elementary schools, because we must strike these blows for the development of our future audiences. But, we can't wait till these youngsters grow up to join our adult audience. Our performing arts institutions must survive *now*, in order to remain there when the kids have matured. So we must not buy ourselves out of subscription selling with these audience development efforts for the future. Ideally, we should work on both levels, but first things first! Above all, we should never accept any statistic as the *best* we can do. We can always do better. If we got 2% of all the people in our area to subscribe last year, and we still have seats to fill, we should set our sights even higher for next season.

# 8

## It's What's Up Top That Counts: Staff Leadership and

*"Some of My Best Friends Are Board Members"*

There are two potential barrels in our campaign leadership shotgun—staff and volunteer—and it behooves us to load and shoot off both of them.

We certainly can expect and often get a high degree of competence and aggressive effort from members of the paid staff of nonprofit performing arts groups. The key people are the general managers, business managers, publicity directors, ticket managers and audience development directors. The latter position is a relatively new one in our organizational structure, but it is one that I have argued for all over the continent. I am happy to see spreading the idea of having at least one member of the staff especially responsible for subscription promotion. This position *does* add another person to the payroll, but if the artistic director needed to hire another actor, he would not likely be opposed. "Audience Development Director" is a fancy title for the subscription-ticket sales promoter, just as "Publicity Director" is for press agent. Whatever you call them, these two employees should be constantly driving toward building a "committed" audience (my own euphemism for *subscription* audience), and they should work in close cooperation.

Until recent years, the publicity man or woman was usually the staff member most responsible for subscription. However, some of the organizations have now become very large operations, and the publicists have in such cases become overburdened, have spread themselves too thin. Sometimes there are two and three people now in the department of publicity and promotion. One of them can be given the audience development portfolio (in which case, we are saved that addition to the payroll), although this assignment does not mean that the other members of that department should not also actively participate in the annual subscription drives. For we cannot remind ourselves too often that obtaining an audience, and an increasingly larger one, is the main reason for having such a department at all.

The general manager or business manager, as an upper echelon executive, must keep the entire staff on its toes with regard to subscription sales, and systems of regular reporting of subscription activities and results should be established. We should not wake up, after it is too late in the promotional game, to find that planned activities did not take place or that not enough of them took place to produce the scale of results that our needs require. All those involved in this responsibility should acquit it in the consciousness and context of time's perishability. Success requires long-range planning and the beginning of our campaigns far in advance of each season, so that momentum can be achieved and so that any failures in the earlier stages can still be rectified in the later stages. As long as we still have the time element on our side, everything is yet possible. But when we begin too late, we have lost our margin for error. When the time slips away from us and, because of procrastination or whatever other reasons, we have not done enough early enough, we go down the drain. It is then too late, and we just do not make the sales.

In some campaigns I have helped to generate, certain staff members have evidenced unusual initiative. Sometimes, the ticket manager or head of the box office, who is usually thought of in terms of processing the subscriptions rather than promoting their sale, will turn out to be of great and even crucial assistance. In one such case, the ticket manager of an opera company that had many unsold seats the year before personally sold 2,000 new subscriptions by telephone solicitation during the summer months. In another instance, a theatre company's ticket man took over and ran the entire promotional campaign which brought in more than 8,000 new subscribers. In still another situation, the stage manager of a ballet company, after his namby-pamby general manager and indifferent publicist couldn't bring themselves to make the effort, volunteered to manage the organization's charter subscription drive and carried it off brilliantly. Then, I think of a large symphony orchestra which doubled its subscribership despite a lackluster press agent, because a strong-willed general manager was supported by a box office manager who gave maximum personal devotion to the campaign, even though she could have demurred, like some waiters, with, "This is not my station."

Effective board-level leadership is a precious commodity for us. Matched to effective professional staff work, it can make all the difference under certain circumstances. When an opera company, threatened with extinction for lack of an audience, decided to enter the subscription arena for the first time, it was a dedicated young board leader who stiffened the backs of the staffers, didn't let himself, or them, or any of the volunteers whom he organized, go to sleep for all of the seven months of the campaign. For a starter, he convinced his own firm to give him a three-month leave of absence. He went to the opera company's office every day and remained every night during that period. Then, for the next four months, although back at his own work, he went to the opera office late in the afternoon and remained through the evening—always driving toward the goal. Although I had originally convinced the board of directors to enter upon this effort rather than give up the ship, and although I had succeeded in inspiring this young volunteer leader and had worked out the plan of battle with him, I had not expected to take an active role in the campaign myself. But, when he inundated me with daily reports and correspondence, followed up by regular telephone calls, I found myself drawn into a personal participation far beyond my assignment. I made many trips to that city during the life of the drive and worked along with him and his people. When somebody keeps hitting the tennis ball across the net to you, it's hard not to keep hitting it back. The happy ending, when the goal was reached and surpassed, turned out to be only the beginning. For that fine subscription audience, established from absolute zero under quite difficult circumstances and pressures, has since grown very much greater, with all of the many concomitant benefits such as huge increases in subsidies, increased length of season, greater importance in the life of that city and much higher artistic levels. That extraordinary volunteer leader gave opera in his community the greatest gift that it has ever received; he gave it an audience, and life really began for that company.

I once found myself assigned to assist a certain symphony orchestra, long in the doldrums despite having a world-renowned music director (who was just leaving). At the first board meeting I attended, I met a businessman, who immediately became very enthusiastic about the promotional recommendations which I projected as the antidote to the problems evident in the general manager's report. It turned out that this unusually energetic and gifted man was vice president in charge of sales for a great commercial enterprise. He agreed to take the overall chairmanship of the campaign. He was able to translate into action all the recommendations made. Although the orchestra was going into a season without any music director, much less a prestigious one, the dynamic effort which our chairman structured and led brought about a drive so successful that a dramatic change for the better took place by the time the next season began. Where one formerly saw empty seats throughout the hall, there were now jammed houses. Since then, on my consulting visits, I have gone straight to this chairman's place of business, rather than to the orchestra's office. It is the nerve center of promotional efforts for that organization.

At a hard-pressed resident theatre company about to give up the ghost, I was present when the harassed general manager notified the board of directors that unless the back electric bill of some hundreds of dollars was paid immediately, the power would be cut off, and their rickety upstairs theatre would have to close down. The board president, who had become very enthusiastic about the possibilities of a special subscription campaign effort which we had discussed earlier in the meeting, made out his own check to pay the past-due light bill and then called for the organization's support in the series-ticket sales drive which he announced would be launched immediately. He proceeded to do a superb job, driving to a 200% gain in subscribership by the time the next season began. That company has since moved twice, each time to a playhouse of larger capacity and better facilities, and is now one of the most highly regarded American theatres. That board president has had a number of successors since. However, all of the good work they have done would never have had a chance to take place had he not acted with such vision and vigor when those chips were down.

Just as we seek the best possible talent for our artistic leadership and performers' roster, we should be constantly on the lookout for professional staff people and volunteers of true excellence, those in both categories who can make positive contributions to the establishment and enlargement of our subscription audiences. Ideally, we ought to cast them for their roles with just as much care as we would when seeking the right actors, singers and dancers for productions.

Experience indicates that it is highly desirable for board officers and members of a professional performing arts organization which is entering into a subscription campaign not only to be much involved in the effort, but that it be initiated at their level. Then the general manager, the publicist and other staff people have a clear mandate to proceed without fear of entering into activities and commitments to which their employers might later object. When the board decrees that the campaign be carried out, when it appropriates special funds for that purpose, and when it assigns its own members to specific tasks in the drive, the atmosphere becomes a basically healthy one; the employees are not in the position of having to "stick their necks out" in implementing this or that phase of the promotional plan. And then, too, they are under orders to make a success of it.

Ideally, the table of organization of boards should include a vice president for audience development and a committee for subscription sales—in effect, a recognition of the true importance of this area in the entire life and destiny of the institution. Unfortunately, many organizations in these fields do not operate like that, and their boards, which have traditionally accepted responsibility for fund-raising, have generally tended to avoid any serious involvement in selling season or series tickets.

Please don't get me wrong. Some of my best friends are board members. I respect these public-spirited individuals who voluntarily assume the obligations and financial burdens which such board membership automatically imposes. Yet, these same dedicated persons, often part of the community's power structure, can unwittingly retard our progress in the bringing of large, new audiences to resident theatres, symphony orchestras, opera and ballet companies. And strangely, these board people are frequently very aggressive in the conduct of their own business enterprises—promotional tigers when it comes to sales of their commercial products. Why, then, are they sometimes unresponsive when it comes to our need to market our products successfully? Why are they frequently sedate, flaccid and placid in the face of our unsold seats?

Perhaps there are some board people who take a measure of snobbish pleasure in the empty seats, because it corroborates their conviction that there are indeed very few people of gourmet cultural tastes like their own. They believe they have already done their civic duty, raised all that money for the building, paid for the best in artistic direction, casts, sets and costumes, and provided all of the expensive accoutrements of theatrical production and presentation. They protest that it's the audience's duty to come down and buy the tickets! Imagine one of these men, who happens to be a merchandising tycoon, building a magnificent new department store, stocking it with the finest goods, just *hoping* that the public will show up, and if they don't, shrugging it off, saying, "Well, I suppose the residents of this area just aren't ready for a store this fine." You can be sure that he would act differently; that he would, in fact, have been promoting his head off long before the place opened its doors to be sure the store would be jammed with customers from the very first day!

Today, apathy in the face of our ticket-selling needs might be the result of so many years of poor attendance at arts groups' performances that many board members, thinking it a normal condition, just don't get excited about it. That is, they don't look at the unsold capacity in terms of potential revenue, and they do not realize that they have suffered an additional and even more important loss, a failure in terms of people who did not fill the seats, who were not brought in to appreciate the art.

Unfortunately, too, not all board members are genuine enthusiasts for the art on behalf of which they are doing their civic duty. For sometimes a man of no music-going background agrees to serve on the symphony board only because somebody who is important to him in his business has asked him to do so. This new board member is, let us say, a widget manufacturer. He *knows* that there is a big demand for widgets, and he believes, with total faith, in the salability of *his* widgets. He is not afraid to compete for his fair share of the market, and he's more than willing to spend all that is necessary for him to obtain a lion's share. However, he does not have the same confidence with regard to the salability of our performances, and his own experiences (at the concerts to which his wife has been able to drag him) have left him with the secret conviction that nobody in his right mind would willingly buy a ticket. Thus, in his heart of hearts, he believes that any money and effort spent to promote ticket sales will just go right down the drain. How many times have I been told about this man (and his myriad counterparts) who says, "I'll contribute generously to the fund drive and I'll get others to contribute, but *please* don't ask me to go to the performances!" He does, however, admit that there are a certain, limited number of pedantic types around who "like that sort of thing" and, being a nice guy, he's willing to continue helping with the project.

When board members lack real conviction as to the community's need for the institution which they serve, they are hardly likely to be enthusiastic in aiding its audience development or fund-raising efforts. Once I called upon the board president of a symphony orchestra association to encourage his leadership in a badly needed subscription drive, only to find him in a despairing mood. It seems that he had just read a report which informed him of the small number of people who actually attended the concerts. Those figures were the reason the organization's manager had requested my assistance. The board president told me that he was distraught, saying, "I am supposed to appear before a committee of the state legislature later this week to ask for a grant, and now I'm asking myself if I have the moral right to appeal for public funds for a cause in which so few people are apparently interested." It took me some time to improve his shaken morale, and, of course, I did point out that a truly successful audience development effort could provide a great deal of the missing justification for financial support.

Once I was asked by a board member of a symphony orchestra which had endured close to a hundred years of lackluster attendance and zero expansion, "Mr. Newman, maybe we're rather conservative here, but we've been going along the way we have for a long time now. Wouldn't you say that you're being kind of radical in recommending all of these promotional activities which we never went in for previously?" I replied, "Not at all, sir. In my way of looking at it, it is *you* who are the radical, and it is I who am the conservative. I would consider it not only radical but unsound and irresponsible, in the face of clear evidence that it is necessary to organize regular and committed attendance in advance of each season, not to do so. When I recommend that ambitious subscription campaigns be entered into, utilizing those methods which have proved successful in our field, I feel that I am being truly conservative, genuinely sound and responsible. Actually, I don't think that dependence on single-ticket buyers is as radical as it is improvident and foolhardy. I would liken that course of inaction to walking on the high wire without nets. *I* wouldn't have the nerve."

It is exactly this kind of board member who is always proposing that ticket prices be raised still higher. Believing as he does that there is no hope of ever adding anybody to the present audience, he favors making the ones who are now attending pay the freight. "They're the ones (he really means the *only* ones) who want it, so let them pay for it!" Only recently, I received a long distance phone call from the manager of a small opera company that has long been guaranteeing that it will remain small by refusing to enter the promotional mainstream that has boomed subscription audiences and lengthened seasons for many other opera companies. The manager was panic-stricken, because the board was about to raise the ticket prices 100%, despite the fact that they had recently been performing to 50% unsold seats. Such a drastic price rise in a recessionary economy, he said, would almost certainly drive the percentage of unsold seats up to 75% or more—so why have an opera company in that city at all? I suggested that he have the board president call me, and when he did, I pointed out that if he left the prices the way they were, or raised them only the amount that the current inflation indicated, and then entered into an all-out subscription-ticket sales campaign, he would assure the sale of the other 50% of the capacity. He not only would get the money he sought, but he would give new life to what had been a dormant project. In his own business, you can be sure that he would not double the prices when sales were at low ebb. And, to do so in this case would be almost an act of vengeance toward the people who *do* attend the performances. If it turned out that they didn't pay and that the new, doubled prices kept new people from joining, it could have meant a quick demise for the company. In that case, the board man might self-righteously proclaim, "It is apparent that this city isn't ready for opera." Well, I must rein in my gloomy thoughts and hope that this gentleman has now begun to act upon the advice I gave him and that he will carry through a very successful subscription campaign.

Lest it be interpreted that I am against raising ticket prices under *any* circumstances, I wish to point out that I am not against such a move when the economic situation calls for it, but that I think it is unwise unless there is a sellout or near sellout. All ticket price rises must be considered within the context of our ideology as nonprofit organizations which seek to bring art to the people at a price that will not deprive too many of them of the possibility of ever attending, thus forcing on us the additional burden of fund-raising to close the gap between those ticket prices and the real cost of maintaining the institution.

Should a company's economy require additional funds, *after* such a successful series-ticket selling drive, I would certainly not be opposed to a ticket price rise at that point. For I would have good reason then to believe that the higher prices would be obtained in the context of a season which was in the sold-out category. However, an increase in ticket prices should not be shocking in its size. It is better, in an inflationary era, to increase prices each year or every other year, but in reasonable escalations. Thus, the ticket price scales of many companies I know are currently about 100% higher than they were a decade ago. Had any of those companies catapulted to the entire 100% in a single season, they would have been knocked out of the box.

I sometimes run across the type of man whose years of hard work have won him such influence and affluence that he has been appointed to the board of his city's distinguished resident professional theatre. He mistakenly thought that board membership meant exciting involvement in artistic decisions, that the director would seek his opinions concerning casting and repertoire, that playwrights would be reading scripts to him, that designers would be showing him models of stage settings and swatches of silks and satins for costumes, that he would be immersed in a wonderful, magical world. Instead, he arrives for his first board meeting to find that an audience development consultant from Theatre Communications Group is outlining a proposed subscription ticket-selling campaign. "Selling? But that's what I've been doing all these years in my own business," he says dejectedly. He feels let down, but selling most often *is* the area of his greatest competence, and that is where he could really help us.

Another reason board members may shy away from audience-building activities is that they fear it will detract from what they see as their central role, really their reason for being on the board at all, and that is, fund-raising, the sacred cow—or the golden calf, if you will—of American performing arts organizations. So much emphasis is placed on this function of board members and so many of their deliberations are concerned with this admittedly very important subject, that it is almost always dealt with out of context with the larger picture, and without reference to its direct and truly indispensable relationship to subscription promotion. In fact, selling the subscription is most often the *prerequisite* to obtaining the contribution. In stating that, it is then implicit that I believe the most likely people of the entire society to become our contributors are those who are going regularly to our performances—our subscribers. Because the need for this point to be understood, and then to be acted upon, is so great, and because it is a concept that needs to be understood not only by board members, but by management as well, I will discuss it further and more fully in a separate chapter.

While I believe that there are strong similarities between arts organizations and commerce in the need for successful, efficient business practices, there are also many cases of board people failing to take into consideration certain very basic and crucial *differences* between the economics of the businesses in which they, themselves, are engaged and those of nonprofit organizations. As I said earlier, there are many shrewd businessmen who call the promotional shots wisely on their own turf, but who flub 'em for us. When they do apply the experience of their own enterprises to our situation, their criteria do not always fit us, though there are many analogies in service businesses like the airlines or railroads, both of which share with us high levels of fixed costs, not variable in relation to the number of patrons or passengers. Thus, whether we use 10% or 100% of our capacity, our costs, predetermined by the special nature of our enterprises, remain fixed, although our potential income is variable indeed. The point is that we must be able to run a businesslike operation based on many of the sound economic principles employed in commerce, but we must also recognize the ways in which the nonprofit arts are different.

Let us say that I am the owner of a successful furniture store and also board president of the local theatre. I have been advertising aggressively, and today I am racking up an impressive sales record. By closing time, I have actually sold 50% of all the merchandise displayed in the store, and when I lock the front door that evening, I do so with a sense of satisfaction that I have done my best day's business ever. I am the envy of every merchant on the street. I will certainly relish my dinner and will later surely sleep like a baby. For not only have I turned a fine profit on the 50% of the merchandise that I *did* sell, but the 50% which remained unsold still retains its intrinsic worth. It has a wholesale value, a retail price. I can sell it the next morning, the next week, the next month—and can keep trying to sell it until it's finally all sold!

Now, between my dinner and slumber, I decide to go over to see what's doing at the theatre of which, you will remember, I'm board president. By the time I get there, it's just past curtain time. I head straight for the box office, where the ticket count has been completed, and I learn that half of the tickets have been sold and the other half have remained in the rack. Now, a farmer can throw his rotted fruit to the pigs, but what can I do with the 50% unsold bits of pasteboard? Nothing. Nothing at all. I have suffered a complete, irretrievable, irrevocable final loss of the value of half my merchandise. Where I could afford to smile smugly when half my furniture went unsold, I ought to be tearing out my hair in anguish and despair when half my tickets go unsold. Have I not failed this organization for which I have taken a great responsibility? Should I not have instituted a major subscription campaign long before the season began, and seen to it that it was fought through to such success that a debacle like this could not have happened?

Unfortunately, such soul-searching by board leaders exists more in my romantic fantasy than in actual experience. Now, let us assume that I, as board president, continue to analyze this problem of 50% (or any percent) unsold tickets further, now bearing in mind our special economics. I look at the pattern of attendance not only for this performance, but for all performances of the season to date, and I look back to the record of past seasons, too. I see that playing to half empty houses is the norm. I resolve that this will change, and that I am going to sell 100% of my tickets for the next season. I will put on a big subscription drive. And then, it hits me, and it's beautiful. I have a fantastic incentive for promotion. Since our special economics have already forced me to pay *all* the costs of production and presentation for the 50% who have been buying the tickets, everything that comes in from that point on is gravy (only, of course, on the basis that if we didn't sell those tickets, our loss would be much greater). For, looking at it that way, my remaining merchandise—the tickets—has cost me nothing. So, if we consider how much money I can afford to spend in advertising, direct mail, etc., to sell *all* the seats, it turns out that I can afford to spend a great deal.

Let us say that the unsold 50% of the tickets, if sold, has a value of $50,000. Where in the furniture business my economics might limit me to 5% promotional cost, in our nonprofit performing arts business, there is practically no limit. If it takes $25,000, or 50% of the value of the gross to sell the entire $50,000 of remaining seats, that's a terrific deal. Even if it takes the entire $50,000 (plus a lot of volunteer effort) to sell the $50,000 worth of tickets, we would not have lost a penny on our promotion. And, for the first time in our history, we would have a sold-out season, our theatre jammed at all performances, maybe 65% of all those new subscribers renewing for the next season (and we who created the juggernaut that sold the 100% season would now know how to replace the dropouts).

It must be pointed out that nonprofit groups have the ability to call upon many levels of volunteer assistance from their communities and that such assistance, if it is significant enough, can cut down the amounts of money that might otherwise have to be spent in various kinds of mailing efforts, in the advertising media and in extra sales personnel. In most cases, a combination of money carefully spent and dedicated volunteer aid is required to do the job right.

On the day I began to write this chapter, I spoke via telephone to the competent promotional director of a very large performing arts organization which had, because of board-level blindness in refusing to institute subscription, suffered losses in sales running into millions of dollars during the first five years of its existence. When, belatedly, subscription was begun there, more than $400,000 worth of series-ticket sales poured in immediately, despite very limited promotional expenditures, and the overall attendance rose 22 points from 37% to 59% that season. They got back their money and a profit of about 1,600% on $403,818 of subscription sales for promotional costs of $23,012. Now, one would assume that with 41% of the capacity still unsold, and following an experiment which had paid such fantastic dividends, the board leadership would not only authorize but demand of its staff a much larger campaign—that the 250,000 mailings of the first campaign would now be boosted to a million for the new campaign, that the board itself would throw itself into the drive on various volunteer levels, etc. *Not at all!* A campaign, more or less, of the same, limited nature as the previous one was ordered. The reason? "We can't afford to do more than that." This answer really does drive me up a tree. For did their experiment really cost them anything at all? The *new subscribers* paid for the campaign 16 times over and would continue to make the deal even sweeter in direct ratio to how many of them renewed in succeeding seasons.

A symphony orchestra board president I remember couldn't have timed it worse when, based on the attendance records of past seasons, he argued with his musicians that they should forego a long anticipated raise in pay. He based his argument on the claim that no one in that city wanted to go to concerts, and then he found out I had just assisted the staff to achieve a 75% rise in series subscribership. While there is undoubtedly a humorous aspect to this story, it isn't really funny that the board president of an organization, which exists for the purpose of bringing its art to people, should become angry when it does so. And he did become quite upset.

I am coming to the belief, after so many years of dealing with board officers and members of a very large number of performing arts groups, that there is some mischievous angel who touches some of these men and women of goodwill with a special wand every time they come to our offices, with the result that they temporarily lose their common sense. The moment they return to their own offices, the same angel touches them again so that the judgment upon which their business careers depend returns. For example, a board leader of an opera company (he runs a very successful commercial enterprise) came to the management with the recommendation that it ought to deny the subscribers a considerable portion of the best seats in the house so that they could then become available to the single-ticket buyers, and he recommended that this policy be advertised strongly. Now, the reader will have to know that this particular opera company had tried for 15 years to sell tickets, including its best locations, to single-ticket buyers and failed to do so. It had had no subscription audience at all and, in fact, it had been at the point of bankruptcy when a wiser board leader saw to it that a series-ticket system was introduced.

This move proved to be quite successful and the company prospered, increasing the length of its season in the hundreds of percent and maintaining a fine overall level of attendance, with single-ticket buyers either converting to subscription in order to get better seat locations, or accepting the less desirable locations.

Board leaders, by the way, are often abetted in myopic decisions by arts organization employees titled either controllers or comptrollers. No matter how you spell it, this species remains a sort of natural enemy of the promotional arm, very often inhospitable to its concepts, rarely grasping the forest for the trees. I recall the campaign of a theatre company which resulted in the sale of $175,000 worth of previously unsold tickets with the astonishingly low increase in promotional cost of $12,000 over the year before. The zealous controller, his compartmentalized mind deeply disturbed at having to show $12,000 more outgo than the previous year, simply couldn't link the cause of the promotion to the effect of $163,000 more in income. He kept repeating to me, "You must think money grows on trees." In another situation, a major dance company's controller, who didn't see that the more than 50% unsold tickets were any concern of his, became enraged when $39,000 was expended to bring a new $250,000 in sales (a neat $211,000 gain on the deal) for tickets which had remained unsold during the preceding season. While all other officials of that company were thrilled at the huge improvement, he leveled the accusatory question at me, "What are you trying to do, bankrupt us?" In neither of these two cases, could the tunnel-visioned functionaries I have described see either the obvious, immediate, large cash gains or the even greater advantage of so many more people being built into their audience-bodies. Both organizations went on to flourish as they continued active programs of promotion. Had they heeded the advice of their "watchdogs," they would have been left on first base.

In other instances, we often find that board people are unduly overawed by the art itself, leading to preoccupation with the dignity of the institution, and resulting in a stuffy and stilted approach to the public. They feel that we must never be caught in the stance of selling anything to anybody and that promotion for the arts, if it should be found necessary, should be done artistically through approaches in aesthetic consonance with the high level of the art itself. I know that this argument sounds nice, but it is not very logical. To board members and to some artistic directors, managers and publicists who think that way, I wish to suggest that the producing of the art and the promotion of the art are two entirely separate activities. That is not to deny that the latter activity may not be some kind of an art in itself. The subscription brochure's purpose is not to provide an artistic experience, something like the effect of the performance of the art to the people who receive it in their mailboxes. The brochure's purpose is to intrigue, entice and convince them to send in their checks immediately. Only then are they likely to be in the seats when the curtain goes up at performances. Only then can the artistic experience begin for them!

Are the attitudes of Canadian performing arts leadership on the volunteer level very much different from those of their American counterparts? Well, the much larger role of governmental subsidy—federal, provincial and municipal—in Canada has, in the past, conditioned their trustees to a rather less intensive preoccupation with fund-raising and ticket sales than might be likely found among board members in the U.S. where private funds play a major role. Until fairly recent times, a very important function of Canadian boards seemed to be that of acting as legal conduits through which government passed on subsidy to professional arts organizations. (After all, you couldn't very well give all that money to the artists directly, could you? They, being impractical, improvident and childlike, as we all know, might spend it all in one day. So, "solid citizens" had to be found to receive the monies and then to supervise their orderly disbursement throughout the season. And in that manner, the logistics of matching expenditures to income were soberly and properly implemented.) With government paying so much of the difference between what the box office brought in and what the annual budgets were, this watchdog function was often the most important role which Canada's board members played. However, into this equation we must now mix inflation and an enormous proliferation of institutions—new ones, in all of the performing arts disciplines—largely, I think, inspired by the success in building subscription audiences experienced by the previously established projects. Thus, countless new hungry "customers" have shown up at the government's tables. The pie must now be cut into smaller pieces if all are to share in it, against a background of inflation which, if not raging, still shows no sign of stopping. So, Canadian board leadership has been, for some time now, very much in a transitional process, becoming more like their counterparts in the States in having to accept and discharge responsibility for giving and getting contributions from the private sector, to a degree which had previously been unknown in their country. This change has required a widespread reappraisal of the scope of board involvement resulting in a far greater appreciation of the necessity for their participation in subscription audience development.

In concluding this chapter, I would like to explain why I have given so much attention to the attitudes and actions of board officers and members, so many of whom, in so many places, really *are* my friends. I know that this handbook will be consulted by many administrative novices on performing arts staffs. Willy-nilly, those attitudes and actions of officers, directors or trustees of their respective boards are undoubtedly going to be constant, everyday, important considerations of their professional lives. Because the audience-building missions, which have been my work for so many years now, require their cooperation, I have, by the time of this writing, met with an extraordinary number of performing arts board officials. If I seem to have, in the foregoing pages, complained about some of them, it has been without malice, and in the hope that I may—through the power of the written word—successfully proselytize others of their tribe whom I have, somehow, not yet personally encountered. I am proud of the "conversions" which I have achieved in boardrooms on several continents. And, confident as I am of the ultimate perfectibility of Man, I do believe that there is still hope for errant volunteer leaders (those board members who are not out building subscription audiences). I have, in this same chapter, listed a number of good examples, too, of their peers who could well serve as role models. And, I salute those fine board people who gave both inspiration and commitment to some of the outstanding subscription campaigns in my memory—certainly among the best such efforts which have taken place anywhere. And, as a final admonition in this area of concern, I urge all performing arts organizations, in pursuing their board recruitment activities, *to think of audience development needs as well as those of fund-raising*. And, once that recruitment has been accomplished, I would further stress the importance of truly involving the board in the *process of audience building*.

# 9

# Rummage Sale vs. Subscription Sale: The Role of Guilds, Associations and Auxiliaries

A great many performing arts organizations possess such auxiliary arms as women's guilds, associations and committees, which boast very large memberships, ranging from the hundreds into the thousands. In some cases, these supportive groups play an important role in subscription drives. In most cases, they do not. That is not to say that they do nothing at all for the sale of season or series tickets, but that their contribution is often limited to making the telephone calls to remind the old subscribers about renewal when the deadline is in sight. When it comes to selling new subscriptions—participation in the big push for the larger subscribership that begets our expansions— they are often unwilling to become involved. There are, of course, reasons for their foot dragging in this area.

For instance, all too many of the women who belong to our symphony orchestra guilds do not themselves subscribe to the concert series and very infrequently attend individual concert events. It is not unusual to have fewer than 50 ticket subscribers in a guild of 500 members, even when there are very inexpensive mini-series of four, five or six concerts available. Motions to make subscription mandatory for members are not only voted down, but voted down angrily, in almost every such attempt to bring about this personal commitment on the part of people who are presumably dedicated to the best interests of the performing arts institution with which they are affiliated. This seemingly perverse attitude can probably best be explained on the grounds that auxiliary and guild members would be put into a morally untenable position if they had to go out and sell subscriptions when they themselves didn't subscribe. The solution, of course, would be for them all to subscribe. "But, Mr. Newman, isn't that asking too much?"

It is not that they are unwilling to work hard for the cause, for they will do all sorts of difficult things, as long as it doesn't involve selling subscriptions. Fund-raising is what they much prefer to do, and they will ask 12 people in a row for a contribution rather than ask 2 to buy series tickets. However, for many of our organizations with great numbers of unsold seats, the subscription sales would bring the needed money—and the *people,* too. For, looking at it in a certain way, the money by itself is sterile, but the money accompanied by people to attend the art is vital.

Several years ago I found myself meeting for the first time with the board of a women's association in support of a large new theatre project that had in its recent initial season, performed to $700,000 worth of unsold seats, a catastrophe of no small proportions. I exhorted them to take the lead in a counterattack for the next season, to go out and do a big job of subscription-ticket selling. I outlined a plan which called for many levels of volunteer participation to back up the efforts of the professional staff and of the theatre's board of directors. After the meeting, the president of the association told me she was very sorry that her members could not possibly take on the active role I had called for, because they already had a most demanding assignment: raising $12,000 in the theatre's fund-raising campaign. To accomplish this goal, they were holding a continuous round of rummage sales, fashion shows, bazaars and card parties, plus an opening night supper. I replied, "Madam, don't you see that this is a misuse of your womanpower? Surely, if the amount of energy and devotion that you have now begun to put into all of these fund-raising activities were put into a subscription drive, it would result in a lot more than $12,000 in ticket sales (would you believe $50,000?), and you would have all that money and the audience, too." The lady said, "You know, you're right," and at the next meeting she succeeded in getting the bylaws of the association changed so that its primary purpose became audience development. I'm happy to say that the entire organization, including the professional staff, began to bestir itself, and the position of this project improved considerably in the seasons that followed.

I don't think we should be unrealistic about our considerable problem of motivating a large number of the people who have joined our volunteer organizations. Certainly, a performing arts cause simply doesn't have as strong an emotional appeal as other kinds of philanthropy which more easily obtain dedicated response from volunteer workers. It is understandably much harder to generate a do-or-die fervor on behalf of the show that must go on (or the show that must go on with an audience in attendance) than it is to evoke sacrificial devotion to the issues of poverty, flood, famine and disease. However, these volunteers have joined us of their own free will, and presumably they have done so because, on some level, they wish to assist the art and artists. If so, then how could they possibly help more than by bringing us new subscribers, since so many wonderful things develop for us from that starting point, including the basis, the credibility and the all-important excitement factor for successful fund-raising.

When volunteers do pitch in and play a significant role in audience building, they are able to achieve great satisfaction in their accomplishments. I have in mind, for instance, the euphoric victory celebration of one such group when the world-famed pianist Van Cliburn played a special dress rehearsal performance with a symphony orchestra on the day prior to his public one, with the 400 volunteers who had just waged a record-breaking subscription campaign in attendance. A special souvenir program was printed for the dress rehearsal, containing a list of the various components of the campaign and the names of the volunteers responsible for their successful implementation. Awards to outstanding workers in the effort were also listed under the designations, "Standing Ovation," "Ovation," "Bravo" and "Applause."

I would recommend that such auxiliaries engage in internal subscription drives so that the majority of their total members become subscribers. Only then will more of the members become zealous and effective missionaries to others on behalf of our ticket drives. If 10% of the total membership is "active" (and that is the norm I have found), the activists can be employed in our in-house effort to convert the maximum number of recalcitrant members.

Many of these support groups have in common the problem of a stagnant membership, in which little "new blood" has been enrolled for some years, and in which leadership has become self-perpetuating. Every effort should be made to change this picture for the better, as a prerequisite to a new era of productivity. I have found audience development by subscription, and the challenges which are inherent in it, can sometimes have a salutary, revitalizing effect on such groups. Sometimes, but not all the time.

For example, I helped initiate a subscription drive for a major symphony orchestra which had 1,600 members in its guild. Despite the fact that detailed, careful plans had been made for the guild's participation, and despite assurances from its leadership that its assignments would be successfully carried out, we were disappointed by the group's showing in an overall effort which was very successful despite this weakness. When I later remarked to the symphony manager that the ladies certainly had let us down in the series-ticket department, but that they were probably making their real contribution in fund-raising, he showed me the figures which indicated that they had brought in only 1.2% of the orchestra's budgeted needs. However, the manager spoke to me with genuine appreciation of the women's association of a symphony orchestra which he had previously managed in a smaller city and which had fewer than 300 members, every one of whom subscribed to the season and who, in the aggregate, raised a considerable amount of funds in relation to the overall budget. The most important thing, he told me, was that it was mandatory in that small women's association to be season or series subscribers in order to become members of the association, and this is a prerequisite that I never stop trying to effect in the organizations with which I consult.

In speaking of the assistance we receive—and often do not receive—from our volunteers, in connection with subscription-selling efforts, I should also like to register a protest against the widespread "kit syndrome," which is rampant in the performing arts. Let us say that we have been fortunate enough to evoke what appears might well be a significant participation on the part of our volunteer unit. Letters have been sent out and followed up by telephone calls to assure that there will be a big turnout for the campaign kickoff meeting. Several hundred volunteers arrive and are handed huge kits, containing a wide assortment of printed matter about the institution, along with the subscription brochures, order forms, etc. The covers of the kits have been especially designed by the art department of a major advertising agency whose owner is the husband of the women's guild president. It is a beautiful and expensive kit with pockets to hold the materials. It is made of fine, laminated card stock and is printed luxuriously in three colors. On the front of the kit, there is the lovely logo of the arts group, and a pleasant admonishment with which nobody is likely to quarrel, like "Preserve Civilization" or "Support the Arts." The leadership, once having distributed the kits to everybody present, assumes from that point on that the campaign has been successfully carried out and does nothing further about it. And, judging by the lack of subscription sales which so often follows such kit distributions, I have my private vision of the recipient volunteers going promptly home with their kits, getting up on stepladders and putting them permanently away on high shelves, where they will never have to see them again.

By what I have just been saying, am I arbitrarily ruling out the preparation and use of kits as a useful tool in our subscription drives? No, not at all. What I mean to say is that we should not just go through motions and then later, after failure, solace ourselves with, "Well, we did our best . . . everybody took our kits at the meeting." We must give our volunteers inspiration, a sense of involvement, incentive (nothing wrong with prizes), continuing supervision, leadership, and we must try to find, out of the many methods by which we may be selling subscriptions during the campaign, the ones that individual volunteers will respond best to and then "cast" them for their proper roles in the overall drive. We must give considerable thought and planning to the entire volunteer participation aspect of the campaign, both before our kickoff meetings and afterward. Direct contact with each volunteer on the part of the leadership at regular intervals throughout the selling period is a must. The knowledge that there is an ongoing reporting procedure, and that their results or lack of them are being checked and noted, is of importance to the volunteers and will have an affirmative effect on our sales. Conversely, if there appears to be an unspoken, tacit gentlewoman's agreement between the leadership and the volunteers that, "We'll give you the kits and from then on its strictly up to you," and, "We'll come to the meeting and take the kits if there are no questions asked later," then you can well assume that our campaign will suffer.

When a support group of a performing arts group fails us, it is especially harmful to the project, because frequently, when we are under the illusion that we are getting help, we do not make any other moves to cover that particular promotional front, thus setting off a chain reaction of failure in our campaign.

On the other hand, when volunteer efforts succeed, the benefits to the performing arts organizations involved can be considerable. Space limitations do not permit me to mention all of the women's volunteer units which have impressed me with their ability to generate successful subscription-selling campaigns. However, I feel that the women's committee of the Cincinnati Symphony Orchestra deserves an accolade for its efficiency and aggressive spirit. For, as I write this, it has recently made a splendid, sustained contribution on a number of levels to a drive which has brought that orchestra from 11,800 to 17,000 subscriptions, a new, all-time high in its 80-year history. My hat is off, too, to the remarkable women's association of the Columbus (Ohio) Symphony Orchestra, which makes subscribing a membership requirement, has already found 1,000 members, and is sparking the orchestra's expansion plans. And, I have always been rapt in my admiration for the Ravinia Festival Association (Highland Park, Ill.) women's ticket book committee, now 900 strong, which annually accounts for more than a half-million dollars worth of pre-season sales and has been doing this remarkable job for more than 40 years now. Certainly, too, we must admire the beautifully organized Seattle Repertory Theatre women's volunteer force in the subscription destiny of that company since the first season-ticket sale began there in 1964. Their "Ring the Rep" telephone blitzes could well serve as models for this kind of promotion. They have done their fair share in building a vital, committed subscription audience in Seattle of more than 20,000 theatregoers.

I do not suggest that those guilds which may be bringing in substantial sums of money in fund-raising efforts stop doing so in order to work on subscription. For instance, the women's board of Lyric Opera of Chicago, continuing to bring in more than $600,000 toward annual operating costs, is currently honorably exempted from a major role in series-ticket selling, but would participate if the company were not enjoying a succession of sellout seasons which are the result of earlier years of concentration on audience building. But those auxiliary groups which are not out fund-raising, or may be doing so only in a minor way, ought to get into the subscription-sales promotion area as *the* big way in which they can support their respective performing arts organizations.

Two special characteristics of those women's auxiliary groups which seem to succeed best in audience-building drives are: (1) basic recognition on their part that this activity is the primary level on which their performing arts organization ought to be assisted, and (2) a very high percentage of their membership should be enrolled as subscribers. The image of the Billie Burke clubwomen, charming but insipid, functioning largely as party givers for visiting maestros and other arts celebrities, is just a stereotype. Members of many more of our various guilds, associations, committees, etc. can make great contributions to our subscription-ticket selling.

# 10

## *A New Building's Going Up— "Dower It Like a Bride"*

Is your organization about to get a new home, a magnificent, luxurious structure that you've dreamed about, prayed for and worked toward all these years? If so, do not assume that all of your audience development problems are about to be automatically solved. The mere knowledge in the community of a new playhouse or auditorium in the offing with all of the allure that it promises to the public, will not necessarily cause thousands of new season subscribers to come out of the cracks by themselves, without any special effort on your part.

Unquestionably, a new building possesses an inherent excitement factor which, if exploited, can result in an immediate subscription gain for an ongoing performing arts group. For a new organization, which is to function for the first time in the new building, it could mean starting life in the new home with a very large subscribed audience. If the factor of the new building is exploited a little, there will be mild results. If it is exploited a lot, you will sell subscriptions in ratio. And, though you might find it hard to believe, if not exploited at all, the new building might get you virtually *no* new subscribers and even fewer renewals than you achieved the year before. One well-known orchestra managed to turn that trick. It moved into its multimillion dollar structure and promptly performed to a smaller subscription audience and less overall attendance than it did the year before when it performed in "the old barn." This disastrous beginning set off a seven-year cycle of continuously declining attendance which was, at long last, emphatically reversed through a major subscription drive that finally filled the building in its eighth year.

Other symphony orchestras, long in advance of moving into their new buildings and aware of the special opportunity which should not be missed, put on a very large-scale effort. Such big increases were achieved in subscription that major expansions of performance seasons became mandatory, leading to further subscription gains in the hundreds of percent and a succession of sold-out seasons ever since.

The failure of one resident professional theatre to generate a successful enough subscription campaign in conjunction with its move to a long dreamed-of new playhouse, combined with a failure of its fund-raising activities, put itself out of existence in short order after it had survived for 20 years in its old quarters. On the other hand, at least half a dozen resident theatres have used their new playhouse opportunities to double their audiences immediately, while another half-dozen, born at the same time as their buildings, began their producing lives by promoting tremendous attendance, the momentum of which has brought them continuous growth and development in the seasons that followed.

Thus, it is clear that it can go either way with a new house. You can miss the boat, and suffer the consequences. Or, you can start out on top. It depends very much on what you do about the special audience development possibility that is built into the new building. However, if you have missed the boat but are still somehow there for the next season, experience has shown that you can still salvage your situation.

One case in point, for example, where a new building's subscription-selling potential was not originally taken advantage of, but in which this unfortunate neglect was later redressed with excellent results, was that of the Dallas Theatre Center. Thirteen years after moving into its splendid Frank Lloyd Wright-designed playhouse, the theatre made a major move to increase its subscribed audience and succeeded in doing so, to the tune of an immediate 221% gain, leading to a succession of gains in the seasons that followed.

A basic component of its intensive campaign was the large-scale distribution of a brochure which devoted its center spread to depicting in photographs and delineating in strong wordage the marvels of the physical setting in which this company's plays were presented—and reminding the public that its architect was not just any architect, that he just happened to be one of the legendary gods of this field. Below large, panoramic photographs of the theatre's interior (showing a packed house and a performance in progress on its thrust stage) and exterior (showing some of the landscaping), there was a large panel, containing a photograph of Mr. Wright, with a caption reading:

**We're proud of our stunning, luxurious theatre center, containing one of the most perfect chambers for the enjoyment of playgoing ever conceived and constructed on this continent.**

And then, the panel stated:

**All of the genius of the late, great Frank Lloyd Wright is reflected in this striking building—this perfect synthesis of this creativity and inspiration, plus stone, metal, wood, fabric and the vaulting aspirations of a dynamic, burgeoning American metropolis. This adventure in architecture has brought an endless stream of visitors from throughout the world to marvel at our Dallas Theatre Center's Kalita Humphreys Theatre. For this giant among twentieth century architects set our dramatic, cantilevered playhouse, with its superb staging facilities, perfect visibility and remarkable acoustical properties, in a grassy glade, in the heart of a green, wooded area—so that here, in idyllic surroundings, but only minutes from the heart of town, you can find the relaxation, excitement, entertainment and exaltation that only the living stage at its best can provide... in a setting that is in consonance with the center's widely respected artistic standards.**

One of the reasons we sometimes don't really put on that all-out subscription campaign for the new building is unwillingness on the part of the people in charge to consider the cost of doing so as an integral part of the capital investment in the overall project. We do not blanch at raising and spending millions of dollars for the bricks, mortar and equipment required. For this, we understand to be necessary expense. But the idea of making a concomitant capital investment in organizing an audience that will be committed to attend all the performances which are going to be presented in that building—an audience large enough to fill it, from the opening night on—is something that rarely finds acceptance. By allocating sufficient funds, we could dower the building like a bride, but with a house full of audience instead of a house full of furniture. Thus, we can establish instant success on the attendance level and begin the process of drawing dividends on the investment in the form of annual subscription renewals for years to come. However, subscription campaign funds for the first season in the new building are not usually provided on a capital basis, but must come out of the operating budget of that first season, and artistic needs will most often take over the majority of available funds. Artists' fees, staff salaries, costumes, scenery and all the demands of the art simply eat up so much of the budget that only a minor percentage of the overall expenditure for the season will remain to be allotted to the promotion of ticket sales. Yet, the lack of audiences may be the most continuing, nagging problem that the performing arts organization will face in its new building. That symphony orchestra, with the seven-year continuous drop in attendance (Three more years of decline at that rate and they would have only been able to perform at rehearsals, since there would have been no audience at all!), boasted a world-renowned conductor and 90-some handpicked instrumentalists, performing its excellent programming with famed soloists, in an $11 million concert hall. It had everything—*except* an audience. It had not invested in a great subscription effort when it first moved into the new building and, to make matters worse, it had continued to make insufficient promotional expenditures in subsequent seasons. And, attempting to sell single tickets from concert to concert is a very frustrating experience—just ask any symphony orchestra manager.

We have seen some new buildings go up, with all of the costly ingredients: marble from Carrara, splashing fountains in the courtyard, massive abstract sculptures in the lobbies, dressing rooms more luxurious than the Istanbul Hilton, theatre seats so deeply cushioned that patrons, once sunk in, may disappear forever, turntable stages and electronic, computerized lighting installations so complex that it may take years before anybody learns how to make them work. And then there are the generous complements of artists and technicians and the lavish physical productions for the ambitious repertoire planned. All of this requires fortunes and years of advance planning, fund-raising, hiring and firing successive platoons of architects, constructing, equipping, and so on, ad infinitum. Finally, it is a few months or a few weeks before the opening, and somebody might (or might not) ask the question, "What about the audience that is supposed to fill up this place? What has been done about that?" Here, years have gone into the bringing about of that happy day when the building will open, and the audience, presumably for whom we have done all this, is the last thing to come into our calculations.

It seems that arts-folk tend to depend upon miracles, and producing an unending series of hits would certainly fall into that category, not only for nonprofit companies, but for commercial show business as well. Miracles, like when the Red Sea parted and my ancestors walked safely through, come few and far between. And to be reasonable, doesn't an even benign Providence have more important miracles to perform, in our troubled generation, than filling theatres and concert halls with recalcitrant single-ticket buyers? So, I argue for making a capital investment in audience building and not only in money, but in the energies of all those to whom our projects are dear. A combination of promotional monies well-spent and a barn-raising scale of cooperative effort on the volunteer level in the community is necessary.

While I have been arguing here for an increased understanding of the special opportunity for major subscription promotion that is given to us whenever we are in the process of moving to a new building, I have not spoken about an opportunity of virtually equal dimension, in the one that is present if we move to a remodeled building. The fact that it is not entirely new from the foundation up makes little difference in its potential for sparking an enormous rise in an ongoing performing arts company's subscribership, or for assisting a beginning organization in signing up a big, committed following before it ever presents its first show.

Some of the most successful "new" performing arts buildings on this continent have been remodeled ones. For instance, Actors Theatre of Louisville made successive conversions of an old railroad depot and an old bank; the St. Louis, Pittsburgh and Vancouver orchestras converted Powell, Heinz and Orpheum halls—all magnificent former vintage vaudeville houses. All four of these organizations have enjoyed considerable subscription success in their "new" homes, not only because they made the moves, but because they exploited the selling power of the moves.

How do you talk about your remodeled performing arts home in your brochure and in your other advertising? Here's some of the prose from the Pittsburgh Symphony's brochure, which was circulated on a scale which had, up to then, been unprecedented in its area. It certainly boasted no less of the wonders of its "new" Heinz Hall than have other performing arts institutions of their 100% new-from-the-ground-up structures, when it said:

**Here, in a miracle of reconstruction, is the home of the Pittsburgh Symphony Orchestra. In this acoustically perfect, climate-controlled auditorium, you will enjoy perfect audibility and visibility from every one of its deep-cushioned, spacious, red plush-covered seats . . . luxuriously appointed . . . in the heart of downtown Pittsburgh, with ample parking and restaurants nearby. . . . Picture the splendor of the new Concert Hall as you enter the Grand Lobby. Magnificent crystal chandeliers and lighting fixtures are set off against off-white walls decorated with richly colored panels. Gleaming marble columns and great gold-leafed Baroque pillars add to the luster of the 42-foot, four-story high Grand Window, sure to become the landmark of the new Concert Hall. And as you leave the Grand Lobby, you'll proceed through luxuriously carpeted auditorium lobbies and foyers, enriched with gold and red velvet draperies and sparkling crystal. The auditorium's warm, white interior glitters with gold leaf and crystal, setting off that red plush**

**seating. Every one of the 2,700 seats has an unobstructed view of the great stage. The new Concert Hall is certain to be the showplace of Pittsburgh....5,000 parking spaces are available within a two-block area of the theatre. And, of course, public transportation to all parts of the city is nearby. No matter where you live, you'll find getting to the new Concert Hall is easy....You are invited to become a Charter Subscriber.**

For more nice words and apt phrases that might assist you in describing the physical facilities of your new or old "new" building, please see the chapter later in this book on methods of writing brochure copy.

Whether your new performing arts home is a really spanking new one, or a new building only in the sense of its being, like Heinz Hall, "a miracle of reconstruction," the ways by which it can be dowered with those big "charter" subscription audiences right from the time you move in, are the same ways, in the main, which are proposed, examined and explained in other chapters of this manual. However, in your case there is a promotional advantage that those organizations not having new or remodeled homes cannot share. If you utilize this boon imaginatively and aggressively, you will most likely achieve hitherto undreamed-of success in series-ticket sales.

When should you start beating the drum about the new building? Even years ahead, if you know definitely that it is going to happen. Each season, as you approach the one when the actual move will be made, is another opportunity for you to sell more subscriptions than you would otherwise by offering permanent priority seating in the magnificent new playhouse or hall, to those farsighted subscribers who have the intelligence and initiative to "get in on the ground floor," thus staking out their claims far ahead of time. Let us say that it takes three years from the time of the initial announcement to the completion of the promised new facility. The brochure in that year can trumpet this good news strongly. The brochure of the second year might contain architectural renderings and photographs of the artistic director and board leaders, wearing their rakish "hard hats" as they are inspecting the building under construction. Then, in the third year, just prior to moving in, you go all out in the brochure outlining all the "goodies" awaiting charter subscribers. Tell them that the opening will be "the talk of the town," describe some of the gala opening social events for subscribers only, inform them that the names of charter subscribers will be listed in the commemorative program, and point out that a new "culture bus" route will service the new hall from the main residential areas at performance times. If your season is already close to sold-out, warn them that even though the palatial new hall is 50% larger than the old one, they may not get a seat if they don't subscribe. Show them pictures of the best features of the new or remodeled facilities. One company even went so far as to provide in the brochure a designer's rendering of the soft, swiveling, reclining seats in which audience members would be able to wallow while watching the performances.

In a contrasting situation, I was once assigned to consult with a more than 100-year-old organization which had, by the fell clutch of circumstance, been forced to announce that for the next season the concerts would be switched from a beautiful, recently built auditorium to an older, much less desirable one, which had the ultimate in defects where their comfort-loving subscribers were concerned. It had wooden seats! Perhaps an adjective is lacking in that last sentence. It had *hard* wooden seats. The subscribers dropped out in droves and single-ticket buyers, normally scarce as hens' teeth, disappeared from the scene entirely. It is human to find reasons to justify our failures. When those reasons are admittedly pretty good ones, they can lead to promotional inertness and "Why even try?" becomes the call to disarm.

When I arrived there, I wondered why portable seat cushions had not been placed atop the slats of the chairs, but above all, I wondered why the management and board, knowing that they faced this handicap, had not compensated with a subscription campaign on a much larger scale and of much greater intensity, which seemed to me only logical. Stopping to think about it, the staff and board of this organization agreed. With the hard, wooden seats still to look forward to for the following year, they geared up for and carried out a subscription-selling effort that, by their past standards, was tremendous (including large-scale brochure distribution). In so doing, they not only boosted subscription by 74%, but went "clean," selling out entirely in advance; whereupon they proceeded to increase the number of performances for the next season by 100%! So, here we see that promotion hath power to sooth the ravaged backside, too. Or is it simply that when the house is full, the audience tends to think that everything is better than it might really be?

Should a carpenters' or a plasterers' strike—or any other catastrophe—stall the opening for another year, why, you just go on selling even more subscriptions, on the ground that paradise may be postponed but that when the gates finally do open, it will still be paradise and will have well been worth the wait. During that anxious year, you will tell all of your subscribers—the old-timers and the new ones who have been signing up in response to the promise of the new building (drawn as moths to the flame)—that you will, like an aging actress doing still one more farewell tour, perform for yet another season at your beloved, old location. And when you finally *do* move into the new, wonderful home, they will appreciate it all the more—and, do you know what? So will you.

# 11

# Treatment of Subscribers at the Ticket Wicket: Exchanges

Subscribers, for all of the countless reasons spoken of in this handbook, deserve and ought to get the best of treatment in any contacts they may have with our subscription department and box office. All personnel dealing with our cherished series-ticket holders should be strongly, and affirmatively, indoctrinated on this point. We are likely to have many direct contacts with a considerable number of the members of our extended subscriber family for, hopefully, many years after they have initially signed up. We will be talking to them and seeing them in the process of their renewing from season to season, when they may be negotiating for improved seat locations or for a change in the night of their series, when they want to exchange their tickets for another night, or when they invoke their subscriber's privilege of obtaining priority treatment for their own relatives and friends whom they may wish to bring in as new subscribers. It is conceivable that one of our hard-pressed box office staff might find himself unreasonably badgered by a subscriber bent on obtaining his heart's desire, for example, no less than a switch to the seat locations belonging for many years to somebody else, who is possibly our largest financial contributor. It is not easy for our man in such sticky situations. Diplomacy, tact and charm are of the essence. The abilities to please, placate and defuse, are very important in the box office of ongoing nonprofit performing arts institutions which sell tickets to seasons rather than to individual attractions.

When an organization needs to hold the sale of subscriptions open until very close to the beginning of the season, or right up to the first curtain—or even, in the case of some resident professional theatres, right through the run of the first play—it often means a hassle with the box office employees, who chafe under any such extensions because they want to clear the decks for the handling of single tickets. This problem is especially true in situations where large-scale subscription promotion is a recent innovation, and the box office ticket sellers tend to look at it as an intrusion on their normal way of life. When we sell enough subscriptions, it finally dawns on them that the business of selling individual tickets has become a very minor part of their work, and they then make the adaptation in their thinking.

However, some performing arts groups have their tickets sold through privately operated, commercial, central box offices, which may serve a number of projects. In these cases, the box office employees may be bitter enemies of subscription, which they feel is detrimental when a hit does come along. From their viewpoint, it is better for us to have few or no subscribers and to take a beating for five shows in a row, as long as the sixth one is a hit. While corruption at the wicket is rare in our nonprofit companies, it has certainly not been unknown—particularly in some of the larger cities. However, the best insurance against this kind of hanky-panky is when most or all of the tickets are in the hands of subscribers before the season begins. The chances for such skullduggery may well increase in direct ratio to the number of tickets not sold in advance on subscription.

Often, simply for their own convenience, box office personnel may insist upon cutting off renewals or new sales long before they should. I recall the case of a harassed theatre company manager who foolishly permitted his ticket-selling staff to decide for him that they already had all the subscriptions they needed, and despite the fact that sales were coming in heavily, they stopped taking orders. Thousands of subscribers were turned away in the crucial period just before the initial season of this new project was to begin. The young and quite inexperienced box office staff's arrogant error almost closed up the theatre since single-ticket sales later did not develop to anywhere near the volume they had predicted. Those turned-away subscriptions were sorely missed, and only heroic exertions on the part of the company's leadership closed the resulting financial gap and enabled the theatre to continue. In another case—a classic, I should say—a strong-willed promotional director successfully fought back the box office staff's insistence on a premature deadline date, got a last minute reprieve from the general manager, and went on to sell an additional 4,100 subscriptions.

In still another situation, where there had been a late start in the subscription drive because the list of plays had not been definitely decided in time to get enough brochures into circulation, the audience development practitioner defied the box office staff, sent out an additional large mailing, and thus brought in 1,700 more subscriptions than would otherwise have been sold. Although the box office employees screamed, they found ways to accommodate those late subscribers. These 6,800 seats might have gone empty. Instead, for a four-play season, they were filled, and 1,200 of those late subscribers renewed for the season that followed, at the negligible sales cost, by the way, of 30¢ each.

The problem of exchanges—that is, when a subscriber is unable to attend on one of his scheduled dates and would like to exchange his tickets for another performance of the same presentation—is one that vexes many box office employees. There are, of course, certain situations in which exchanges of tickets are not possible. For instance, in a series of concerts where there is only one performance of each event. In the cases of many opera companies, where there are only a few performances of each work, options for exchange are very limited. Thus, exchanges are virtually never mentioned in the brochures of symphony orchestras, concert managements, opera and dance companies. However, in the case of resident theatres, which may run each play of the season for three, four or five weeks (or more), for seven or eight performances per week, there are often fairly good possibilities for exchanges to accommodate subscribers. Even when there is a very high subscription rate in relation to the capacity, additional exchange possibilities develop when a Monday night subscriber asks for an exchange to Thursday night, while a Thursday night subscriber is trying to get Monday night tickets, and so on. The exchange privilege, when it can be offered, is highly prized by subscribers and is undoubtedly a factor in many decisions to subscribe. For even when the privilege is rarely, if ever, invoked, it is a psychological escape hatch for some people who would otherwise feel locked into an inflexible schedule of attendance or feel that they might sustain a loss if they couldn't use a ticket to one of the performances because of illness or having to be out of town. Many box office employees tend to become annoyed by the traffic in exchanges and their resentment is felt by the subscribers who are, after all, only asking for what has been promised them—that our theatre will exchange for another performance *of the same play* if tickets are available on the requested date. It should be pointed out to the box office crews of theatres where the bulk of the season's tickets are subscribed (meaning that the amount of work they have to do in selling single tickets is minimal) that once the season is in progress, they will have precious little to do but handle the subscriber's exchange requests, and that this procedure should be carried out with grace.

One kind of request we do *not* wish to accommodate is that calling for an exchange to a performance of a *different play of the series*. To honor such a request would strike a blow at one of the vital concepts of our subscription offer—that the subscriber contracts with us to attend all of the plays of the series. If he is to be permitted to ignore some of the plays and to double up his tickets for others (taking along friends or relatives on those occasions), we are back to the evils of single-ticket buying, and how will we ever develop an audience with an appreciation of a wider repertoire? However, we should try our best to effect virtually any other kind of request for an exchange, and to do it with a smile.

The telephone operator who answers all the calls coming in to our switchboard is a goodwill ambassador for our organization and a nonprofit performing arts institution certainly needs all kinds of goodwill in the community. But it is specifically the subscription-processing department and our entire ticket-selling apparatus, usually summed up in the two words *box office*, that is directly responsible for the success or failure of our relations with those people who are so important to us, our subscribers.

# 12

## Clipping Coupons:
### Renewal, Conversion of Single-Ticket Buyers and Recovery of Dropouts

The initial order of business in a subscription campaign is the renewal of the current season's subscribers for the season to come. However, the fact that we usually begin this phase of our drive first does not mean that we have to wait until the renewal is over, which might be a matter of months, before beginning the sale of new subscriptions. In the past, many arts organizations have thought that they could only offer new subscriptions after they had come to the end of the renewal period, and could thus tell the season- or series-ticket purchaser exactly what seat locations had become available, as a result of unrenewed subscriptions. More and more, we have begun soliciting new subscriptions within a few days and up to a few weeks following the launching of renewal, thus taking renewal and new orders simultaneously. This method enlarges our time element for new sales, which is a very important advantage. We have found that we can just take new subscription orders as they come in and assign the seat locations later, following the completion of the renewal effort. Of course, for those groups having a form of subscription which does not offer specific seating, there is no problem at all. There are always some purchasers who will want to know, before committing their money, exactly where they are going to sit. However, once it is known that an arts organization deals fairly on seat assignments, according to the date of application arrival (and within any system of priorities which may be stated in the brochure), pressures of this kind tend to lessen. And above all, the demands concerning specific seat locations diminish in direct ratio to how sold-out the performances were last season.

The number of weeks or months during which the re-enrollment of established subscribers is taken, will vary according to circumstances. One group, needing subscribers badly, might hold its renewal open much longer than another group which is very successful, and can thus afford to enforce an early deadline date.

Overall, continuing good relations with the subscribers are a logical prerequisite to obtaining the largest possible annual renewal. I would suggest that it makes sense to maintain some regular communication with the subscribers through newsletters, or through a journal or house organ at least several times during the year, containing news, photographs and feature material concerning the performing arts company, its productions, its plans. In this way, we heighten the sense of our subscribers' involvement with us, increase the level of their interest and commitment—for we are then not just dealing with them as customers with whom we communicate only at the time we need their renewal.

Because our already hard-won subscribers have been winnowed out of the chaff, or in a few cases might have voluntarily revealed themselves as members of that minority with a special willingness to accept what we have to offer, we must approach each renewal drive with the resolve that we will not, by any omission on our part, lose one subscriber more than is dictated by the effects of transiency and mortality.

What is a good renewal rate? It naturally tends to be higher where the subscriberships are older and more established and where the artistic success is the greatest. And not unreasonably, renewal can easily be affected negatively where there is subscriber dissatisfaction. We know that even within the elite taste represented by our subscriberships, a more popular repertoire and an element of increased star strength for the coming season are likely to elicit a higher renewal response. The existence of a new building or the appointment of a new artistic director could, if exploited well, bring a higher renewal than in the past. There are really so many varying circumstances involved that one cannot specifically answer the question about a good renewal rate, any more than one can give a single, specific reply to the question, "What is a good rate of return for direct mailing?" However, I will say this: A good renewal rate, according to the various conditions found in different performing arts groups, could be anywhere between 60% and 90%. I was most recently thrilled to learn that the Baltimore Symphony Orchestra has achieved a 99% renewal figure, possibly an all-time record in our field, indicating that the subscribers love their orchestra and are impervious to the transiency of our times; that the symphony management has carried out a superb renewal drive; and that death has indeed taken a long holiday in that area.

A definitely bad return would be anything below the 50% mark and if it were to become a pattern, season after season, the survival of the organization would be highly doubtful. For, implicit in my entire concept of arts subscription is that a larger or smaller majority—but a *majority*—of the subscribers will renew each year, and then we will replace the attrition and acquire many new ones, too. Only then can the project function in a healthy way. Only then can the expansion of operations, the increase in length of season, the new buildings with their better facilities, become possible. Faced with the almost impossible task of annually replacing more than half of the subscribers, just to get even with the previous season, the promotional arm (even a very effective one) might not be able to cope. After all, in what we know is a somewhat limited potential for "our thing" in the overall population, we will soon go through all the possibilities for new blood candidates and will not be able to balance the inordinate drain on our subscriber base caused by such a large percentage of dropouts.

For an organization which wants to achieve a higher renewal percentage than ever before, there can be no cavalier treatment of the recalcitrants who have not yet been heard from in the latter stages of the drive. To begin with, we should prepare our materials carefully for the struggle. I have introduced to many organizations a type of printed renewal form which was first suggested to me by a bright fund-raiser some years ago, and which is now in very wide use. It is not a bill but has the appearance of a statement and is a clear form for reordering. Its effect is one of assuming rather than soliciting the renewal. It is most often made in triplicate, with carbon sheets between each of the three copies which are printed in different colors (say, white, pink and yellow), and it can be sent at three different stages of the renewal drive, each time accompanied by different letters, subscription brochures or other inserts, according to our individual promotional plans. The white one might have boldly printed on it, "Renewal Notice," the pink one "Second Renewal Notice," and the yellow one, "Third and Final Renewal Notice." The statement or notice has the subscriber's name and address on it. It contains such information as his specific seat locations and the price. It also has places for him to check whether he is making partial payment, enclosing the full amount or asking to be billed, and so on. It even contains a place for him to ask for a switch in the night of his series, a different price or location of seat, etc. All the information is typed once on the first copy, which, because of the carbon sheets, suffices for the second and third copies, too. Through the use of window envelopes (which do not have to be the standard number 10 size, but can be obtained to fit the statements and enclosures without folding them, if we want it that way), no further typing is necessary.

We must bear in mind that we have made a previous investment in expenditure of money and energy in obtaining almost all our subscribers, and it is through their annual renewal that we obtain the interest payments—the audience dividends—that are due us. In effect, our continuing subscribers are the accumulated audience capital from which we "clip coupons" in the form of assured attendance for our performances each season. I estimate that it costs 10 to 30 times as much in promotional expenditures to obtain a new subscriber as it does to obtain the renewal of a previous one. For instance, in a subscription campaign in which a total of a million dollars worth of series tickets were sold, $750,000 came in on renewal at a cost of $4,400, while the next $250,000 was arrived at in new sales, at a cost of $45,000. It was certainly well worth it for that organization to "buy" that quarter-million dollars worth of new subscriptions for $45,000, but what made it an even sweeter deal was that just one year later those new subscribers became eligible to join that $4,400 club, to be renewed by us for peanuts.

It is important to foster in every possible way a consciousness on the part of the subscribers that renewal time is at hand. For example, in a theatre, beginning with at least two plays before the current season's conclusion, the printed program should contain, ideally at its center spread, a double-page ad for the season to come, with the idea of renewing one's subscription strongly put forth. If the early edition of the brochure is ready, it should be inserted into the program. There should be attractive subscription booths set up in strategic locations in the lobbies, with volunteer workers or staff members manning them, so that when the subscribers arrive, come out for intermissions, and leave, we can sign them up right there. The Alley Theatre of Houston, for instance, annually renews thousands of its subscribers in this manner. At each performance during this period, short and effective talks about renewal should be made from the stage by the artistic director, the general manager or a member of the acting company. In some symphony orchestra organizations, it has been the custom to present orchids or roses to subscribers whose renewal has already been received, or who re-enroll at a particular concert, prior to the current season's end. Sometimes, special bonuses are devised as extra incentives for early renewal, which leaves room for much individuality and originality—two things highly prized by so many people connected with the promotion of the performing arts. However, in the remainder of this section of my book, I shall try to suggest that along with the kind of renewal

# Lyric Opera
## OF CHICAGO

SUITE 648
312-346-6111

20 NORTH WACKER DRIVE
CHICAGO. IL 60606

Please indicate change of address below:

_____

_____

_____

☐ **Please renew my subscription seats**

| Series | No. of Seats | Location | Price Per Subscription |
|--------|--------------|----------|------------------------|

## RENEWAL DEADLINE:
## May 3, 1977

**1977 RENEWAL ORDER FORM**
Please <u>do not</u> request individual performances at this time.

Mr. and Mrs. Homer L. Smith, Jr.
3271 Orchard Street
Oak Park, Illinois  60303

RESIDENCE PHONE          BUSINESS PHONE

**TOTAL AMOUNT DUE: $_____**

Although your present seats will be held for you until the renewal deadline date, we would appreciate receiving your renewal order at the earliest possible date to expedite processing.

**TO RENEW YOUR SUBSCRIPTION**
Please check the box above.

My check for *$ _____
is enclosed, payable to Lyric Opera.
* Minimum 50% payment required.
No refunds or exchanges after September 8.

☐ I will NOT be renewing.
   You may release my seats.

**DO NOT WRITE IN THIS SPACE**
(For Office Use)

Date _____

Amt. $ _____

Contr. $ _____

IF you wish to change your series or section please list both a first and second choice. If you select a different series from your 1976 series, we cannot guarantee the same or comparable seating.

| 1st Preference | | 2nd Preference | |
|---|---|---|---|
| Series | | Series | |
| No. of seats | | No. of seats | |
| Location:<br>**Check**<br>√<br>**One** | Main Floor<br>Box<br>First Balcony<br>Upper Balcony | Location:<br>**Check**<br>√<br>**One** | Main Floor<br>Box<br>First Balcony<br>Upper Balcony |
| Price per Series $ | | Price per Series $ | |

Contributors and Guild Members receive priority in seating locations contingent upon availabilities.

**THIS FORM MUST BE RETURNED WITH YOUR PAYMENT**

*The first page of a sample renewal form, printed in triplicate* activities just described, we should have an ongoing process of careful, and in-depth mail and telephone follow-ups to all subscribers to the current season who have not yet been heard from concerning the upcoming season.

Let us say that an arts company begins its renewal drive on March 1 and concludes it on May 31, after which the new sales continue until the beginning of the coming fall season. In that case, the mailing of the original white copy of the statement should be sent on March 1, along with the brochure (or if the brochure for any reason is not yet ready, then a letter from the management and a sheet containing basic information about the season to come). By the end of March, we will already have a certain number of renewals. So, in effect, we take their record cards out of the current season's "shoebox" and put them into another "shoebox" marked "next season." (I do realize that many of our arts groups are very sophisticated in their record keeping—perhaps even computerized. However, the "shoebox" example is very basic, and I tend to think of the process in this simplistic way.) Now, as the campaign progresses, simply by looking into the two shoeboxes, and comparing the number of cards in each, we know how we are doing on renewal, on a day-to-day basis.

On April 1, the second or pink copy of the statement goes out to all those subscribers who have not been heard from yet, along with a brochure and a letter exulting in the extraordinary number of renewal orders which have already come in (assuming that the facts support the claim); the letter should respectfully remind the recipients that this is the time for renewal and perhaps explain that their early reordering will help us, their favorite nonprofit arts producers, in preventing a bottleneck in the final days and weeks of subscription processing, thus saving us money for extra manpower in that department. Another type of enclosure, by the way, which can go into any of the three statement mailings would be a photo reprint of a favorable article about us which might have recently appeared in a newspaper or a magazine.

On May 1, we issue the third or yellow copy of the statement, perhaps accompanied by another edition of the brochure. Perhaps, up to this point, as many organizations do, we have been sending our established subscriber group a brochure especially created for the renewal purpose. Now, the third time around, we might enclose the other, much more powerful brochure which we have been using on another front in the campaign to bring in new subscribers. We have, up to this point in the renewal effort, treated our own subscribers quite gently, and the brochure we have been sending them may have been a very low-key one, since it assumed that they didn't have to be convinced about us as strongly as a stranger.

Each time we go to the well in a renewal campaign, we find that we get still more results. We should not give in to the amateurish concern about annoying people with persistent efforts in this connection. We must school ourselves to think that the only sins we can commit in our renewal drives are those of omission, when we do not go often enough to that well. We might find that for every person who expresses annoyance, there might be many others who will thank us for our keeping after them, saying, "We just sort of let it go. We didn't realize that we were so close to the deadline, and we really wouldn't think of giving up our subscription." Or, "We were out of town a great deal and would have forgotten if you hadn't been so conscientious in reaching us." Our experience is that the majority of the recalcitrants (those we don't hear from as the campaign has progressed to a later stage), are very pleasant and do express appreciation for being reminded when we begin to telephone them, after the final statement has presumably been received and some days have passed.

Thus, going back to the chronology of our renewal push (statements having been mailed on March 1, April 1 and May 1), we take to the telephone on May 15 and in the two weeks from that date to the campaign's official conclusion on May 31, track down each recalcitrant, either at home or office (the subscription forms on which they have ordered in the past asked them to fill in both daytime and nighttime telephone numbers). There are some people, however, whom we simply can't reach by phone, no matter how often we try. Ideally, had we enough volunteer and staff workers, we ought to visit them in person. They are not strangers to us. They have been attending our performances. They have a taste for our art form. They even know the way to our playhouse, opera house or concert hall. Some of them may have been subscribers for years. We have much in common with them, and they with us. How can we just let them go without doing everything possible to prevent it? We should only reconcile ourselves to their loss if we have proof that they have moved to another distant city or, unfortunately, if they are deceased.

By the way, we have obtained excellent results in reaching people who never seemed to be in when we tried to get them by phone, through the use of facsimile telegrams or Mailgrams. Regular telegrams are now impractical because of their high cost and the difficulty in getting them delivered. In phoning renewal prospects, it is best to set up a routine and then to supervise a methodical calling to both daytime and evening telephone numbers, to see to it that every person not reached on the first call is followed up on until reached. Each still recalcitrant subscriber's card should be clearly marked with the pertinent information after each call is tried so that we will know exactly what has transpired in each case. Many subscribers who may have been intending to drop out can be won back to us after they have had a chance to get complaints off their chests to our sympathetic telephone operators.

### SAMPLE TIMETABLE FOR RENEWAL CAMPAIGN

| | |
|---|---|
| March 1 | First mailing to full subscriber list |
| April 1 | Second notice mailing |
| May 1 | Third notice mailing |
| May 15 | Telephone campaign to recalcitrants |
| May 31 | Official conclusion of campaign |
| June 15 | End of "grace" period (if appropriate) |

In one of my projects, a famous American symphony orchestra, a very experienced, sophisticated, professional telephoner has been employed for those phases of the subscription drive having to do with the gathering of renewals and the retrieval of dropouts. He tells me that his most effective line of approach has been "listening." By listening carefully, he is able to respond to each case on an individual basis. By hearing them out if they have criticisms (perhaps they wanted Tchaikovsky and they got John Cage, or they felt there were too many piano soloists and they happen to lean toward violinists), he provides the catharsis which earns their gratitude, thus leading to the sale. Also, while listening, he has the time in which to think over a response to the points they have raised. "Listening," he says, "is as great a selling tool as any 'pitch' can be."

While I would not recommend it in all situations, when there is a larger than usual number of dropouts from the subscriber lists, it may be advisable to create a "grace period," much as the insurance companies do, so that even though the subscriber has technically lapsed his subscription by not renewing in time, we find the small type in the policy, so to speak, that justifies this extension of time. We write to the lapsed subscribers, explaining that we look upon them as members of our subscriber family, that we find it hard to accept their withdrawal from our subscriber ranks, and that the door is still open to them until the end of the grace period, say on June 15. To those whom we never reached by phone, we might say that something must have gone wrong.

Maybe they were away on a long overseas trip, didn't receive their mail and have just returned. Or perhaps they moved without letting us know, and the post office did not forward all our letters to their new address—the idea being, though not stated in so many words, that nobody in his right mind, unless he somehow never found out about our forthcoming season, would possibly have failed to resubscribe, not only to all the goodies that we have to offer, but to an organization so worthwhile as ours.

Even when it appears that a recalcitrant subscriber has fallen into the classification of a full-fledged dropout, meaning that he has not been heard from by the original deadline or even by the conclusion of any grace period which may have been extended to him, I would still not consider him irretrievably lost and would approach him again in the late summer or early fall. At that time, I would offer him, not his old seat locations (which he let lapse and which we had probably already assigned to one of the thousands of new subscribers who had been beating down our doors), but the best seats available *at that late date,* on a priority basis over orders from the general public. For as long as the curtain has not yet gone up on the first performance of the season, in our hearts we think of him as a member of the subscriber family who can yet be saved from making the mistake of dropping out.

I have found a tendency in many performing arts groups to place the blame for a poor renewal percentage on the transiency of their population. In city after city, I'm told that *they* have the highest rate in the country of people moving away. They insist that there isn't much use in intensive renewal efforts; the subscribers just move to other cities in such large numbers that their efforts would be wasted. On one occasion some years ago, I was informed in a major city that they were the "transiency capital" of America, and this fact was responsible for their tepid 50% renewal level. I replied, "Let us pretend that we don't know that we have a transiency problem. Let us proceed to carry out a really intensive renewal drive, just as if nobody were going to move. Let us cover all the bases." And so, for the first time in the history of that organization, a really good renewal job was done. The renewal level went up to 70%!

While, in the foregoing pages, I have spoken of March 1 as a kickoff date for renewal efforts, I have only done so because that is often the earliest date upon which many of our organizations with seasons starting in the fall feel that they can or should begin. However, there is a great advantage in commencing renewal drives even earlier, thereby increasing the time in which to do the job and getting the money into the bank where it can earn interest over a longer period. Acting upon this suggestion, the Minnesota Orchestra began its renewal activities several months ahead of time, shooting off a simple, inexpensive "letter brochure" to its constituency on January 11. Three months later, it was happily drawing interest on the $451,000 already received. The advance letter brochure has proved, over many years of use in countless projects, to be a useful, practical tool in the early stages of renewal campaigns. It is a folded 17" x 22" sheet of paper which gives us four 8½" x 11" sides on which to give the basic information. The first page is the organization's regular letterhead and contains a communication about the season, signed by the general manager or artistic director. The second and third pages offer the pertinent series information. The fourth page has room for special features, announcements and a built-in order form in those cases where an automatic renewal order form is not enclosed with the mailing.

The worst renewal percentage I know of took place in the case of a resident theatre company where the audience's rejection amounted to an attrition of 86%! This loss meant a renewal of only 14%! This situation remains an atypical case in our field. The miraculous survival of this particular project (it did considerably improve its artistic standards and eventually reached a 70% renewal figure), was possible only because of unusual subsidy circumstances plus extraordinarily effective, strongly applied, resuscitative subscription sales strategies. On the other hand, almost as I began to write this paragraph, I received a happy phone call from another theatre management which has just achieved a rare 90% renewal rate, sparking a sharp rise in their overall subscription figure. For, only 10% of all that company's new sales must now go to replace attrition.

Unquestionably, we have a chance to convert some single-ticket buyers into subscribers. On the face of it, these sometime theatregoers are ideal prospects. They do like our arts. They do attend performances, even if irregularly. They do know the way to our opera houses, concert halls and playhouses. However, we must realistically face the truth that many of these people, despite their tendencies in our favor, will be very hard to bring into the subscriber-fold. They *like* being single-ticket buyers, in the way that some men *like* being bachelors, and they resist subscribing like those bachelors resist marriage. But not all single-ticket buyers feel that way, and they are especially good prospects for us. We must woo them by writing personalized letters, in which we let them know we know they go to some of our presenta-

# Minnesota Orchestra
## Seventy·fifth Anniversary Season
## 1977·78

Stanislaw Skrowaczewski
Music Director

January 11, 1977

TO 1976-77 IMPERIAL AND ROYAL CONCERT SERIES HOLDERS <u>ONLY</u>--

First chance to renew your seats for the Gala 75th ANNIVERSARY Season!

As one of our full season subscribers you are receiving early notice
of the forthcoming season--a year of celebration for us as the
Orchestra enters its 75th season.  Our renewal brochure will not be
going out in general circulation until the spring but we thought that
an earlier notice would be helpful to many of you and it will also
assist us in getting an advance start on processing our huge season
ticket list which now numbers more than 20,000.

<u>A Season of Beethoven</u>--In tribute to this anniversary season, the
Orchestra will present a complete cycle of Beethoven's nine symphonies.  The <u>Missa Solemnis</u> will also be performed during Easter
week.  (Note:  The Ninth Symphony will be performed on special nonsubscription concerts, September 23, 24 and 25 to which you will
receive an early opportunity to purchase tickets.)

Guest artists appearing with us this season will include violinist
Isaac Stern, pianist Claudio Arrau, cellist Leonard Rose and French
horn virtuoso Barry Tuckwell.  The heralded Soviet pianist Lazar
Berman will be making his area debut with the Minnesota Orchestra
after a truly triumphal year of concertizing throughout the United
States.

The phenomenal Eugene Ormandy will lead a roster of distinguished
guest conductors during this anniversary season including Klaus
Tennstedt and Neville Marriner as well as Leonard Slatkin.  Making
his debut with us will be the remarkable young Soviet conductor
Yuri Temirkanov.

Inside this letter you will find a listing of concert dates and
performing artists scheduled so far.  You will receive notification
of programs and the entire artist roster in March.

You help yourself and you help us by sending in the order form on
the back of this letter RIGHT NOW.  You can relax knowing your seats
are secure and assigned even before other subscribers are given this
announcement.  Orders received now will receive immediate attention.

I would like to take this opportunity to wish you a happy, healthy
and fulfilling New Year.

Sincerely yours,

Richard M. Cisek
Vice President and Managing Director

*A sample letter brochure*

tions and, because they have been exhibiting this good judgment, they might just be ready to go the rest of the way by becoming full-scale series or season subscribers. We suggest a number of reasons why *now* is the logical time for them to make that move—reasons like a new artistic director; a remodeled auditorium; a new building; the great season we have just had in which the usually blasé critics have raved their heads off; the celebrated guest artists playing key roles in the coming season; the selection of an unusually attractive repertoire; the enormous recent growth of the subscribership which clearly shows that *everybody else* is subscribing; the extra "For Subscribers Only" benefits we have only now begun to offer, such as free subscriptions to a performing arts magazine or free recordings to new subscribers; and so on and on, to the point that the single-ticket buyer who receives our letter really would have to possess phenomenal sales resistance not to capitulate.

And then, there should be follow-up letters and telephone calls to every single-ticket buyer. If some of them cannot be found at home, their office telephone numbers should be obtained if we do not already have them in our records, and they should be called at work. And, under certain considerations and in certain places, they might be visited in person. After all, they are not total strangers to us. They do attend some of our presentations, even if not all of them, and they will most likely react in a friendly manner to our efforts. The most friendly they can get, as I look at it, is to subscribe!

When we try to ferret out and obtain the use of prospect lists that will have special relevance for our subscription campaigning purposes, we should never forget that we are hardly likely to find one that is as rich in possible sales for us as our own list of dropout subscribers, going back for the past several seasons. Certainly, some of those dropouts have moved away to other cities, others may even no longer be alive, and still others may hate us so bitterly, because of some progressive programming which they feel we outrageously forced down their throats, that they may be like the salted soil of Carthage for us. However, there are usually a considerable number of our dropouts from the past several seasons, who may now be ready for a return whirl at subscription. They may not generate the movement toward us by themselves, but, if approached, they might well capitulate. For instance, there may have been a certain number of young couples who did not renew their subscriptions when they had a new baby and felt they had to stay home for the next year or two in the exercise of their parental responsibility. Now the baby is old enough, they feel, to leave for the evening with a dependable sitter. Now the couple could well re-enroll. As in the case of our single-ticket buyers, whom we are seeking to convert, we must deal with our dropouts via personalized letters, telephone calls and visits. We must remind them that, even though they seemed to have gone off somewhere without us, we still think of them as members of our extended subscriber family; we feel that there still exists a relationship between us; and we point out all of the wonderful ways in which our project has progressed and developed during the time they have been away, as well as all of the fine things that are going to be happening for the season to come.

We have managed to restore dropouts of from 5% to 20% by intensively directed efforts for this purpose. For an organization that has not been doing this work annually, there can be a potential bonanza of subscription in records of dropouts. Let us say that a performing arts group, on a plateau of about 15,000 series- or season-ticket holders, has been having a yearly attrition of 25%, which it has been replacing. Going back three years, there are then 11,250 people who have dropped out. A successful push to bring back just 15% of them, would mean a campaign component resulting in almost 1,700 subscriptions, certainly a solid contribution to the overall success of a subscription drive. Now, the job of reaching these 11,250 dropouts is not as hard as it may sound at first. To begin with, since every two subscriptions are held, on the average, in one name, we set out to contact really only half as many people as we intend to reach. Our records may show who has moved to other cities, and we are entirely spared going after those people. Because of the value of our dropouts as a campaign component, it is imperative that we should be able to go into our records and immediately identify these lapsed subscribers. Too many times I have found that there were no clear records kept, and that these names were simply thrown in with the other names on general mailing lists. We are then unable to mount this component of our campaign.

When we do a thorough job on the levels of renewal, conversion of single-ticket buyers and restoration of dropouts, we are operating at a high level of efficiency, amortizing over the years to come all of the financial and energy investment which has gone into originally bringing these people into our orbit.

## 13

## *How Can We Best Spend Our Promotional Monies?*

For many performing arts organizations, measuring out their often meager and insufficient promotional monies in an eyedropper, so to speak, the directions in which these monies are spent—and the knowledge that they are well spent—is of extreme importance. We should be constantly reviewing the criteria that influence our decisions in these matters.

But first, I think it is important to underscore that whatever decisions are made in this area, these funds are best and most efficiently expended in the pre-season subscription campaign, rather than afterward. For, as I have pointed out elsewhere in the book, it is at that stage, when the tickets are in their subscription package, that they are all salable. Considerable wasted advertising goes into fruitless attempts to sell individual tickets to attractions which the public has its reasons for not wanting to attend. That these reasons are not always valid, and that we believe the non-buyers would have found merit in these very attractions had they attended them, is beside the point.

I recently encountered a classic case which illustrates this unwise use of promotional funds. I was assigned to assist a most distinguished arts institution which had suffered years of barely 30% of its capacity on subscription, resulting in a general audience insufficiency. Upon leafing through the figures presented to me, I was shocked to find that for the previous season only $10,000 had been spent in the subscription drive, while *$87,000* had been allocated for largely futile advertising efforts to sell the huge quantities of unsubscribed tickets, $270,000 worth of which, it turned out, remained unsold. It will surely be proved during the organization's forthcoming campaign that a reversal of these expenditures—the vastly larger amount for the subscription push and the smaller sum held in reserve for single-ticket promotion—will bring about a happy, new situation. And perhaps it will not require all of the $87,000 to achieve a subscription sellout, particularly if the additional campaign components which were not previously employed, are implemented by the new management team. At any rate, a better use of the promotional funds will certainly bring in a large part or all of that missing $270,000 next season. And that money will represent a huge, new complement of subscribers. People will be going regularly to the art, where there had previously been not only the heavy financial loss but the painful morale loss for this worthwhile project, which had been deprived of its rightful audience—not by outside forces but by its own failure to initiate and maintain sound promotional policies.

## Newspaper Advertising vs. Direct Mail

While radio and even television advertising are sometimes utilized in subscription campaigning, most arts company managements will usually think in terms of their largest investments as in either direct mail or newspaper advertising. This attitude is quite a change from not many years back when major expenditures for mailings or other large distributions of brochures were virtually unknown to the promoters of nonprofit performing arts organizations.

Newspaper advertising has particular effectiveness in getting a quick box office and mail-order response for the kind of major attractions that the commercial theatrical field has to offer, far more often than it does for nonprofit performing arts groups. A commercial hit with a big-name star, taking to the road after a long run in New York, during which time it has received continuous publicity on a national level, often depends mainly and successfully upon newspaper advertising to do the selling job. However, if the press agent of a resident professional theatre established in one of those same road cities attempts to follow that same formula, it would most likely fail to get similar results for him. For, except in rare circumstances, the resident companies do not consistently produce the type of work that can compete on the naked box office draw level. And, on a subscription basis, an offering of, say, half a dozen attractions of limited box office potential will bring similarly unsatisfactory results.

Thus, newspaper advertising for subscription campaigns must be applied in most of our kinds of projects with special planning and care and as only one element in the overall promotional picture, which has additional dimensions for us that the commercial producer lacks. He may have his Carol Channing and *Hello, Dolly!* to blazon across his full-page ad to help him draw sellout crowds in all of the road cities where our companies are in residence, but we have advantages denied him: the possibility of calling upon a wide range of volunteer participation and the tremendous economic advantage in the non-profit third class postal rates (in the U.S.) that permit us to profitably utilize direct mail on a considerable scale.

Newspaper advertising can be used to buttress large-scale subscription mailings and all of the other components being brought to bear at strategic points in the campaigns. That is, in early stages, at midpoint and to clean the bottom of the barrel. But expenditures for this advertising must be carefully controlled, with three questions in mind: (1) What are the direct results we have obtained in the past from its uses? (2) What do we judge to be the indirect benefits? (3) Are the costs involved tolerable and justified in light of those direct and indirect benefits? Advertising cannot be placed on the basis of "It's cheap here because this is a smaller city than some others." We pay for advertising according to the size of the circulation, but the lower linage rates in the smaller cities may not be the bargain they seem to be, while the linage rates of the big city papers, with correspondingly large readerships, may be a reasonably good buy, even at their seemingly high linage rates, if the sales results are good.

Generally speaking, newspaper advertising for nonprofit performing arts organizations is more costly than immediately meets the eye. To begin with, we don't get a third class, nonprofit rate, like we do from the post office for our direct-mail advertising. In fact, it is much more costly for us than it is for, say, a department store which finds its market for everything it seeks to sell (clothes, shoes, hardware, food, sporting goods, television sets, jewelry, etc.) in virtually 100% of a newspaper's readership. We, on the other hand, are attempting to sell products which, let us say, up to 98% of the newspaper's readers are *not* actively in the market for. Thus, when a department store buys an ad, listing its various wares, it not only pays a lesser rate than we do (since it buys huge amounts of space, it gets wholesale rates), but it is effectively getting up to 98% more chances to sell for its money than we are. That is one of many reasons department stores can profitably run continuous, large, daily advertising—a course of action that would certainly be impractical for most theatres, ballet companies, opera companies and symphony orchestras.

Our newspaper advertising, when we employ it, should contain the basic selling elements that we would use in our mailing pieces. When we have a brochure that has been fully written, covering the entire range of reasons that buying our subscription is a wise decision, we have a fund of already prepared material from which to choose the copy for our ads. Because of space costs, we cannot usually use everything that the brochure contains, so we must carefully select the best points, and then arrange them in a balance that will be most effective for our program.

Ideally, subscription ads should contain order form coupons to ease and organize the process of ordering the subscription. There are cases where such an order form is unnecessary, for instance, when the newspaper ad's sole purpose is to invite readers to send in requests to obtain the subscription brochure for the forthcoming season. A proper order form coupon, especially where multi-series offers are concerned (more a problem for opera and ballet companies, and for orchestras, than for theatres), requires a good deal of space and can thus be very costly to place in a newspaper ad. However, if the ad is being used as a promotional instrument, and we have made the decision to spend our money on it, we must then take care that it is the kind of ad that can do the job for us.

There are very few newspapers of daily circulation which are known to have a special concentration of performing arts readers and, even in the cases of the strongest of those publications (from that standpoint), most of the results in subscription sales tend to come from the initial ad and to peter out after it is run a few additional times. The New York Philharmonic, relying mainly on newspaper advertising, was able to find only 2,230 new series-ticket subscribers for its 1974–75 season. When it switched to a large-scale, mail-oriented promotional approach for the 1975–76 season, it found more than 10,000 new subscribers. As part of its intensive subscription drive, a major theatre company spent three times as much money on brochure distributions as it did in newspaper advertising and reported that it got 10 sales from the brochures for every sale made from the ads. One could argue, with some justice, that the newspaper advertising created a better context in which the brochures could do their job. By the same token, would not the mailings conversely have enhanced the pull of the ads?

It seems to be the nature of subscription campaigns that they require the cumulative effects of months of continuous mailings, along with a measured input of newspaper and other forms of advertising and a wide range of supportive volunteer components, in order to achieve the goals we set for ourselves. In addition to the paid advertising, we are, of course, always seeking to obtain the maximum amount of free space in the press for our activities.

A case in point would be that of a symphony orchestra in a smaller American city which had its dream come true, when a magnificent, luxurious new civic auditorium was built and would provide, at long last, a fine home for good music in that community. Although a sound, variegated plan had been worked out for a charter subscription drive, aimed at starting the orchestra off with a sold-out first season in the new home, the autocratic board president made a last-minute decision not to proceed with the recommended mix of large-scale mailings, strategically placed ads and a backup of volunteer committees. He simply put what was practically the entire budget of $25,000 into a series of newspaper ads, with the result that the orchestra opened its first season in the new auditorium with an audience not much larger than it was in previous years. One year later, the board president listened to reason and carried out the original plan, with the result that they got their sellout season, albeit a year late.

One of the most continuously asked questions is: How much should our promotional budget be? It is somehow assumed that there should be a certain set percentage allocation for promotion in the overall organizational budget. It is impossible to make a blanket prescription for expenditures that would fit all performing arts companies' promotional requirements, there being such a wide variance in individual circumstances. It would certainly be advisable for organizations to consult with others very much like themselves, to share experiences and to learn from them. I would also counsel that, when in doubt, make small-scale experiments which could, if they pan out, safely lead to the larger-scale promotional investments which are often so necessary in developing greater audiences.

Promotion is one area in which the answers must be custom-made to the situation. A new company, with no established audience at all, would certainly require a larger expenditure than one which has already built a following. A company with a sellout season and no plan to expand the number of performances for its next season will certainly need to spend less than it did during the years it was promoting itself up to full capacity status. A company which has just suffered a disastrous season from the standpoint of artistic acceptance, resulting in large subscriber attrition at renewal time, would be foolish not to increase the size of its promotional budget to fight the battle of obtaining replacement subscribers. A company making a move to larger quarters would have to, by all logic, spend more to assure that the increased seating capacity would be filled. And one could go on and on, listing all sorts of varying circumstances which would influence the amount of money (and extra volunteer efforts) that would or would not have to be poured into meeting sales goals. We must also be prepared, under certain circumstances, to think not only of budgeted amounts which are related to the potential expenses and income of a given season, but (and here comes another one of my leitmotifs) of additional amounts, to be thought of as capital investments in long-range audience development needs, which could be amortized over many seasons.

## Can We Afford the Luxury of Institutional Advertising?

While I believe that we should never begrudge necessary expenditures for audience development and that our promotional arm should be backed in its experiments just as the artistic leadership is, we should be wary of just putting money down the drain in nebulous "institutional advertising," when we really know, by all the patterns of our common experience, that there are few direct benefits to be derived. Institutional advertising, whereby the reputation and stature of a performing arts organization is promoted, rather than its specific productions and performances, is a great luxury which only a few old-line nonprofit arts organizations with tremendous endowments can manage. However, for most performing arts projects, particularly the newer ones holding on to survival by their teeth, it is painful to see promotional monies diverted from the immediate need to accomplish direct sales of subscription tickets (and even single tickets), in order to achieve amorphous future benefits, usually referred to as creating its "image."

I cannot imagine a greater exercise in futility than investments being made for these vague purposes when, at the same time, the playhouse or concert halls of the organizations involved are half empty, and their records show little or no expansion. If it's image they're looking for, I submit that the best image a performing arts company can project is that of being sold-out, of people clamoring to get in, of seasons being extended. Nothing is likely to be achieved by a series of full-page ads, all white space except for three words in tiny type in the upper left-hand corner of the otherwise empty page saying only:

Mid-U.S.A. Dance Theatre

Or even through the "hard-sell" version of an institutional ad, where there are three more words added, in the lower right-hand corner reading:

American Retrospective Season

When I have questioned the wisdom of putting good money into useless advertising (useless, if you need results *now*), I'm told things like, "But, don't you see, people will become curious about what this Mid-U.S.A. Dance Theatre is all about, and if we keep running the ad long enough (that'll bankrupt 'em for sure), eventually we'll be the talk of the town. *Then* we'll do business." This is nonsense in the case of fragile, young organizations. And why such slogans as "American Retrospective Season" are supposed to convince anybody of anything, I've never understood at all. If we are looking for things to say about such a performing arts company, why not something with more substance, like:

**At Long Last This City's Own Resident**
**Professional Dance Company!**

Follow that with affirmative copy about the artists involved, the dances being presented, the playhouse in which it will perform, the manifold advantages of subscribing, etc.

Nonprofit arts companies have, I believe, learned about institutional advertising from commercial enterprises. Let us say that the board chairman of International Sparkplugs has an enthusiasm for modern abstract painting, and his corporation, having paid a fortune in income taxes last year, now decides to run a series of ads in all national magazines and major newspapers. Instead of giving all that money to the government this year, he'll spend some of it on an image-building campaign, not expecting to sell a single sparkplug thereby; after all, why not go down in the history of commerce as a man of good taste in art, when the Internal Revenue Service allows such expenditures as legitimate deductions? So, the tycoon commissions a number of famed contemporary painters to create the original works required, and eventually a series of striking ads appear. They are splendid examples of the best in the art of our times, printed in full color. At the bottom of each ad, in tiny agate type, is the statement, "Art provides the spark that ignites the flame of civilization. This advertisement is sponsored by International Sparkplugs." The ads are widely admired, and there is an article in the *Wall Street Journal,* praising the enlightened board chairman of International Sparkplugs, and pointing out, "There is now a new breed of businessman, equally at home in the marts of trade and the Museum of Modern Art." Whereupon, owners of much smaller companies enter upon similar campaigns, taking their cue from their betters or, shall we say, their biggers. But, unlike the giant International Sparkplugs, if they don't sell their product on a day-to-day basis, they don't eat. Following the leader in this situation can well bankrupt them, for their promotion money will be spent with no practical results. For the big, wealthy corporation, it may be a permissible and effective gesture; for the little operator, the same course of action can spell disaster. Our nonprofit arts organizations are mainly in the category of those small businessmen; they cannot yet afford the luxury of institutional advertising.

## Shall We Look an Advertising Agency's Gift in the Mouth?

Many board members, big-time businessmen themselves, have difficulty understanding our needs. Such a situation can occur when an enthusiastic board member owns a flourishing advertising agency. He may throw a monkey wrench into our machinery, unwittingly and with the best of intentions, by volunteering the services of his staff in the preparation of the brochures and other materials which are to be important instruments in the effort. Of course, his generous offer is invariably and enthusiastically accepted, and he returns to his agency's offices to tell the news to his chief copywriter and to the head of his graphic arts department—both of whom are high-priced, top men in their fields. They are overjoyed to learn that they can apply their talents to something as creative and fine as, say, our local opera company, after years of drudgery on behalf of deodorants and other commercial products for which they can summon up little fervor. They promise their boss that he'll be proud of them when they come up with their copy and design approaches.

Let's say that the copywriter has long been unhappy and frustrated. He feels that, but for the cruel circumstances of life, he might well have been another Fitzgerald, Faulkner or Hemingway. But instead of writing the great American novel, he joined the advertising agency, lives well and still harbors his secret dream. The art director perhaps fancies himself a potential Picasso, maybe a Chagall, if only he could ever get the time to give it a real try, but the demands of his important job at the agency have never permitted him that chance. Suddenly, like manna from heaven, comes this challenge to both of these spiritually afflicted men. Here is not a commercial client but one that stands for true art—a superior opera company. Writer and artist's minds begin to race with their muse, their creative juices begin to flow and turn to torrent.

For the various products which they normally serve, they had presumably proceeded on tried-and-true agency principles, and their high salaries indicate that they must have established enviable records on behalf of the wares they advertised. They have achieved favorable image, market penetration, product identity, and all those things so often referred to in their special, Madison Avenue, gray-flannel lexicon, which succeed in selling their client's merchandise. Now, however, with their new assignment (us), they abandon their proved, sound techniques and boldly strike out to create a campaign which is totally in consonance with the art of opera itself. They labor with love and come up with brochures, posters, newspaper- and display-advertising materials which are literarily impeccable, aesthetically unimpeachable and artistically inspiring, but which are useless for our purpose of *selling* subscriptions. However, because their services are contributed, we are sometimes too embarrassed to reject them. So, we use the unsatisfactory materials, to the great detriment of our subscription sales drive.

However, in fairness to the agency people, there are often cases where they are encouraged in their error by members of our own staff and board, who have a weakness for pretty but ineffectual approaches. I recall receiving a "posthumous" letter from an administrator of a performing arts company which had just gone out of existence, partly as a result of its failure to attract a large enough audience. In closing the letter, which told the sad story of the group's demise, there was a poignant, self-solacing statement: "But we thought you would like to know that our promotional materials won first prize for excellence in this year's Advertising Council contest."

Certainly, all donated services by advertising agencies are not harmful, and can even be very useful, *in direct ratio to how much we can make our special needs understood by their employees.* Ideally our own staff members should participate all along the line in the process of creating the promotional materials which are so important to us. This advice, of course, assumes that our own people are competent and are able to make a knowledgeable contribution in this area.

# 14

# *The Discount Factor: "8 Plays for the Price of 6!"*

The discount factor is a formidable one in the promotion of subscription. Some snobs are apt to denigrate discounts with such straight-through-their-hats statements as, "Nobody I know would possibly make his decision to buy or not to buy on the basis of a discount." Yet, all experience is to the contrary. It is not unusual to have a known millionaire inquire by phone or in person at the symphony office, "How do I get those four concerts *free* if I subscribe?" or, holding in his hand the list of the entire series, asking, "Which ones on this list are the four *free* concerts?"

I was once assigned to work with a theatre suffering a bad case of subscriber malnutrition, which performed to 50% empty seats regularly. It had built up to all of 1,200 subscribers in the 15 years of its bare existence. Its board and staff's feeling was that, after all those years of fighting the battle, they had reached all of the people who would possibly subscribe to a theatre of good plays in that city—all 1,200 of them! I proposed an in-depth season-ticket campaign, offering:

**Five Plays for the Price of Four,
a Smashing 20% Discount,
One Play FREE to Subscribers.**

The business manager was keeping the place half full by desperately selling theatre parties at the last minute to company employee clubs and other organizations at *50% off* regular ticket prices. He unreasonably opposed this subscription offer; so did a prominent board member, who seemingly had no objection to giving 50% off to club and benefit-ticket buyers, but who was horrified at giving 20% off to subscribers. He could only keep repeating that we would be giving away plays free when the company was struggling to survive. . . .

Fortunately, the decision maker of that company, its founder and artistic director, sided with the subscription discount offer, which was then exploited well enough to achieve an immediate 125% season-ticket gain. Thus a chain of gains was set off that mounted, within six years, to an overall 700% gain, a considerably longer season, a magnificent new building—which set off a new campaign that soon escalated to a 1,600% gain—reckoning all the way from the original 1,200 to 20,288 subscribers! I would point out that we even offered *two* plays free at this theatre when the total number of plays increased, and that this offer evoked tremendous response. The difference in ticket sales income alone was over a half-million dollars per season, and the general success of the project inspired considerable additional monies in contributions.

Since that experience, I have met a considerable number of managers and board members of similar mold, with visceral feelings against the idea of offering subscription at a discount in advance of the season. Yet, once the season is in operation, as each play opens and does not do a terrific single-ticket business, this type of manager will gladly sell 'em at cut rates much lower than the subscription discount prices would have amounted to. Or, he might even "paper" the house with complimentary tickets, because only at this stage does he really feel it's right to do so. To make a conscious calculation, based on the track record of previous years, not to sell individual tickets to each performance as the season unrolls, and to make a discount offer many months before the season begins, as a bargain feature of the subscription offer, is something that is unthinkable for some unthinking practitioners in our field. Perhaps they feel they would somehow be selling short the drawing power of the season to come, by selling subscriptions at a discount. Later, when the season is in progress and most of the plays fail to sell their individual tickets in sufficient quantities, they feel there is nothing wrong in dumping the tickets at any price (or at no price) because they now know that the tickets won't sell any other way. The way I recommend is the way of the "educated guess," based upon all the facts and figures of the project's past seasons and of other performing arts sales patterns which show that all-out hits, capable of selling out via single sale on their own steam, are just as rare in the nonprofit professional field as they are in commercial show business. In theatres with large subscription audiences, there is, of course, little thought on anybody's part about hits or flops, and the subscribers tend to think in terms of entire seasons. Hopefully, they will say, come renewal time, "Well, we've had a pretty good *season*," or even "a darn good one," or in that most happy of instances, "a really great *season*."

Suppose you have a nonsubscription theatre which produces eight plays as its season offering, and two of these are hits, actually selling out on single sale. The other six plays do an average of 40% of capacity, meaning that the overall sale was 55% of capacity. Had you offered two plays *free*, backed this offer with a great campaign, and sold out on subscription, you would have a gross equivalent to 75% at full price. Having been sold-out before the season began, you could have turned people away for months on end and thus become a "sensation." You would then have been in a position to cut the discount to *one* play free for the next season, in the confidence that your momentum had become so great that you could replace those subscribers who might have dropped out as a result of the lower discount. You might have replaced them from right off your waiting list. If this sellout situation continued for another season, you might drop the discount entirely. On the other hand, at either of these two stages, or at both, you might decide to launch expansions (to add on performances), keeping the discounts for the time being, as you simultane- ously want to have your renewal at the highest possible level and attract the needed new subscribers. Thus, I wish to point out that discounts are not necessarily fixed irrevocably and can be manipulated, maneuvered and orchestrated according to different conditions and situations—sometimes de-escalated and, under certain circumstances, eliminated entirely.

For example, in certain situations where the weeknight sales are lagging, although the weekend nights are invariably sold-out, the sales balance can often be righted by lessening or entirely taking away the discount for the latter. Thus, a number of Friday and Saturday subscribers, who don't *have* to go on those nights but prefer to do so as long as there is no price differential, make the switch to Monday, Tuesday, Wednesday or Thursday evenings. Then, people who can only attend on weekends, and who were previously being turned away, come in to fill those vacated places at the higher subscrip- tion price. And should there not be enough subscribers to do that, there might even be some single-ticket buyers, since all experience indicates that when and if they do materialize, it is usually for weekend performances.

In another example, San Francisco's American Conservatory Theatre, on the threshold of its second decade, dropped its discount offer entirely after having wielded it like a big sword in building its subscribership up to the 20,000-plus category. During one of its early seasons, subscribers had been able to obtain as many as 6½ plays free, which was a 50% discount for what was then a 13-play season. Over the years, both the outsize annual repertoire and the discounts diminished, and with the past few seasons virtually sold-out all the time, the theatre—confident in its catbird seat—has simply invoked the prerogative of the seller's market. It has raised the price of its wares by eliminating the discount and yet has succeeded in retaining the volume of its subscription sales. However, should sales fall off at any future time, the management would be well advised to get its old discount policy out of the mothballs and begin to use it once more.

Symphony orchestras have been among the biggest discounters in the performing arts spectrum, but they haven't always admitted it. They would tell how much a series of 20 concerts cost, not pointing out that this price was a big bargain compared to individual tickets. Thus, they got little advantage from their attractive, but unexploited offers. Within recent years, many symphony discounters have come out of the closet, have made much of their discount offers, and have achieved marvelous results in sales. One orchestra I was assigned to assist sold its 20-concert main series at a price of $100 in the box seat section of its luxurious hall, with prices of other locations scaled down from there. Nowhere in the brochure did it point out that these box seats cost $10 apiece if you bought them individually, so that those 20 concerts would have cost *$200* if not purchased on subscription. Stating this discount factor would have been an extraordinary enticement to potential series-ticket purchasers. One would have to be insane—or anti-music—to turn it down! Actually, they were *giving* a straight 50% discount in all price and location categories, but not *offering* it. Previous subscribers were aware of the bargain they were getting which, no doubt, kept many of them resubscribing each season. However, potential subscribers never found out about it until the management changed its approach entirely and blazoned across the face of the brochure:

**A Smashing 50% Discount to Subscribers!**
**20 Concerts for the Price of 10!**
**10 Thrilling Musical Entertainment Events FREE!**

The brochure copy very plainly, very clearly spelled out on the order form the 50% savings for each price and location category, and new subscribers poured in. Within one season, the audience more than doubled.

Dance companies everywhere have found a tremendous attraction in *The Nutcracker,* an attraction even capable of selling single tickets in great volume. The same dance companies usually find an entirely different public reaction to the announcements of their regular repertoire. By putting *The Nutcracker* into the company's subscription series, the regular repertoire finds an admittedly captive audience, but one which often stays to cheer the programs they would have ignored were it not for *The Nutcracker's* allure in combination with the discount that was offered. Let us say that one of these balletic series is for four events, with one dance concert offered free. This offer can be stated, "See *The Nutcracker* Free," for we are entitled to interpret our discount that way if we wish to!

Opera companies must charge the highest ticket prices of all the performing arts, for the simple reason that their costs are a collective of *all* the types of costs incurred in producing all those arts. For, opera companies, in order to function, must employ symphony orchestras, ballet companies, choruses, principal singers, conductors, directors, small armies of stagehands and special technicians. They must obtain stage settings, costumes, lighting equipment and all the elaborate accoutrements required to create the grandeur of grand opera. Opera impresarios are caught between the traditional tastes in repertoire of the majority of that minority who go to opera at all, and the special tastes of that fraction of the minority which hungers for esoteric revivals, contemporary and avant-garde works. It is the discount dynamic which is often the determining factor in the decision of the traditionalist majority to go along with the subscription package that offers a larger or smaller quotient of unusual repertoire selections, according to the decisions made by the artistic director. Certain opera companies have built large subscription audiences, achieved major expansions via the discount route, and have since either gone to lower discounts or have withdrawn them entirely. When an audience is big enough, and when the "Were *you* one of the thousands turned away last season?" advertising for subscribing is credible enough, the discount may no longer be necessary. At that point, the main reason for subscribing becomes the fear of not getting in at all—the assurance of having seats when others must stand in line, only to be turned away.

One of the greatest problems in developing new audiences for many symphony orchestras has been the tremendous number of events to which new subscribers must commit and submit themselves. The subscription series will sometimes consist of 20 or 24 concerts. It is not too likely that very many people who have not yet been subscribers will start out by going to all 20 or 24 concerts. Therefore, I have urged orchestra managements to use the half-series as well, so that there will be, let us say, the Saturday Night "A" Series of 20 concerts, and the Saturday Night "A-1" Series of 10 concerts. Accompanied by strong subscription-selling campaigns, this packaging has opened up a new, much larger audience market for many orchestras. A considerable number of the new half-series ticket holders graduate to the full series within a season or two after their initial indoctrination to the joys of regular concert going. And success along these lines has encouraged many orchestras to create additional series of special interest and of various sizes, so that orchestras which had only one or two series not many seasons back now boast an entire "Chinese menu" in their season brochures.

Where series packagings offer different numbers of symphony concerts, the discounts should be set up so as to create incentive for the potential subscriber to take the larger series. At the same time, the discount for the smaller series should be attractive enough to give pause to the man who is tempted to wait and buy single tickets to the few big-name soloist concerts and special programs that he especially favors. To illustrate this point, I would suggest that the sponsors of a 20-concert series might offer 6 concerts free to subscribers, while giving 2 free to those who purchase the 10-pack. One of my projects, the Scottish Opera, launching subscription for the first time in Glasgow (its home base), offered 3 free for their full series of 10 operas and 1 free for the half-series of 5 works. The campaign was very successful, with 60% of the charter subscribers unable to resist the better offer, and thus taking the entire 10, while 40% took the series of 5, managing to avoid the alternative of waiting for single sale. The subscription, thus initiated, sold so well that the company was immediately able to *double* the length of the season. The Scots may have a reputation of being thrifty, but I suggest that, when it comes to discounts, we are all bargain hunters!

Obviously, a tremendous impetus to ticket sales is the use of nationally or internationally renowned stars on the artist roster of opera companies, or as guest soloists with symphony orchestras and ballet companies, or to perform leading roles in plays presented by theatre companies. However, the stars we seek are not always available, or the artistic policy of the specific performing arts organization may preclude the employment of artists who are not part of the permanent ensemble. In such cases, the *discount* may be the star. The discount may provide that extra ounce of drawing power that sells the subscription. And the combination of big-name, big-talent artists *and* a discount could mean *double* drawing power for our offer.

Sometimes, we must stop and ask ourselves, "Why *should* people buy our subscription?" It is certainly very hard for us to be objective about our own work. Yet, when the people stay away from our performances in droves, we ought to be able to get the message that there is resistance to what we have to offer. If our company is devoted to an artistic policy that is especially hard to sell, then it especially cries out for a big discount to stimulate the sale. Maybe people who are successfully wooed by the discount may find out that what we offer has real merit, and then we can begin to build a real audience. A good-size discount may be necessary for some years, to inculcate the renewal habit and sell more and more new subscriptions. An opera company I know, bravely presenting a largely avant-garde repertoire to usually minuscule audiences, dramatically increased its attendance and its box office income by making, for the first time, a good discount offer and strongly promoting it. Despite the enormous benefits derived from this campaign, the board begrudged the discount, cut it from 25% (one opera free out of four offered) to only 10% for the next season, and promptly lost its head of steam. The momentum of subscription gains stopped in its tracks when the significant discount offer was cut down too early in the growth game. I have never quite been able to understand the stubborn stinginess of these anti-discount board members of arts groups with heavily unsold season capacities, particularly *after* clear demonstrations of the discount's efficacy. It is almost as if there were a machine in which you could put quarters and out would come dollars, and you refused to put in the coins because you said you couldn't afford it.

I recall one instance where the discount principle was attempted in reverse. That is, instead of six plays for the price of five, the offer became *five* plays for the price of *six*, with the public asked to pay the full price for all five of the season's plays, and then the equivalent of the full price for a sixth one—in effect a contribution. The result of this fund-raising experiment was that 50% of the then existing subscribership failed to renew. The loss engendered had to be somewhere between 5 and 10 times the contributions brought in from those who did pay. *They* were, of course, too few, and the subscription fell to an all-time low. That theatre company's management later wisely jettisoned this innovation, restored discounts, and has made considerable strides in building a much larger subscription audience. It has also been employing much more effective methods of fund-raising.

The discount, creatively applied, remains one of the most effective promotional instruments we have in audience building, and I would wager that a
very large percentage of the subscribers to the performing arts have originally
come to their subscribing decisions because of it.

# 15

## *The Central Instrument of Our Campaign: The Brochure*

I consider the brochure to be the central instrument of most of our subscription promotion campaigns. While a well-balanced campaign will draw its sales from a number of different sources, each contributing to the total, it is almost always the direct sales from the distribution of brochures which turn out to be the single greatest factor in our success. However, the power of the brochure to accomplish these sales is much enhanced by the mesh and scale of all of the activities involved in the overall subscription-selling effort. We can and sometimes do achieve remarkable results from direct mail in the absence of other promotional components, but it is running a risk that we ought not to run to have all our eggs in this one basket. Developing additional campaign components will not only bring direct sales from those extra sources, but will, from all that we have learned, positively affect the level of returns from the brochure mailings as well.

It would be absolutely ideal if the management and the volunteer complement of our performing arts groups were all gifted, supersalesmen and there were enough of them so that we could personally call on each of the hundreds of thousands of people in our area whose names are on our mailing lists. We would probably do an unprecedentedly great job of bringing in new subscribers to our organizations. The next best thing to do, in order to reach a very great number of people within the allotted time element, is to send them brochures of such excellence that there is a good chance we will accomplish our purpose.

### Making the Point

The brochure itself can be of all-around value in the campaign; it is not only used to obtain new subscriptions, but is effective, too, in garnering the largest possible percentage of renewals. It also becomes the working manual for the staff and volunteers. It should, of course, contain all of the basic information concerning the planned repertoire, the artists involved, the series being offered, the dates and the prices—all stated with clarity. This clarity can be of crucial importance in whether or not we get the sale. I have found (fortunately, more often in the past than currently) that potential subscribers can become confused by the way in which the series information is given or by the order form itself. This confusion presents a real block to making the mail-order sale. In the case of a certain musical organization which mysteriously went into an attendance decline, I found that the root of the problem lay in the inability of the people who received its brochures to find out how to order any of the series being offered. They assumed that the fault was theirs, that they were too stupid to understand the form, and since they were too embarrassed to admit it, many of them didn't call the office to make further inquiry. They simply threw away the brochure, and our chances with them ended then and there. This problem did not affect the renewal of subscription, because the old subscribers had only to check the place where it said, "Please renew my subscription." But there was a pattern of annual attrition amounting to 20% of subscription in that organization and, with no new subscribers coming in to take their place, within a few years the audience was simply withering away. A new brochure was put out, with the series information outlined in a manner that a baby could follow, with the order form clarified and in large type. Overnight, there was a big upturn in subscription sales.

The New York Philharmonic recently added 10,500 new subscriptions, as against only 2,000 new ones the year before. The major factors which brought about this more than 500% gain were the use of greatly increased distributions of brochures, a less institutional and more sales-directed tone, *and the employment of extra clarity in displaying the 11 different series of varying sizes that were being offered.* If there were two series of 13 concerts each alternating on Thursday evenings, they were not listed together just to save space; each package of 13 received a clearly separate display—and the same for all of the series which the brochure successfully sought to sell—enabling the prospective subscriber to easily discern the dates on which *his* series would be performed.

There should be no question in the mind of the person who has received the brochure as to what we want of him. We want him to *subscribe* and, ideally, the entire brochure should lead him inevitably and inexorably to do so. Arts organizations have often sent out instruments which are the opposite of this, leaving the person who reads it (*if* he does) in doubt as to what the sender wants of him. One can imagine him perusing one of those enervated "institutional" pieces, where the writer and designer have not come to the point at all, and saying to himself, "You know, it was nice of these people to send me information about their organization. I suppose I'll eventually get *another* brochure, asking me to subscribe." But, of course, he never does.

However, a brochure should give much more than just the plain information. It should contain many other elements, mainly enticing ones. It should offer the strongest, most affirmative and attractive statements concerning who we are, what is so special about our project, what is so great about the productions we are listing, and why *subscribing* to them and to us is so desirable. It should contain so many good reasons the man reading it should buy the subscription we are offering that halfway through, he should excitedly call out to his wife, "Helen, where's my checkbook?" At least, we should feel when we send it out that it does have this power to attain for us that "consummation devoutly to be wished," that is, another ticket subscriber brought into our fold.

If we are sending a self-mailer type of brochure (and most of our third class bulk mail is in that category), we must be certain not to lose the battle at the initial skirmish. By that I mean we must first get the person who receives it, to open it and begin to read it. It is at this level that many arts organizations strike out. In most cases the person receiving our brochure didn't send for it. He is probably not already a member of our audience. Although it is sometimes painful for us to admit, he may never have heard of us. Or, if he has, it didn't excite or inspire him. What makes us think that he will not regard our brochure as just another piece of "junk mail," and simply throw it away without reading it? A brochure which has only our name and address plus a couple of Greek drama masks, or a musical clef, or a ballerina in a tutu on its address side, is just too weak to do the job. If we offer star soloists on the inside, then their pictures and names should be de rigueur on the outside. If we have a smashing discount for subscribers, that is money in the bank when placed out front. If one can enjoy:

### 24 Thrilling, Memorable Musical Entertainment Events
### for the Price of 16!

with this boon equaling "8 Concerts Free," it belongs right out there—next to, above or below the name of the brochure's recipient. If "the entire season of seven great professional legitimate stage plays" can be purchased for "as little as $14," this inducement certainly demands to be seen at first glance. If there is a new playhouse in the offing, a tenth anniversary season coming up or the news that we've just hit 20,000 subscribers, this fact is all-important for the front of the brochure.

Since the postal regulations permit a surprising amount of the surface of the address side to be used for our message, we would be foolish not to take advantage of such a perfect showcase. And let us not forget that the back of the brochure is another "front," depending upon which way the recipient takes it out of his mailbox. Thus, the back should be used very effectively. I recently received a brochure with an order form covering its entire back. Now, this doesn't make sense. The man hasn't yet opened the brochure, and he is already confronted with the order form. He hasn't yet read about the repertoire, the artists, and the many arguments for subscribing that are to be found on the inside. For instance, the back of the brochure is a good spot to run the architect's glamorized rendering of the magnificent new building that will be ready in time for the coming season, with an appropriate caption like:

**Become a Charter Subscriber in Our Magnificent, Luxurious, New Concert Hall—Obtain a Permanent "Leasehold" on Your Own Choice Seats in This Most Perfect Setting for the Enjoyment and Appreciation of Fine Music!**

Or, the back is a fine position for a beautiful photograph of a scene from our biggest hit of last season, with a big, bold caption over it, reading:

**Were you one of the thousands turned away from our production of *Zeisler's Revenge*? Well, not one of our cherished season subscribers failed to get in. They not only had tickets to this smash hit—and to all our other highly praised productions last season— they enjoyed better seats than any single-ticket buyer could ever hope to obtain—but they paid far less than box office prices!**

Then, below the picture, the follow-up statement:

**So subscribe now to the forthcoming season, using the official order form on the inside of this brochure!**

The most logical position for the order form is *inside* the brochure. It might well be placed so that it is on the reverse side of the front of the brochure where it was addressed to the recipient, thus facilitating the processing of the order. However, I would not insist on this placement in all cases, as the selling need must outrank the processing problems in our overall considerations. A very bold, broken line (dashes) should mark off the form, so as to subliminally suggest that it be torn out. Abbreviations in the form should be used with great care, for the potential subscriber may not be as familiar with box office terminology as we are. The type should be of a style that is plain, eminently readable and, most important, large enough so that people possessing less than 20–20 vision will see every word clearly. The form's contents should conform carefully to the ordering information and descriptions of the offering in the main body of the brochure. The form should *not* be used as a questionnaire to obtain information not directly pertinent to getting our order. It should not be cluttered unnecessarily.

Sometimes, in planning sessions concerning brochures, I hear the term "hard sell" used in a pejorative way. Basically, I really don't think very much in terms of hard or soft sell, but rather in terms of "effective" and "ineffective." And, surprising as it may seem to some people, I *can* conceive of "soft sell" as being effective under certain circumstances, particularly in some renewal situations, where our already enrolled subscribers are quite well indoctrinated in our strong points and the advantages of subscribing.

Some skeptics have made the wrong assumption that many of the great subscription gains which have been achieved by so many performing arts groups have been solely the result of the greatly increased scale of brochure distributions which I have recommended so extensively, and they will say— with no facts to back them up—that the appearance, content and thrust of the brochure is not a factor, that a lovely, dull, institutional one will get the same or better results than the kind of effective brochure that I am describing in this handbook. I believe that we should strive to create instruments in good taste, attractive to the eye, but with the selling thrust we need, too. I would rather err on the side of being too strong than too weak. One symphony orchestra recently took it on the chin when an expensive, exquisitely designed, understated brochure, sent out in the hundreds of thousands, elicited little response. Fortunately, a new management took over immediately following that debacle and had the aggressive spirit to put out, overnight, a plain, low cost but aimed-for-the-jugular brochure. It was sent out in large quantities to lists of the same characteristics as the first mailings, and got a return of four to one over the earlier batch.

One of the most gifted and thorough promoters of subscription for theatre companies I know of, operating in one of the largest markets in the country, prepared and simultaneously sent out four different brochures for the same series to mailing lists of virtually identical characteristics. They were all aesthetically acceptable brochures, written and designed in clear gradations of convincing power with varying approaches to the promotion of their subscriptions, ranging from the purely informational take-it-or-leave-it attitude to eloquence and showmanship. Need I say that, when the results of his test were in, the brochures which could easily have been designated in advance as "most effective," "not quite as effective," "even less effective" and "ineffective" came in first, second, third and fourth in sales volume?

The cardinal sin in preparing a brochure is to offer both subscriptions and single tickets simultaneously. When selling subscriptions, we do not mention the existence of single tickets other than that there will not be any left at all, after subscribers have had their pick. Or, that if any *are* left, they will be the least desirable seat locations or much more expensive than subscriptions because of the subscriber discount factor. If, along with the subscription offer, the brochure's reader learns that he can order single tickets, he will likely pick the one or two events that most attract him, and the percentage of subscription sales will likely be badly affected. The proper approach is to sell subscriptions *exclusively* for months. Only if there are tickets left at the campaign's end should single tickets then be offered for sale. To offer both, evenhandedly and at the same time, will only foster the presumption that whether the purchaser buys one or the other, the seat locations will be of equal quality—thus betraying the primacy of the subscription.

### Designing the Brochure

There is no one perfect physical format for a brochure. I myself have written and helped design between 50 and 100 brochures annually for a wide range of professional performing arts organizations for many years now, and I use about a dozen different, basic formats, with variations of these, depending on all sorts of circumstances.

The brochure should be neither very small nor overly large. It should be of conventional size. It should not have "cutesy" complicated folds which retard the simple process of opening it quickly and easily. It should not be in the form of a book which requires turning many pages before reaching the order form on page 12. Too few people ever get that far. The order form ought to be right next to the main elements of information about the season and in an outside edge position, so it can be cut or torn off easily. I have sometimes favored a sort of lip or flap at the bottom of the inside spread of a brochure, as it provides special showcases on its front and on its back, for extra display of featured elements. If the brochure folds down to too small a size, it lacks impact and importance to the eye of the person who receives it. Also, it may fall down, horizontally, to the bottom of the mailbox and remain there for months before it is discovered. If the basic sheet of paper on which it is printed is not large enough for the amount of material which we require to convey the basic information, plus the excitement and enticement factors, the brochure will become a procrustean bed in which we will have to lop off the head or the legs of our message. Or, each panel will contain type so tiny that it will not only impede, but discourage, reading. A too-small brochure frustrates the obvious need to have large, easily readable type with enough space between the lines so that reading will be invited rather than repelled. If, on the other hand, the brochure is too large, it becomes unwieldy when opened to its full spread.

In cases where special letters will accompany a few thousand, out of hundreds of thousands, of self-mailer brochures, I wince when I'm told that the brochure must fit a number 10 envelope, simply because the organization has a supply of them. I would never plan the size of my brochure according to the limitations of an envelope. I would buy a larger size envelope for those few thousand brochures and make my sales instrument the size that I thought would be most effective for my overall purposes.

The design of brochures to function as posters has become quite popular in recent years, and I have found that there is often a great self-satisfaction on the part of the arts people who put them out, when they contemplate the savings they feel they are achieving through producing this double-duty instrument. I wish I could share their enthusiasm, but I cannot, because these dual purpose brochure-posters invariably fall between two stools. Neither as brochures nor as posters are they as effective as they ought to be. I am not so much concerned about the posters lacking effectiveness, since in most situations I find them an anachronistic, often self-indulgent, form of promotion anyway. However, I *am* very much concerned when a *brochure* lacks full effectiveness, for it is not a matter of indulgence or of image, but of specific sales—in effect, whether or not we eat, whether or not our projects live and live well. The brochure-poster bears a similarity to an all-purpose auditorium, which generally turns out to be unsuitable for any of the purposes it was supposed to serve.

Unusual, special, highly decorative typefaces which might be admired for distinction and originality, but which repel reading, should be avoided like the plague. The much contemporarily used sans serif grouping of Helvetica, Optima and Univers typefaces are all useful for us, along with the more traditional and formal serif styles such as Caslon, Bodoni, Times Roman and Baskerville. This dictum does not rule out a custom-made typeface for the name or logo of the organization. However, for the body of the brochure's copy, we require the solid, standard type fonts. The judicious juxtaposition of reverse printing and black-on-white, as well as the utilization of various "screens" can provide the brochure with extra eye appeal.

A photographic element in a symphony brochure would include a picture of the full orchestra, with conductor in action, guest soloist flailing away at the piano (hair flying), taken either from the back or from the side corner of the hall so as to show the audience, too—in effect, a photograph of the "experience" of a concert event. More often, for no other reason than there being no such photographs available, separate photos of the orchestra and of the audience are used. However, in planning ahead for next season's brochure, the all-embracing kind of photograph I have described can be taken at one of the current season's performances. Be sure, however, that you tell the photographer to come on a night when you have a sold-out house, so that this happy condition will be apparent in the completed picture. If you are preparing for a theatre brochure, then you might suggest that he shoot during a scene when the stage is especially well lit, so that the spillover light will partially illuminate the audience which is sitting in the darkened playhouse. At a musical concert, where the house lights are usually at least partially up during the performance, his job is an easier one.

If you are laying out a symphony orchestra brochure, the biggest-name soloists' pictures might well be used on the front, and then repeated inside in the full spread of all the soloists. Depending upon the reader to find out about your star power *after* he gets to the inside of the brochure is not very wise. He might throw the piece away without ever getting to the inside.

Let us say that we can get a fabulous deal from our printer, so that we buy a two-color brochure for the same price as the one-color job we had last year. What then should the two colors be? I know that there have been positive opinions on this given out by motivational researchers. However, I think that entirely too much time and discussion goes on about the selection of colors. I don't really think it matters that much. Any reasonable, attractive combination of colors will do, as long as they are not weak or too pale. We need strong, full-blooded, bright colors. I do admit to a personal tendency to favor the good old theatrical reds and blacks for brochures. However, people will not buy our subscriptions because of the mesmerizing shades of chartreuse and magenta in which our message might be printed. They *will* tear out and send in our order form because of the intrinsic value of what we have to offer and what we say about it—and *how* we say it!

Managers should never permit themselves to be buffaloed by graphics designers or fall victim to their pretensions. Some years ago, when I was sent to assist a certain dance company, I was appalled at the total impracticality of the subscription brochure that was being employed there with understandably little success. They'd been stuck with a fortune in unsold seats during that season, meaning a smashing defeat financially and a stunning blow to the morale of the artists. Furthermore, the potential number of dropout subscribers increased, as they saw that there were always plenty of seats at the last minute. When I enumerated to the general manager the changes that would be required for the next season's brochures, if we were to have an effective instrument for the purpose of getting people to subscribe, he became so obviously uncomfortable that I could not help but notice it. I asked him why he appeared so upset, whereupon he blurted out, "I can't even suggest one of these changes to our graphics designer. You see, he wants season-to-season continuity of the image he has created for us (that ol' image & logo syndrome raising its ugly head), and if I interfered with that, why he would just resign!" I quickly got the idea that this general manager didn't care at all about such "minor" matters as building an audience, expanding seasons and turning unsold capacity into money. No, he was hung up on "important" things like keeping graphics designers happy. Now, I am about to say something which may sound cruel, but *I* wouldn't hire that man (the general manager) as an usher. Because I am persistent, I finally convinced him to tackle the designer. He did so, with much trepidation. As he had predicted, the man did resign, whereupon we found another man who did a fine job on the next brochure. We also did a great deal more business for the next season.

Let us assume that we, the planners of the brochure, have a very definite promotional line in mind as we write the copy and that we have very definite ideas as to which elements we wish to give special emphasis and display. We must then be very careful in selecting a practical designer who will carry out, in the type selection, in the graphics employed and in the overall layout, *our* intentions. Too many times, our responsible staff people have found themselves frustrated and traduced by designers who ignore our needs, while achieving their own self-expression at the expense of our subscription sales. We are then put in the position of accepting a brochure that we don't want, or having to start all over again with another designer. From the standpoint of the kind of commercial artist or graphics designer who creates this kind of difficulty for us, it is *we* who are wrong. He wants us to subordinate all our considerations to his design, which would be reasonable only if we had commissioned him to do a painting for the wall in our lobby. We must be on the alert to see to it that he doesn't design us down the river.

For our direct-mail selling purposes, such a commercial artist or designer is in about the same position as a draftsman who does the detailing for an architect, and it is we, the managers, publicists and audience development personnel who are the architects of our campaigns. The promoting of subscription sales via brochure mailings has its own effective strategies and approaches, already tested and developed through countless campaigns. What will work and what will not work, and what will work better for the amount of money spent, are all fairly well established by now. So, it is important that we get the kind of design assistance that will give us what we need—brochures that are simple in design and do the job. Fortunately, there are many practical yet highly talented commercial artists available, practitioners who even take pride in the number of subscription sales racked up by the brochures they have turned out for us.

### What's the Price Tag?

Must brochures be expensive to get results? The answer is no! Actually, there seems to be some sort of correlation between expensive and ineffective in this connection. Perhaps one of the reasons is that when such a heavy investment is made, it is usually accompanied by a very lofty, no-sell approach throughout. I recall a particular case where a theatre must have pawned its board members' jewels in order to pay the costs of publishing a large, aesthetically magnificent brochure, produced in so many hues of the rainbow that it undoubtedly would have put to shame Joseph's coat of many colors, and printed on paper of the highest rag content. Not only were the returns abysmal for the number which were mailed, but the extremely high cost of each piece inhibited and indeed forbade any distribution but on the smallest scale. With the theatre company almost put out of existence by the failure of this work of art to sell subscriptions, the board called me for succor. A new brochure was issued, at one-fiftieth the previous cost, printed in only one color but with a very practical, no-nonsense approach saying all the right things about the plays offered and the advantages of subscribing. It was written in my hotel room overnight and sent to the typesetter without benefit of a designer's ministrations. The results, of landslide proportions, happened because the brochure drew very well for the percentage of its distribution and could be distributed on a large scale, since the basic cost of its production was so low. Subscription was increased by several hundred percent over the previous season, setting off a chain of future gains, with the collaboration of staff members and volunteers making additional components come to life, too.

The performing arts "business" has been victimized because of its special economic circumstances even more than conventional commerce, by that "old devil" inflation. So, the ingrained reluctance on the part of our boards to approve expenditures for promotion (a subject dealt with in another part of this book) has now been aggravated and compounded by such factors as the sky-high cost of paper and other related charges reflected in our printing bills. In light of these conditions, it is incomprehensible that we would simply call up a printer, and without regard to what the eventual bill is going to be, just order brochures in the hundreds of thousands. But that is what has sometimes been found to be the modus operandi in arts institutions. As those responsible for the survival and, hopefully, the success of these institutions, we must not forget that we are acting in a fiduciary capacity when we expend these funds.

I would recommend that old relationships with printers who have had our business "sewed up" for a long time be re-examined; that no sizable order be given without competitive bidding for the job; and that, along with the information on our requirements, we precondition the bidders to understand our determination to cut costs. Naturally, the less expensively we can buy the printing, the larger our circulation can be. And it is important that, at the time of the bidding, we have already come to certain advance decisions on the scale of our distributions. For the price can be lower per brochure in direct ratio to how many we order at the same time. It may be advisable to discuss our plans in advance with the printers we are thinking of using. For sometimes, a minute concession on our part as to the dimensions of the planned brochure will make possible considerable savings in cost. Involved, for instance, may be the size of the printer's presses and how many brochures can most efficiently come out of one piece of paper of a certain standard size. We must not forget that the cost of printing often varies widely, from city to city and region to region.

Sometimes, astonishingly, there are great disparities between the price of a printing job with the same requirements in communities which are not all that far from each other. One west coast city seems to have what are probably the lowest average printing costs in the country. Thus, it more than pays performing arts projects in another city of that region, more than 400 miles away, to have its brochures printed away from home. The cost of shipping the completed brochures is peanuts compared to the savings effected. While every aspect of mailing costs should be carefully considered and controlled, certainly a major factor in those costs will be the printing. In the case of one large project I recall, costs for the same size, quality and number of pieces mailed were over $23,000 less from one year to the next (despite inflation) because a new man was placed in charge who was simply more knowledgeable, conscientious and thorough.

In our efforts—certainly laudable—to save money, we often seek out a private or corporate donor who may own a printing plant (or give a great amount of business to one), with the idea of getting the brochure contributed. Sometimes this works out well. However, I urge care in making such arrangements. I have seen more than one case where, because the printing was a contribution, the arts organization had no control over delivery dates. Thus, one group launching a crucial subscription drive, was almost forced out of existence when the contributed brochure finally arrived from the printer exactly *two* days before the season began. I have also run into many situations where board members, through their connections, obtained very low paper and printing prices, but ended up getting delivery too late for our needs. In such circumstances, our groups would obviously have avoided huge losses in sales which could never take place because the ammunition arrived after the battle was lost, if they had not tried to get the brochures for free or at wholesale prices. I am by no means suggesting that we should never try for the latter advantages (free or wholesale) but that when we do, we make clear that the time element is crucial for us; that there is a double loss when the printer delivers too late; that the entire cost of the paper and printing then goes for naught; and that we also lose all the distribution. Even when we pay the bills directly out of our own funds, we are in danger of such mishaps. So delivery dates must be specified by us in the contracts we make with our printers, or the costs of direct-mail campaigns become much higher than the price tag on printing our brochure.

Are there any conditions under which you should stop making expenditures for brochure printing and distribution and for other promotional aids? Well, one such condition would be where you are already at 100% of your present capacity and you are not able to expand the number of performances at the moment. However, even if it appears likely that you will hit your 100%, in a combination of big subscription and the incremental single-ticket sales which have been generated by the far-reaching effects of your all-out season- or series-ticket campaign, it still makes long-range sense to continue expenditures which are aimed at getting the virtual or actual sellout by subscription alone. It has been my experience over and over again that such situations create that instant, dynamic climate in which we have our best chance for success in immediate expansions of number of performances and length of season. An arts company can go along for many years, coming very close to selling out its limited number of performances with a combination of, say, 75% subscription and 20% single sale, and never achieve the momentum for expansion. Yet the same organization, bestirring itself and running a campaign which brings its subscription up to the high 90's or even to the 100% mark overnight, seems to find the courage, the ability, the mandate, to successfully schedule additional performances for the season that follows. I cannot help but decry the cases where such victories for our greater good are lost or delayed by lack of vision or by such immediate financial concerns that we settle for what might cost less in promotional expenses today, but will prove much more costly in loss of opportunity for our projects to fulfill their audience-serving potential tomorrow—and for all of the days and years after that. Such an attitude is shortsighted.

## Advance Planning and Listing the Repertoire

The plays offered by a theatre must be given a central and dominant position on the inside of the brochure—along with the all-important statements we make about each of those works. For what we say about them can evoke a scale of negative, tepid or positive reactions on the part of the reader. When all is said and done, when all the arguments have been made, all the advantages of subscribing pointed out, those plays remain the heart of the matter. It may be largely on the basis of how attractive these repertoire selections are to the subscriber that the direct sale will or will not be made. This problem has plagued the promotional stewards of many theatre companies because in-depth subscription campaigning must take place over a considerable period of time each year, with the spring phase of the effort beginning in March or April, very often before the artistic director can come up with definite choices for the season to begin in October. Maybe he is hoping that the production rights will be released for a play which is still doing well Off Broadway, and this decision won't be made until July or even August. Maybe he will do a certain play if he gets a certain distinguished actor to appear in a principal role, but will switch to another play if the deal doesn't work out. In that case, this would affect the balance of the season he had in mind, and might force him to alter some of his other choices up to that point. He desperately seeks to keep his options open as long as possible. Because of this blockage, many theatres, in the past, did not begin their subscription drives until disastrously late, paying a big price in lost sales.

In attempting to reconcile the artistic director's dilemma with our need to get on the market in time, we made some experiments many years ago, which proved out to the extent that this problem is now solved for a great number of theatres. They now employ the following approach: In the spring, they publish a brochure which might have a caption over the repertoire section which says:

**Aiming for the most ambitious and exciting season in our theatre's history, we are considering these 12 outstanding classic, contemporary and avant-garde plays for inclusion in our 1974–75 7-play offering.**

Then, below this heading, they not only list each of the 12 plays which are uppermost in the artistic director's mind, but also describe them, interestingly and colorfully, in a compact but penetrating paragraph about each work. In all other ways, the brochure is the same type they generally use and contains the best statements they can make, in full detail, concerning all aspects of the offer.

Both renewing and new subscription buyers have accepted this solution beautifully, and have unhesitatingly made their spring and summer commitments to us in vast numbers everywhere, within the framework of that compromise. The artistic directors have usually made their final choices well within the plays proposed in their early listings, and where they have deviated, the subscribers have rarely quarreled with the final selections. It is a heartening and quite wonderful thing to see the development of the subscribers' faith in the theatre to which they adhere. I have always felt that one of the reasons for the wide acceptance of this plan has been the sporting instinct of the subscriber. There are, of course, some people, and they are in the minority, who simply won't make any buying decision at all until just before the season begins, not only because they want to be assured of the specific plays, but because all during the previous months of our efforts to bring them in, they somehow haven't heard us or seen us. That is why we have vigorous fall campaigns, too (with the later edition of the brochure giving the final play selections)—sweeping them into our net right up to the moment the first curtain goes up, and even beyond that to the end of the run of the season's first production.

Not all theatres have put to use this all-repertoire-options-left-open-as-long-as-possible compromise approach, because they don't need to. And not all artistic directors are cut of the same cloth. Some *do* make up their minds very definitely about their seasons long in advance, having either been temperamentally geared to the advance planning demand that subscription does make, or having disciplined themselves thereto. Then there are some situations where the management knows definitely in the spring what the first play or the first two plays are going to be, but not the remainder of the repertoire, so the brochure states just that and then goes on to present a list from which the other plays of the forthcoming season may or will be chosen.

Can theatre subscriptions be sold through a brochure which does not contain any list of plays at all? There have been a few cases where large, established, successful organizations, under unusually favorable circumstances, obtained a reasonable renewal response in their early solicitations without any kind of repertoire mentioned. Later in the game, when plays were announced, many more subscribers renewed. However, I know of no case where any substantial number of *new* subscriptions were sold without some plays either given as possibilities or definitely promised. For most theatre companies, it would be disastrous to attempt to sell subscriptions with no plays listed at all. In one particular instance, an artistic director took the stand that it was demeaning to him and to his project to have to reveal any of his artistic plans for the next season to existing or potential subscribers. He believed that the will to renew should be generated by the theatre's past performance and by the subscriber's faith alone. He thought that new subscribers should be willing to buy solely because of "what the project stood for." So, the brochure explained his artistic credo and told of past productions but contained not one title or description of a play being considered or already chosen. There was also an order form. The results were catastrophic. In the overwhelming number of cases, it requires a combination of subscriber faith *and* the attraction of the coming season's plans to lure the renewal. And above all, to bring in new subscribers who have had no opportunity to develop faith in us, we must have a brochure which exhibits as many characteristics of a normal offering as possible. And there have been a few cases of companies having excellent artistic reputations or well-recognized policies of producing only original scripts, where they have, by most intensive efforts, managed to sell respectable amounts of subscriptions within relatively small seating capacity situations.

Unlike theatre, the soloist requirements inherent in symphony programming have usually forced the longer range planning that has made it the norm to include soloist listings in the spring subscription campaign. In most cases, opera companies also make very definite repertoire plans, often a few years ahead, not only because principal singers are in short supply and have to be pinned down considerably in advance, but because of the advance planning necessary for the outsize physical production demands of that field. Dance requires the most intricate and complex advance planning of all, with its problem of having to avoid duplications of ballets to subscribers within the same season, with three or four separate dance works often offered on the same program and with limitations on the number of new works that can be produced in any one season.

As I said before, experience has taught us that the more restrained approach has insufficient power to affect the person who has not yet begun to subscribe, or who may hardly be aware of our existence at all. For those people—and they would be our main targets in large-scale brochure distributions—we know that we must hit harder. I have always thought that a certain floridity of style and extravagance of phrase is not only good for us but is expected of us, and that the public is somewhat disappointed when such colorful expression is absent from our pronouncements. For after all, we are not in some staid and stuffy business. We are the performing arts. We are entertainment. It is a mistake, I think, to become overdulled with dignity and thus to give the impression that our performances must be as lacking in verve as our brochures.

In writing the descriptions of the plays, operas, ballets and symphonies for our brochures, we must avoid an uninspired academic tone, not because such statements are incorrect or inadequate from the informational standpoint, but because they do not strike strong enough blows for our purpose—which is to put our best possible foot forward. We must convince a prospective subscriber that what he might think is a musty classic is really full of contemporary meaning and will provide him with a great evening of superior entertainment; that a work he might have considered to be trivial and not worthy of his attention does possess merit on a number of levels; that an avant-garde listing in the repertoire which he would ordinarily avoid at all costs promises to be an intriguing, exciting and welcome new experience for him. Through these descriptions, we know that we can influence decisions to buy our subscription tickets—which is great for us, and for the customer, too. For, put off by preconceived, unjustified, negative notions about our repertoire, many people might not buy, unless caught up in our brochure's thrust. More often than not, the literal telling of the play's story defeats our purpose, particularly when limited by the space allowed in a brochure. Thus, we are usually better off giving images and impressions of the work, its spirit, its mood, presented with a vigor in contradistinction to the dead hand of the play catalogue writer.

One *could* write about Shakespeare's *The Tempest* as follows:

**Many critics consider this last work of Shakespeare an allegorical autobiography—a probing of human nature in loveliest poetry.**

I would certainly have no objection to this spare description for the purpose of a school class, but in a brochure designed to sell subscription tickets, I would much prefer the following:

> Here's one of the Bard's most scintillating works of genius, offer-
> ing in quicksilver profusion a procession of frolicking goddesses,
> clowns, faeries, sprites and spirits, weaving mythically and magi-
> cally through the tangled, tropical jungle of our subconscious in this
> pre-Freudian splurge of richly poetic fantasy—all enthralled by the
> limitless wonders of sorcery—in short, "such stuff as dreams are
> made on."

Supposing one is describing a play about a subject that is painful to contemplate, a play that people might well not want to attend. A case in point might be Peter Nichols' play, *Joe Egg*. We believe that once in attendance, the audience will find it fascinating and inspiring and that the artistic policy of our company which embraces drama of every facet of the human condition will be honored by its production. Yet, if we describe it flatly, we might not get the audience for it. It might weaken our entire season, as subscription links the basic attendance at each of the plays being offered. One might write the following about *Joe Egg*:

> The tragic dilemma of young parents trapped by the reality of
> their brain-damaged child.

While the oversimplified information would be correct, the effect on prospective subscribers would almost certainly be negative. However, the balance might swing over in our favor if we suggested more of the mood and content of the play itself in greater depth, saying something like this:

> Vivid vaudeville and sawdust circus provide the fascinating
> framework for this sensitive and vastly talented playwright's
> rampant black humor and ruthlessly honest, razor-sharp insight
> —while a jazz combo syncopates his unrestrained, undisguised
> scream of personal agony—in this immensely moving, profound
> and provocative drama about the multi-levels of love, marriage and
> parental responsibility. Already applauded in London, New York
> and wherever theatre of the highest quality is treasured.

How does the brochure writer handle the often great swings in the balance and composition of the forthcoming season's repertoire, which is presented to him by the artistic director and which he must now promote? For, having to write the descriptions of plays of varied genres, he fears that the potential subscriber for some elements of the offer, let us say the Restoration comedy, the revival of the 1930's hit-farce and the turn-of-the-century Russian drama, will be turned off when he sees the more progressive or avant-garde element in the programming. What does the writer do about that? He must have faith in the diversity of taste in enough of the people who will receive the brochure. He must proceed to write the brightest, most attractive descriptions that he can about all these plays. He tries to make the plays stand up and talk for themselves. He may not always succeed, but he should try to achieve a high degree of reader interest and involvement. I am not suggesting that the following statements about four plays in the categories mentioned above are the best possible descriptions, but they will give some idea of what I mean:

### *She Stoops to Conquer* by Oliver Goldsmith

This delightfully delirious divertissement parlays its playwright's ploy of mistaken identity into an uproarious high comedy of errors about a girl betrothed to a man she's never met. It's rich in rapier riposte, bubbling with wit and laced with grace—while languishing ladies, fatuous fops, bumbling bumpkins and bawdy barmaids cavort in all manner of pastoral jollification—and it's filled with all those marvelous, preposterous absurdities of an era of elegant entertainment.

### *Uncle Vanya* by Anton Chekhov

The compassionate Russian dramatist whose works have inspired platoons of playwrights, brilliantly illumines a human comedy in which powerful passions are stirred and brought to slow boil under the deceptively placid surface, while bittersweet humor cannot assuage the pang or stop the pain of love unrequited. A moody masterpiece of private grief and muted laughter, in which the yearning heart forgives man's follies and foibles.

### *Room Service* by John Murray and Allen Boretz

Here's a laugh-laden lampoon of "shoestring" theatrical producers, impecunious playwrights and actors "on their uppers," set in an inhospitable hostelry of the fleabag genre. This fast, funny, mile-a-minute farce, riotous with mad mayhem and extroverted,

exuberant, comic confusion—Marx Brothers style—is in the top
tradition of America's pre-existential theatre of the absurd!

### *Marat/Sade* by Peter Weiss

This sensation of the international stage is an eviscerating
event—jeering, jarring, sneering, snarling, mocking, shocking—a
laceration and flagellation of society, proceeding from revelation to
revolution—in the psychedelic atmosphere of a weird, disturbing
dream—meshing music, mummery and song. A modern master-
work of simply stunning theatricality!

I would say that most nonprofit professional theatres have a special problem. An entire generation of Americans has been raised in cities where
professional theatre has always meant the touring companies of last year's
Broadway hits, routed through the Independent Booking Office to the local
"road" legit houses, such as the Shubert in Chicago, the Biltmore in Los
Angeles, the Hanna in Cleveland, and so on. Now, in many of those same
cities, our resident companies have established themselves. They are certainly not like the other theatres just listed. They are not "straw hat"
enterprises. Neither are they old-time stock companies nor present-day dinner
theatres. They have their own contemporary character. In certain ways, they
are different kinds of theatrical producing entities from those our society has
heretofore known. Because they do not fit into the familiar categories or
molds, they often have a hard time in convincing the existing theatregoing
public that they are really professional.

If we were to tune in on the thoughts of those among the citizenry who have
long attended the visiting attractions at the local commercial playhouse, we
might become privy to some skeptical ruminations about our beloved project.
For they have considerable reservations about us. First of all, the artistic
director, the designer, the staff members and particularly many of the actors,
live right here, in the residential areas of the city, next door to ordinary
"civilians." Compared to their fellow actors who work in the visiting bus-
and-truck tour shows performed downtown at the old Bijou Theatre (where
they've sold that watery orange drink for as long as anybody in town can
remember and where cantankerous old Gus in the box office insults you in true
professional style), our resident theatre-folk are simply not exotic. They lack
the mystery of the gypsy troupers.

And besides, the good burghers are certainly saying to themselves, and out loud, too, "They work for an organization that openly admits it's *not-for-profit;* they even solicit contributions and often put on plays which, shall we say, are not 'everybody's cup of tea.' Obviously, these people don't put on good enough shows, or they wouldn't be in that position. Didn't it say in the paper that the famous producer, Harold Herrick, made a million dollars on that big musical, the fourth road company of which played at the Civic Auditorium (the Bijou wasn't big enough to handle the crowds) several years back? Of course, the place was so huge that most of us couldn't see or hear very much, but we knew it was great because the New York critics said it was. Oh, no ... you can't fool us. We know that this local effort isn't really 'perfessional.' We always have the feeling, somehow, that they're just youngsters who put powder in their hair and pretend to be 'real' actors. Come on now, let's face it. They're running a little theatre group—but with pretensions!"

Now this situation is where the brochure planners can strike a strong blow on our behalf—one that will, if we keep hammering away at it, help to disabuse our doubters of their preconceived notions and prejudices about our professional status. Right across the front of the brochure we can run a banner statement reading:

### One of Mid-America's Outstanding Resident
### *Professional* Legitimate Stage Companies!

The words "legitimate stage" added to "professional" also help to give the impression that it's "just like downtown" for those brochure readers who might need that kind of assurance and indoctrination. This motif should be repeated in several strategic spots in the brochure instrument. When we put out our brochures in the hundreds of thousands, often in duplication, we are repeating that message to them. And we can't do it often enough. I am convinced that in some of the strongholds of resident theatre—in the places where we have become consistently successful and have achieved continuity and viability—there are still many people, who ought to know better, but who think of our theatres as not truly professional. I suppose that we must, in such cases, solace ourselves with the adage, "Well, you can't win 'em all." And we can better afford to react this way in those places where we have already won to our theatres large-scale audiences, the members of which renew in considerable percentages annually. *They* know that we are truly professional. They may even have developed prejudices of their own against the "show biz" quality of programming at their city's respective commercial theatres.

*Writing the Copy . . . Opera*

In a large-scale distribution of brochures, there will be many people receiving them who will buy the subscription because several of their favorite operas are included in the repertoire and because a widely known star or several major ones will be appearing. However, for a great many others who will be receiving the same brochure, these enticements will not be enough, if they are not knowledgeable about either the operas or the stars. They will require additional selling points such as testimonials from the experts, an array of arguments about the advantages of subscribing, perhaps the discount and other factors. They will certainly have to be told more than the names of the big stars. Descriptions of the operas themselves can be especially helpful in convincing the prospective subscriber to fill out the order form, often overcoming what we believe are unfair, preconceived notions that what we have to offer is dull. The descriptions themselves should begin to sing arias to the readers! Bearing this in mind, we might describe some standard operas like this:

### *Carmen* by Georges Bizet

**The glint and glow of Iberian grandeur, the rhythmic click of Sevillian castanets, the mystique of the Spanish corrida, the portent of doom divined in the cards by a smoldering Gypsy girl with too many men in her life—and the flashing knife at her moment of truth. All set to the exquisite, haunting musical score that has captivated opera aficionados the world over!**

### *Don Giovanni* by Wolfgang Amadeus Mozart

**The "perfect opera" perfectly describes this supreme Mozartian achievement, this incredibly felicitous matching of divine music to flawless libretto. Here, the great libertine of song and legend lives and loves comically, tragically, furiously—and fatally. To see it, to hear it, is the opera buff's ultimate joy!**

### *Faust* by Charles Gounod

**In this opera, opulent in ravishing arias and duets, man dangles 'twixt heaven and hell and strikes a devil's bargain to revel in youth, love and wealth. Faust jousts with his soul but yields to his flesh!**

*The Barber of Seville* by Gioacchino Rossini

Delightful disguises abound and young love triumphs as pretty Rosina, noble Almaviva and resourceful Figaro bamboozle Bartolo, befuddle Basilio and confound the carabinieri in this charming, comic opera of bubbling champagne music that delights while it intoxicates.

*Pagliacci* by Ruggiero Leoncavallo

Canio pours out his glorious, searing song—then gives murderous vent to his passion. For clown though he be, he disdains cuckold's horns. This compact classic packs a powerful punch.

*Lucia di Lammermoor* by Gaetano Donizetti

A limitless feast of florid melody and vaulting song-bursts, replete with coloratura fireworks, thrusting tenor brilliance, rousing ensembles and thrilling choruses—all that soaring musical beauty that has made this work a crown jewel in grand opera's glittering diadem.

Now, I think we have made the point to the previously unreached brochure reader that grand opera isn't dull at all, although we may displease some members of the lorgnette set who tend to look down their noses at such efforts to attract new audience members. We know by our experience that this approach has been responsible for tremendous increases in opera companies' subscriberships.

### *Writing the Copy . . . Symphony Orchestras and Pops Concerts*

Programming assumes a unique importance from the promotional standpoint when a symphony orchestra undertakes certain special events, larger and obviously more exciting than the usual cycle of orchestral concerts with guest instrumental or vocal soloists. I mean extraordinary efforts like the presentation of a Verdi *Requiem,* Beethoven's *Ninth Symphony,* Britten's *War Requiem,* Orff's *Carmina Burana,* Schoenberg's *Gurre Lieder*—works which probably require, for many orchestras, augmenting the number of musicians, arranging for very large choral forces, and entire complements of fine vocal soloists. This kind of "blue chip" happening can be dramatized in the brochure, given major space and attention—perhaps an entire panel devoted to the subject—with a description which underscores its significance. For instance, if we were doing Beethoven's *Ninth Symphony,* I would suggest a fine drawing of the composer; pictures of the conductor, the entire orchestra, soloists, massed choruses; statements about each of the soloists; and an overall statement about the composer, the work itself, and so on. Something like this:

> **Reverence for the creative gifts of Ludwig van Beethoven is legendary. Paderewski felt unworthy to even touch the piano that the composer-giant had played. Wagner and Tchaikovsky paid him homage that verged on deification. The celebrated conductor Jullien, when performing a Beethoven work, always wore white kid gloves and used a jeweled baton he had brought to him on a silver tray. The world has honored this extraordinary man who could not hear the magnificent music he imagined, as it has honored no other composer—as succeeding generations continue to experience the joys of hearing his immortal symphonies and concertos. For each orchestra that undertakes the interpretation of his stirring works, Beethoven provides inspiration anew. Now, our own symphony orchestra, a superb group of highly trained musicians, each possessing soloist skills, welded into one mighty, finely honed musical instrument by our own beloved music director, with the collaboration of the great choral forces we have assembled and the participation of renowned vocal soloists, rises to the challenge of Beethoven's *Ninth Symphony*—the masterwork of a true genius, in whose work is revealed the rich product of his maturity—as he makes the most profound, most moving of musical statements, addressing himself directly and forcefully to our hearts and minds—yet sumptuously to our senses, too. His timeless theme of human brotherhood, peace and a better world is as pertinent today as it was in his own generation.**

You will note in the foregoing paragraph, the words, "a superb group of highly trained musicians, *each possessing soloist skills,* welded into one finely honed instrument," etc. This is not only a good point for our brochure, but a politic statement to make. For we audience promoters not only have to deal with the idiosyncracies of boards and administrators, but of the performers, too. In the case of a certain symphony orchestra (where several successive, successful subscription campaigns brought about an astronomical gain in the size of the audience, with such accompanying benefits to the musicians as higher weekly pay, more weeks of employment, and a new, acoustically superb hall in which to perform their art), a committee of orchestra members came to call upon the management, ironically to protest that they were not really as good an orchestra as was being claimed in the organization's promotional materials. Significantly, when confronted with the particular brochure they said they objected to, they were unable to put their finger on what was "wrong." The management finally deduced that what they really meant, but weren't saying, was that they didn't think that the conductor and the guest soloists were as good as was being claimed; that *they,* the instrumentalists, the unsung heroes, should be given more credit for the orchestra's recent success, after many years of comparative obscurity. That is not for us, the audience developers, to judge. However, if it will help assuage wounded feelings and boost morale, while at the same time providing extra strength for the brochure, why not look for ways in which to underscore the talents and highly developed musical skills of our players.

In the new climate of expanding audiences for symphony orchestras, there has been a considerable proliferation of the "pops" genre. In an increasing number of situations, such series, begun on an experimental basis, now have become a major element in orchestra programming, with events originally given for one performance each, now in the doubles and triples categories. Sometimes, these series are part of the regular fall-winter-spring seasons which are standard for symphony orchestras. In other cases, they take place in the summer or in special, larger-capacity spaces. One symphony organization has enjoyed much success with its "Summer Festival of Light Musical Entertainment," subtitled "Picnic Pops at Sunset." Like many others of the pops series producers, it has promoted its subscription through special brochures. A wide range of attractions is offered, including renowned guest conductors, country and western personalities, classical ballet stars, pianists and vocalists. When André Kostelanetz conducts an all-Tchaikovsky evening in the outdoor setting, the *1812 Overture* has cannons and fireworks. The brochure states:

**A Picnic-Pops-at-Sunset Event Is Not Just A Joyous Outing…It Is Like a Month in the Country!**

It goes on to say:

> Better still, *six* such joyous events—evenings of relaxation, of lolling on the green, grassy grounds of the serene parklike setting of the San Diego State Open-Air Theatre—bird-watching, girl-watching, fried chicken-munching, cheese-nibbling, wine-bibbing, beer-sipping, seven-upping—and amid these idyllic surroundings, you are beguiled and bedazzled by the entertainment world's most "in-demand" performers, backed by our 90-member symphony orchestra, under the batons of internationally admired conductors. All this can be yours by subscribing to the Terrace Series, the Garden Series or the Promenade Series. Whichever you choose, it's the biggest light musical entertainment bargain around. In fact, you get one great evening of unstuffed-shirted fun and frolic completely *free,* if you subscribe!

The one-color, simple, low-cost brochure also describes the open-air theatre location as "the most spectacular outdoor setting for great shows since the Roman Coliseum!" and shows a photograph of an attractive young couple grilling their shashlik under a tree, while below it says:

> Picnic box-suppers and beverages are on sale, to be enjoyed at tables on the grass before the show begins. Available will be fried chicken, a variety of sandwiches, fresh fruit, delectable pastries, soft drinks, coffee.

Now, that orchestra's pops series is very successful and has attracted a tremendous number of new people thereby. I think that its promotional approach has been as sound as it has been effective and that it has employed what I love to call "whip-cracking American showmanship," a phrase which I purloined some 40 years ago from a brochure written by one of the greats among direct-mail practitioners, Mike Kanter, who is still showing us all how to do it better.

For an orchestra in Canada a few seasons ago, we found a way to feature the comedienne Phyllis Diller in one of its excellent star-pops series concerts, and a large panel in its brochure was headed:

**Did You Know That Phyllis Plays the Piano, Too?**

Then, underneath her photograph it says:

**The new Phyllis is on her way to our town—face lifted, nose jobbed and teeth realigned! A Van Cliburn she ain't, but laugh you will when she sits down to play the piano—and positively underwhelms you with the fury of her Horowitzian attack—and then, back on her arch-supported feet, to prove her billing as "the world's greatest, funniest, female stand-up comic"—La Daffy-Diller herself!**

Evidently there is also whip-cracking *Canadian* showmanship around!

### *Writing the Copy...Dance*

Dance companies' brochures have often assumed a knowledge on the part of their readers that simply doesn't exist, particularly when, through large distributions, these brochures begin to reach many more people than in the past—far more than are within the circle of balletomanes who are well informed concerning the dance field. Many of the dance programs listed consist of three or four different works at one performance, and with all the series offered, there may be listed the titles of many works. Unless the reader is highly knowledgeable, not only about ballet in general, but about the repertoire of that company specifically, the mere listing of these titles will be meaningless to him and will have no effect on what we always hope will be his affirmative decision to buy the subscription. Even in the cases of the already indoctrinated, if some of the works listed have just been choreographed and are about to be presented for the first time, it is necessary to give information about them.

With these factors in mind, I have campaigned, with some success, for the inclusion in dance companies' subscription brochures, statements about each of the works which are being presented. For the Joffrey Ballet's brochure, New York critics provide a great statement about choreographer Gerald Arpino's work *Trinity* when they say:

**The most exhilarating, explosive, continuously inventive of rock ballets...probably the best rock ballet ever created...a positive celebration of life and dance.**

While about Leonide Massine's *Le Beau Danube,* they write:

**A nostalgic look at gay Vienna, bubbling with instant romance, public jollity and perpetual dancing to the rhythms of Johann Strauss...catches the very bounce and lilt of some of the most dance-provocative music in the world!**

For the person who may be considering subscribing to our dance series for the first time, the brochure must not only delineate the advantages of doing so—the entire rationale of subscribership (just as brochures on behalf of other performing arts disciplines would do), but must also exult in what is special and wonderful about *our* dance company, said in such a way that the idea of going to dance itself will seem to be more attractive. For instance, in the New York City Ballet's 25th anniversary season brochure there is prominently displayed a powerful statement under a bold caption, reading:

### A Feast for All the Senses

The paragraph goes on as follows:

**We offer a stunning season of dance-theatre, with our famed principal dancers, crack corps de ballet, top-drawer orchestral complement, opulent stage decor, exquisite costumes, brilliant lighting design, choreography to take your breath away—and all the excitement, exhilaration and exaltation of that perfect synthesis of old world balletic elegance and new world staging style for which this company is renowned—with performances flashing between the lofty peaks of the classic, the modern muse, the down-to-earthiness of jazz—from surging virility to limpid loveliness. In all, an irresistible combination of theatrical, musical and dance elements that are delightful to the eye, ravishing to the ear and, indeed, are a feast for all the senses!**

### *Featuring Artists and Star Power*

To illustrate how easily we can fall into the trap of mistakenly assuming that prospective subscribers know what *we* know, I was stunned when I read the brochure of a certain ballet company to see that not one of the 16 world-famed choreographers represented in its repertoire was even mentioned, although their works were listed. However, there was huge space given over to magnificent graphic artwork. Not only did I mention each of those choreographers in the new brochure I wrote for that company, but I also ran their pictures in a most central position. Their names on that brochure were like sterling on silver. I did not have to wait for the mail-order returns to know that the subscription level would show the immediate gain it did.

Some resident theatres offer "distinguished guest artists" (the euphemism for "guest stars," which better suits the sensitivities of some artistic directors). The star system, however, is the blood and bone of most American opera companies, and guest soloists of symphony orchestras are integral to their audience-drawing power. In all phases of promotion for any performing arts organization which has stars to offer, we should take full advantage of that potential box office boon. In certain situations, arts organizations, finding it hard to admit deviation from their own, oft-stated ideologies, will bring in big-name performers but then mute the point in their publicity and promotion. In their brochures they "have the name, but not the game." Thus, they do not get the full results in subscription sales that should be the "payoff." I think that once the decision is made to bring in a star, every possible benefit should be obtained from that fact, especially in the subscription context, where any extra element of such selling strength for any one of the productions of the series or season can increase the sales for the entire offering.

If a medium-size American opera company pays through the nose to buy the services of a big-name, big-voice, big-talent star like, let us say, Joan Sutherland, I would recommend that La Sutherland's photograph be employed on the *front* of the brochure, the *back* of the brochure *and inside the brochure*. The accompanying statements, considering her reputation, couldn't be too extravagant in their claims. Perhaps, something like this:

**Not since grand opera's golden age has such an incredibly flawless and supremely expressive voice been heard—a voice that can sweep to the high E's of the musical stratosphere—a voice of such purity and perfection that it leaves audiences limp with pleasure and frustrates usually articulate critics who struggle to find words worthy of describing such a phenomenon—an effortless technique that makes the most fiendishly difficult passages, the most cruel tessituras and the most delicate vocal embroidery seem like child's play. She's the greatest!**

However, if an opera company is a very big one, operating on a multimillion dollar budget, with its seasons regularly rich in the participation of the performing greats of the opera world, the emphasis on any one star does not have the same impact as in the case above—and may not even fit into the "billing" policies of the organization. In this situation, the appearance on the front, back or inside of the brochure of the photographs and names of a number of such widely admired opera idols, will have a combined, powerhouse effect on those readers who have knowledge of the opera field. Usually, an opera company that has many big-name stars on its artists' roster has been long and well established; has undergone previous periods of considerable expansion; and has already built up a very large subscription audience. For such a company (and there are very few of them), it is possible to publish more restrained brochures than those which I would prescribe for most arts organizations still on the rise, which still have audiences to build and expansions to achieve. However, the big, multimillion dollar company would be well advised, should its strong audience position suffer a decline, to put aside pretensions and get back into the market in a more aggressive way.

Since the star system is integral to the life of so many opera companies, and since there is always a limited supply of available stars whose services must be bid for in intensive, international competition, the forthcoming season might be weaker in big-name artists than the last several seasons. This situation might have a deleterious effect on both the renewal of subscriptions and on the sale of new ones to replace that attrition, and even on the chances to forge ahead in the total amount of subscribership. However, since it is normal in the grand opera field to make plans and to contract major artists far in advance, it would not be unusual for the management to know who its most important singers are going to be two seasons ahead. Such advance knowledge, when it involves some casting coups of great importance, enables us to help compensate for any weakness in star strength of the season immediately ahead by inserting a panel in the brochure for that future season which is captioned, "Looking Ahead," and which contains pictures of opera luminaries scheduled to appear two seasons hence, along with announcements of the roles they will be interpreting. Thus, subscribers who might be toying with the idea of dropping out for the season coming up, think twice before relinquishing their regular seat locations. For, in a situation of very high subscribership where it is very difficult to obtain single tickets the subscriber's loyalty is strengthened by the sober consideration that, if he

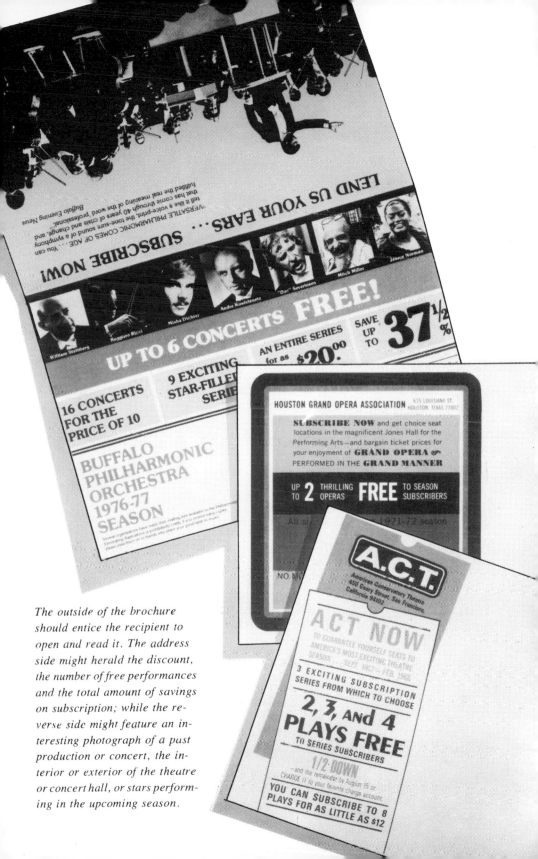

The outside of the brochure should entice the recipient to open and read it. The address side might herald the discount, the number of free performances and the total amount of savings on subscription; while the reverse side might feature an interesting photograph of a past production or concert, the interior or exterior of the theatre or concert hall, or stars performing in the upcoming season.

**an Sand**

*1*

e flaming ardor, th
passion that we ha
ssociate with the tra
ain's great ones. Yet,
he abandoned frenzy
from his steely finger
k the keyboard with the
Flamenco dancer's
heels, he amazes by
n reining in; his
ntrol! To honour the
d of Rachmaninoff
en chosen to per-
orlds most beloved
the Rachmaninoff 2nd.
inner of ten International
npetitions Aloys Mooser,
e," Geneva, wrote "Spain
a performer that will
imself in the glorious line
e, Casals and Segovia."

# FOR THE

**Mario Ber**

MUSIC DIRECTOR
PRINCIPAL CONDU
HIS NATIONAL ARTS
ORCHESTRA
*MAR. 9-10*

In 1969, the vigorous, n
tional Arts Centre Orche
upon the scene, appropri
led by young, Canadian-b
Mario Bernardi, whose adv
musical studies in Italy, late
soning as Music Director of
London Sadlers Wells Opera
outstanding conducting at the
San Francisco Opera (i.e. "A
Masked Ball" with Leontyne
Price, when The S. F. Examiner
critic wrote, "I was bowled over
. . . Bernardi is a find!"), have all
gone into the making of a first
rate Music Director for the
Ottawa-base ensemble. Under his
lively baton, the N.A.C.O. has already savored sweet success in
its 1972 Lincoln Center descent
into the lion's den, with the staid
New York Times going all-out in

**Jerry Jennings,**

TENOR

An American who has "made it"
in Europe, this tremendously

— to c
ouse!

**William Walke**

BARITONE

Whether he's on-stage at
Metropolitan Opera or on
way — or on the T.V. scre
Johnny Carson's "Tonigh
Show," this tall, blonde, h
some he-man of a bariton
ways the supreme showm
booming out his big, bea

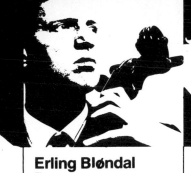

## Erling Bløndal Bengtsson
**CELLIST**
*FEB. 2-3*

Scandinavia's master cellist, a protege of Piatigorsky, is noted for the elegance of his playing, for his impeccable sense of style, as well as for his deep-pile, velvet-lined, brooding tone that sets concert-goers shivering with pure auditory pleasure!

## Byron Jan
**PIANIST**
*FEB. 9-10*

An intangible g
delicacy of phr
thundering py
keyboard mas
glow bursts i
"Nothing she
raved the cr
Yorker," an
distinguish
The Mosc
chestra, w
"One of t
the age!

**The Queen of Song Returns**

VOA Proudly Presents
**JOAN SUTHERLAND**

## S SAVE YOU MONEY

## Cliburn
**PIANIST**
*APRIL 13-14*

Once again, we're to hear that blazing technical brilliance, passionate interpretation and total immersion in the vital force of music, so astonishing that it sets audiences on fire. This extraordinarily talented young man enjoys the greatest following — worldwide — of any artist alive today. His popularity is so overwhelming that only subscribers to our 1973-74 season will be assured of having tickets for this "Must" event of Winnipeg's 100th Anniversary Year!

## Piero Gamba
**MUSIC DIRECTOR AND PRINCIPAL CONDUCTOR**

The spectacular impact of Piero Gamba during the two seasons of his serving our Orchestra as its Musical Director, has set us rocketing to heretofore undreamed of success. Yes, The Winnipeg Symphony Orchestra has entered upon a new era of artistic achievement and public recognition, under the inspired leadership of this prestigious, international Man of Music — already celebrating his 28th year as a conductor of prodigious powers on the podium.

*Nothing sells like star power. Stars should be featured prominently in photos, headlines and copy — on the inside and outside of the brochure. Less well-known artists can be featured as well, by relying on production photos and descriptive copy to build them up, if names and faces are not readily recognized.*

## Welcome to Producing Director, Jon Jory

Actors Theatre of Louisville takes much pride and satisfaction in having secured the services of the brilliant, dynamic and dedicated Jon Jory as its new Producing Director. One of the finest, young directorial talents in the U.S.A. today, he is also a forceful and effective executive, and just the very opposite of the "ivory-tower" artist, and just the man to give strong leadership to our theatre.

A product of the famed Yale University, he went on to found and give artistic direction to the renowned New Haven Long Wharf and has since achieved national recognition staging successes in major playhouses throughout the country. Louisville now looks to him in its pursuit of excellence in entertainment with the own highest aspiration.

## Our NEW

Let me be honest — I love this people are my kind — colourful, e to come home.

A theatre should reflect the and so, as the new Artistic Dire continue to involve Winnipeg a comedies and musicals. My aim best actors, the best directors, have come to expect — so th each production at the "M next season and become a subscriber family. It promi

Mr. Cariou's extr from major musical theatre. His starri A LITTLE NIGHT were delighte M

YOU ARE INVITED TO BECO TO THE SYRACUSE SYMPH

## NEW CONC

Picture the splendor of the Civic Center, the new showplace of Central New York. Here you will be able to enjoy the world's finest music in one of the most luxuriously appointed concert theaters in the Northeast. Fashioned in the contemporary elegance of brick, glass and wood, it will combine a gracious visual environment with the acoustical excellence that is a must for the enjoyment of fine music.

As you enter the Civic Center, you will find yourself in a three story lobby with floating walkways at each level, perfect for promenading and people watching. You can enjoy a pre-concert dinner or a post-concert toast in the Center Restaurant and Lounge, and portable bars will be stationed about the lobby for your intermission refreshment.

Within the concert hall itself you will be able to see and hear perfectly from each one of the more than 2000 comfortable, spacious seats. Continental seating will assure plenty of leg room between rows and the maximum number of seats in the best viewing and

## Our 75th Anniversary Year, The Best of Two Wor
## he Mellow Sound Retained ... BUT NEW COMFO
## W CONVENIENCE, NEW ELEGANCE...

The Grand Foyer

Escalators to the Dress Circle and Gallery

### MUSIC HALL

Many symphony orchestras in no the United States, but all over the have built fabulously expensiv halls, only to discover that the m portant element, the acoustics, ju measure up. Taking no chance keeping the old hall, with its ma acoustics, seasoned by almost a years of great music, giving it a new comfort, new convenie elegance.

## Artistic Director

...y, I was born and bred here. The
...rprising — unique! So I've decided

...ure of its audiences — ours does —
...r of Manitoba Theatre Centre I shall
...ences a balanced season of dramas,
...to present on stage, the best plays, the
...in short the standard of excellence you
...you the audience, will look forward to
...'' and the "Warehouse". Please join me
...ember of the Manitoba Theatre Centre
...to be colourful, enterprising, and unique!

Sincerely yours,

Len Cariou

...dinary range as a theatre artist has o...
...on Broadway to Greek Tragedy in A...
...Broadway performances in Ab...
...USIC each earned him a Tony Aw...
...to have obtained the services of s...
...Cariou, whose early career is s...
...tre Centre, is uniquely equ...
...tinued growth and...
...leased tha...

### ...ME A CHARTER SUBSCRIBER
### ...ONY IN ITS MAGNIFICENT
# ...ERT HALL!

## The Dream is Now a Rea...

The stunning new Playhouse, an adve...
theatrical architecture, is set in a grass...
in the heart of a green, wooded park, or...
overlooking a spectacular, panoramic vie...
great city. Aesthetically pleasing and func...
flawless, this theatre possesses superb stag...
facilities, perfect visibility throughout and re...
accoustics. Here, in idyllic surroundings, but o...
a few minutes from the center of town, you car...
the relaxation, entertainment, excitement and
exaltation that only the theatre at its best can pro...
Here, you will enjoy one of the country's finest act...
ensembles in a succession of excellent, professiona...
legitimate stage productions. Make this theatre and
its provocative program a regular part of your
way of life.

### Subscribe Now

use the order form on the inside of this brochure.

...comfort as well as an open airy feeling. The
furthest seat in the second balcony is only
125 feet from the stage, creating a remarkable sense of intimacy for a hall of this size.
In each of the 14 boxes, the six movable
chairs will offer additional comfort.

Russell Johnson, one of the most distinguished acoustical engineers on this continent, has designed an orchestra shell and
18 motor-operated adjustable velour banners
to create the perfect conditions for orchestral
music in this multi-purpose hall. In the handsome, functional design, even the sound-
reflecting brick enhances the hall acoustically.

No matter where you live in Central New
York, you'll find it easy to get to the new
Civic Center, located in the heart of downtown Syracuse convenient to routes 690 and
81. Within a two block radius there are more
than 3,000 parking spaces available.

The new Civic Center is destined to become
more than a cultural landmark. It will be a
musical showcase comparable to the finest

*When something new is in the offing, your brochure should
capitalize on this promotional advantage. A new or remodeled facility; a new artistic director, conductor or resident
choreographer; or even a new artistic policy can convince
the potential subscriber that he can get in on something
new and exciting by purchasing a subscription.*

# 6½ PLAYS

*The discount, when offered, should be an important feature in the brochure, as should all special privileges and benefits accruing to the season or series subscriber — prizes, priority seating, parking and exchange privileges, etc.*

**TO CHOOSE FROM**

SERIES "C"
8 Exciting New Productions Plus 8
Gold Star Coupons Good to Any Production in the A.C.T. Repertory.

**4 FREE PLAYS**
16 Plays for the price of 12

| Seat Location | Ticket Price | You Pay |
|---|---|---|
| Orchestra | $5.00 | $60.50 |
| 1st balcony | $4.00 | $48.50 |
| 2nd balcony— 1st 7 rows | $3.00 | $36.50 |
| 2nd balcony— last 5 rows | $2.00 | $24.50 |

Prices include 50¢ for handling and mailing

**ENT PLANS**

Many organizations, particularly orchestras, offer a complicated selection of series, half-series and special events, requiring a great deal of space to lay out clearly each separate plan (left). In large auditoriums, it is sometimes advisable to print a floor plan reflecting seats in various price ranges. Organizations with smaller seating capacities and a standard subscription price can get away with a simple listing of offerings (below). Note that in this particular theatre brochure, the management chose to identify two of the most popular offerings as the plays "free" to purchasers of the discount subscription package.

**8 PLAYS FOR THE PRICE OF 6**

SEE THE TWO EXTRA-PRICE MUSICALS
"THE KING AND I" (a $4.50 ticket)
"GUYS AND DOLLS" (a $4.50 ticket)
**Absolutely FREE**

a clear $9.00 saving by subscribing to a series ticket
and have your own regular seat to all eight of the season's productions
a much better seat than single ticket buyers will be able to obtain
for any of the season's plays

THE KING AND I

THE GLASS MENAGERIE

THE TAVERN

BECKET

GUYS & DOLLS

THE BALLAD OF THE SAD CAFE

ANTONY & CLEOPATRA

the Cocktail Party

The order form should provide the subscriber with enough information to order what he wants and your organization with what you need to know about the subscriber. Performance days and times, series prices, return address, and (if applicable) credit card or billing instructions must be included. The series and dates should be so clear in the brochure that the subscriber can simply check them off or indicate them by letter or number on the order form.

(Please Print)

NAME

ADDRESS

CITY_____STATE_____ZIP_____
(Important)

PHONE

**CHECK PERFORMANCE DESIRED:** (Offer expires June 30, 1967)

**EVENINGS (2 PLAYS FREE)**

☐ Tuesday  ☐ Wednesday  $19.25* (YOU SAVE $7.00)
☐ Thursday  ☐ Sunday

**EVENINGS (1 PLAY FREE)**

☐ Friday  ☐ Saturday  $27.50* (YOU SAVE $4.00)

**MATINEES (2 PLAYS FREE)**

☐ Wednesday  ☐ Sunday  $16.75* (YOU SAVE $6.00)

I would like to order_____subscriptions @ $_____each making a total of $_____.
*Price includes 50c service charge.

☐ Full payment enclosed

☐ Charge my C.A.P. Account No.

☐ Charge my C.B.T. Account No.

☐ Bill me directly

SIGNATURE

Make checks payable, and mail to:
**Hartford Stage Company**
**Kinsley Street at Constitution Plaza**
**Hartford, Connecticut  06103**

For further information call 525-4258

Note: The Hartford Stage Company is a non-profit organization. Contributions over the cost of tickets are tax deductible.

I enclose $_____as a contribution.

Refunds cannot be made on individual plays, nor, once the season has begun, on the series as a whole.

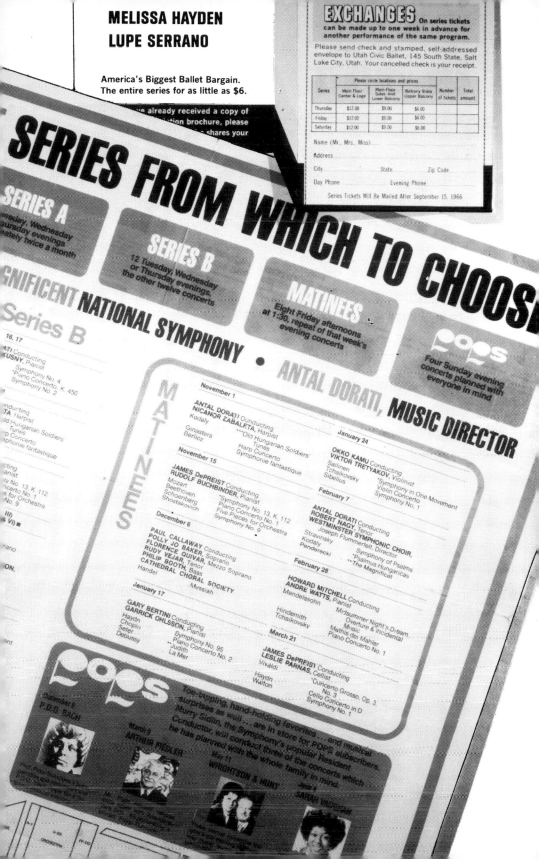

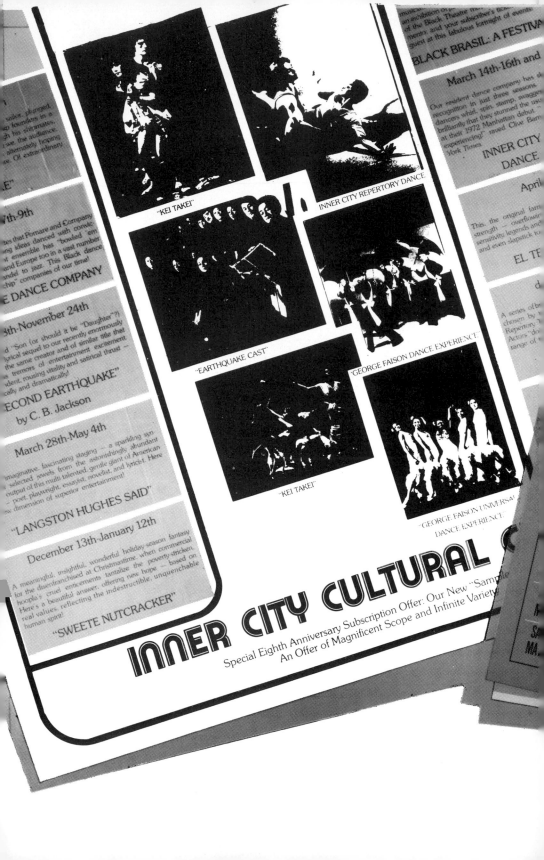

"KEI TAKEI"

INNER CITY REPERTORY DANCE

"EARTHQUAKE CAST"

"GEORGE FAISON DANCE EXPERIENCE"

"KEI TAKEI"

"GEORGE FAISON UNIVERSAL DANCE EXPERIENCE"

# INNER CITY CULTURAL

Special Eighth Anniversary Subscription Offer: Our New "Sample
An Offer of Magnificent Scope and Infinite Variety

"SWEETE NUTCRACKER"

**December 13th-January 12th**

A meaningful, insightful, wonderful holiday season fantasy for the disenfranchised at Christmastime when commercial hoopla's cruel enticements tantalize the poverty-stricken. Here's a beautiful answer, offering new hope — based on real values, reflecting the indestructible, unquenchable human spirit!

"LANGSTON HUGHES SAID"

**March 28th-May 4th**

imaginative, fascinating staging — a sparkling sun selected jewels from the astonishingly abundant output of this multi-talented, gentle giant of American — poet, playwright, essayist, novelist, and lyricist. Here dimension of superior entertainment!

**ECOND EARTHQUAKE**
by C. B. Jackson

d "Son (or should it be 'Daughter'?)
lyrical sequel to our recently enormously
the same creator and of similar title that
tremors of entertainment excitement
rousing vitality and satirical thrust —
and dramatically!

**th-November 24th**

DANCE COMPANY

es that Pomare and Company
ing ideas danced with comic
ensemble has "bodied 'em
Europe too in a vast number
del to jazz. This Black dance
chip" companies of our time!

**th-9th**

BLACK BRASIL: A FESTIVA

**March 14th-16th and**

Our resident dance company has
recognition in just three seasons
dancers who spin, stamp, swagge
brilliantly that they stunned the use
at their 1972 Manhattan debut.
experiencing" raved Clive Bar
York Times.

INNER CITY
DANCE

April

This, the original fam
strength — overflowing
sensitivity legends, and
and even slapstick to

EL TE

A series of br
chosen by
Repertory
Actors "do
range of

Special layout techniques are required for organizations presenting multiple attractions (left) and theatres playing in a rotating
repertory schedule (right). It is essential that the productions and
performance dates are clear so that the potential subscriber
knows what he is buying and when.

"Rush down to the Geary and Marines and see what the American Conservato Theatre has done." —San Francisco Examine

DeAnn Mears and Paul Shenar in Man and Superman.

**JOIN:** The perceptive and culturally aware people in your community who are enjoying "... the kind of theatre available nowhere else, a rich mixture of old and new, classical and commercial, comic and tragic, plays you never tire of seeing, have always wanted to see, and never expected to see." —Oakland Tribune

**HAVE:** "More excitement in a weekend with A.C.T. than a month on Broadway." —Los Angeles Times

**ENJOY:** "The most recklessly imaginative and technically adventurous of all repertory companies." —Saturday Review

**DISCOVER:** "Through the brilliance of A.C.T. what theatre is all about, by its theatricality and its emotional excesses." —San Mateo Times

**PARTICIPATE:** "A.C.T. is an entertaining evening of theatre that shouldn't be talked about, it should be seen." —Palo Alto Times

"I hope you will hasten to see what all the shouting is about." —San Francisco Examiner

*Brochure selling-power is often enhanced by quotes from the press Another promotional technique, exemplified by the brochure at the bottom of the opposite page, is to quote your own subscription sales figures (as long as they are impressive), thank the community for its support, and perhaps follow that with a message from the artistic or managing director.*

# Des économies appréciables.

Économiser de façon appréciable, c'est s'abonner à la saison 76/77 des Grands Ballets Canadiens.

En profitant de cette offre d'abonnement vous épargnerez temps, argent et tracas. Lorsque la saison promet d'être plus que passion-nante, et les places très demandées, n'est-ce pas avantageux d'avoir des billets réservés, avant qu'ils ne soient mis en vente au guichet? Cette saison, s'abonner c'est participer à la sélection des spectacles choisis parmi "Les Plus Grands Succès" des Grands Ballets Canadiens.

Durant la saison, diverses activités seront offertes aux abonnés, telles que des répétitions et classes ouvertes, ainsi que des présen-tations d'ateliers chorégraphiques. Les abonnés recevront égale-ment des communiqués leur donnant des informations sur notre compagnie.

# A beautiful way to save.

Saving is beautiful when you take advantage of Les Grands Balle Canadiens Subscription Series 76/77.

You can save time, bother and money by taking advantage of t subscription offer. Also, as you will see from the highlights of this b chure, this promises to be an exciting and popular season. As a subscriber, you'll be guaranteed seats before the box office ru This season, subscribers will also participate in selecting perfor mances from "The Greatest Hits" of Les Grands|Ballets Canad

Subscribers will be offered the opportunity to participate in a number of special activities during the season. These will rang open classes and rehearsals, special workshop presentation social events where they can meet the dancers and directo will receive a newsletter detailing all the company's activitie

Ludmilla Chiriaeff—Fondatrice et Directrice · Brian Macdonald—Directeur Artistique · Fernand Nault—Chorégraphe Attitré / Ludmilla Chiriaeff—Founder and Director · Brian Macdonald—Artistic Director · Fernand Nault—Resident C

| 1 | 2 | 3 | 4 | 5 | OPTIO |
|---|---|---|---|---|---|
| | | Les Grands Ballets Canadiens. | Le Royal Winnipeg Ballet | Les Grands Ballets Canadiens | Les Gra Ballets Ca Casse-N |

**1**

**TanzforumKöln (Ballet Cologne)**

Le répertoire de cette troupe remarquable est composé des œuvres significatives de la danse moderne. telles que "La Table Verte" de Kurt Jooss et "Tilt" de Hans van Manen. Au rang de leurs créations, on trouve aussi un ballet très populaire, "The Ragtime Dance Company" sur la musique de Scott Joplin. Pour la première fois au Canada, cette troupe susci-tera sans doute un très grand intérêt.

**Ballet Cologne**

Their repertoire retains the works that have given modern dance its special signifi-cance. like Kurt Jooss' famous danse macabre "The Green Table" and Hans van Manen's "Tilt". Their creations include an extremely popular ballet to Scott Joplin's infectious music "The Ragtime Dance Company"

Making their first visit to Canada. Ballet Cologne is certain to attract a great deal of attention

Séries 1 2 3
Octobre 4 5 6

**2**

**Het Nationale Ballet (Ballet National des Pays-Bas)**

Cette compagnie jeune et inventive qui nous vient d'Amsterdam, possède un répertoire classique varié. Elle a été louée pour la façon spectaculaire qu'elle a de traiter les idées et le mouve-ment. Cette compagnie ex-ploite l'ancien et le moderne dans une harmonie merveilleuse

En collaboration avec l'Office des tournées du Conseil des Arts du Canada et Cantour

**Dutch National Ballet**

The young dancers of this inventive company from Amsterdam offer a tremen-dous variety of ballet They have been cited for their pre-sentation of ideas and move-ment that are sure to excite me eye. The company de-monstrate how the old and new can co-exist and thrive together

In collaboration with the Touring Office of the Canada Council and Cantour

Séries 1 2 3
Octobre 28 29 30

**3**

**Les Grands Ballets Canadiens.**

**Lac des Cygnes**

Cette pierre angulaire du répertoire classique n'a que très rarement été historique-ment reconstituée. Suite à des recherches minu-tieuses, cette version fera revivre l'œuvre créée par Petipa et Ivanov en 1895 au théâtre Marie de St-Péters-bourg La demande des billets sera grande. et en vous abonnant vous vous assurez d'avoir un siège et le meilleur

**Swan Lake**

Rarely has historic justice ever been done to this cornerstone of the classical repertoire. Through careful research this version will be entirely faithful to the original created by Petipa and Ivanov in the Maryinsky Theatre in St Petersburg in 1895. There will be a huge demand for tickets Buying a subscrip-tion will guarantee you the best seats before the rush

Séries 1 2 3
Novembre 12 13 18
Soirées du MAURIER

**4**

**Le Royal Winnipeg Ballet**

Ambassadrice reconnue de la danse au Canada. Cette troupe exceptionnelle s'est ralliée l'approbation des pu-blics canadiens et étrangers Elle atteint un très haut degré de professionnalisme qui donne à chaque représenta-tion un caractère inoubliable

**Royal Winnipeg Ballet**

Now established as Canada's ambassadors of dance this spirited troupe has won the hearts of audiences at home and abroad They are a polished troupe who can always be depended on for memorable and warm performances They com-municate the joy of dancing

Séries 1 2 3
Avril 1 2 3
Soirées du MAURIER

**5**

**Les Grands Ballets Canadiens**

**Les Plus Grands Succès**

Au cours des ans plusieurs événements chorégraphi-ques se sont ajoutés au ré-pertoire des Grands Ballets Canadiens. Parce que nous avons la volonté de créer toujours de nouvelles œuvres, la tentation est grande d'ou-blier certains de nos succès passés Cette saison, nous voulons vous offrir à nouveau quel-ques uns de nos chef-d'œuvres, démontrant ainsi l'excellence et le rayonne-ment de notre compagnie Et bien sûr, nous ajouterons au répertoire quelques nouveaux ballets

**Greatest Hits**

Over the years many impres-sive and imaginative ballets have been added to the repertoire of Les Grands Ballets Perhaps because we are always creating new works. it is all too easy to over look past achievements This significant season will redress the balance and clearly show the company's contribution through its most popular successes And we will add a few new ballets to the list as well You'll be voting on the selection See the back of the subscription coupon

Séries 1 2 3
Avril/mai 29 30 1

**OPTIO**

**Les Grands Ballets Ca**

**Casse-N**

Depuis des ann de Fernand Na que Casse-N chanté à l'ép chanté à l'ép des milliers de A n en pas de soirée mêm la famille Si vous n av Casse-Nois vous êtes p jour, faites C est en ent que cette sentée pa Ballets C

Year a Nault versio Chris enc peo able tam

Soirées du MAURIER

**Les Plus Grands Succès.** Abonnés! Participez en sélectionnant 4 de vos ballets favoris.

# Abonnez-vous dès maintenant.

En ce moment, un rabais de 20% est offert sur les abonnements réguliers, et 50% pour les étudiants. Votre série comprendra des billets pour les "Plus Grands Succès".

Des bons seront émis en faveur des abonnés, leur permettant d'acheter au même rabais des billets pour les deuxième et troisième choix des "Plus Grands Succès".

Remplissez dès maintenant ce bon de commande pour des économies appréciables!

**Greatest Hits.** It's up to you! As a subscriber, y of a performance. Indicate your four favourit

# Subscribe now.

There is a 20% discount on subscriptio 50%. The series includes tickets for the

Subscribers will be issued vouchers e the second and third programmes a Fill out this order coupon today.

becomes a dropout, he might not be able to get tickets at all for the spectacular events scheduled a year or two later. Even if he does get in, he might not be able to obtain tickets in the price and seat location category that he had been enjoying previously, as a regularly renewing series subscriber. This approach will also benefit the sale of new subscriptions, because it encourages the potential subscriber to stake out his claim to seats *now,* not only for present advantages but for even greater ones to come.

Every possible strategy must be employed by opera companies to keep subscription at the highest possible level in relation to capacity, considering that their costs of operating are so much greater than those of any of the other performing arts. And because their ticket prices are also more costly, the possibility of selling single tickets to some of their productions is correspondingly less. If it is difficult to get a nonsubscriber to take a chance on an unknown play at $6 a ticket, what do you think the chances are of selling him an unknown opera at $25 a throw?

The list of guest soloists and what is said about them can sometimes be more important in selling subscriptions for symphony orchestra seasons than the programming itself. In fact, some of the most successful spring brochures of recent years have been those in which the full season programming has been absent, but in which the soloists have been stressed heavily, using their photographs centrally, with effective statements about their renown and their capabilities. If the artist is world famous, then there is plenty of excellent material to condense for the purpose. If the artist is virtually unknown, then the statement about him or her must be especially forceful. There are instrumental soloists of outstanding talent who are simply unknown or have not yet developed that special aura that generates instant ticket sales. However, if given a fine send-off in the brochure, they can, in combination with some middle-range and some really famed artists, help constitute a quite salable package in a subscription offer. Sometimes a quote from a critic's review supplied by the artists' managements can make up the entire statement about the artist for the brochure. More often, the brochure writer's own statement about the artist will do a better job. By reading many reviews and much past publicity material, he or she can derive some useful words and ideas to work into the text and obtain a better understanding as to what is special about both the less known and the more established artists. Of course, in the case of the better known ones, the brochure writer may already have excellent impressions, having been present at the artist's previous performances. A recurring problem is one of space, even when much larger brochures than have previously been used are introduced, for often upward of 20 guest soloists and guest conductors must be described. Therefore, the statements should be compact, yet must say enough to convince the reader. Here are some examples of statements about artists at varying stages in their careers in the musical world:

### Van Cliburn, Pianist

Once again we're to hear that blazing technical brilliance, passionate interpretation and total immersion in the vital force of music, so astonishing that it sets audiences on fire. This extraordinarily talented pianist enjoys the greatest following—worldwide— of any classical artist alive today. His popularity is so overwhelming that only subscribers to our forthcoming season will be assured of having tickets for this "must" event of the year!

### Esteban Sanchez, Pianist

Here is the flaming ardor, the pride and passion that we have come to associate with the tradition of Spain's great ones. Yet, for all of the abandoned frenzy that pours from his swift, steely fingers as they hit the keyboard with the power of a flamenco dancer's pounding heels, he amazes by his sudden reining in, his superb control, his change of pace, his poetry and sensitivity. He's already the winner of 10 international competitions.

### Janos Starker, Cellist

He plays with the fantastic dash, bravura, intensity and joyous rapture that only a supreme master of the instrument could ever hope to achieve, though he's suave and subtle, too—and his lush, velvet-lined, brooding tone provides soulful pleasure to audiences fortunate enough to hear him play. "He's the king of cellists," rightly raves critic John Jones of the *New York Chronicle*.

### Pinchas Zukerman, Violinist

"The major violinistic discovery of this generation" is not an exaggeration when applied to this latter-day Israeli Paganini who performs with such dazzling skill, consummate showmanship and unique tonal quality that he simply sweeps his adoring public. He's a protégé of Isaac Stern, who once prophetically stated, "I have rarely heard as richly promising a talent. . . . I fully expect him to take his place among the great artists of our time."

### Kyung-Wha Chung, Violinist

A doll-like beauty from Korea, she's one of the most entrancing violinists to grace the concert scene in many years. She's the epitome of fragile, Madonna-like loveliness, yet she plays like a flaming angel. She's the winner of the world series of violin competitions, the Leventritt. Today, her star is streaking toward the musical heavens.

### Barry Tuckwell, French Horn Player

He has subdued this most treacherous of instruments so that, miraculously, his tone is rich, full and burnished, exploiting all extremes of swift passages, dizzying dimensions of dynamics and variations of color—and then he somehow conjures up a round, warm, infinitely beautiful sound of Caruso-like qualities, a flowing fountain of bel canto songs without words! Without question, he's the greatest living master of the French horn.

### Marisa Robles, Harpist

This dark-eyed beauty from Madrid commands a startling range of colors and subtleties in her playing, turning her harp, at will, into a strumming guitar, a mighty Wurlitzer pipe organ, an entire assortment of percussion instruments—and she can make you hear the tinkling sound of Lisztian piano cadenzas, too! Her recitals are held to be experiences in enchantment.

The arrival of a new director can be treated as the beginning of a new era. Certainly, it can be an important factor for promotion, a "horse to ride." I am, of course, assuming that our man is really terrific. Thus, I wouldn't blanch at starting out with something like this in a symphony brochure:

Welcome to greatness! We are proud that this giant among world maestros has chosen to come to our city, to our orchestra. He arrives here at the peak of his powers and at the height of his international career, the much honored bearer of music's most revered traditions, yet so exciting and innovating that he will undoubtedly attract a burgeoning young audience while also bringing a new dimension of listening pleasure to our mature following. In his previous guest appearances here, we have been thrilled by his crackling dynamism, his own cachet of conductorial charisma, as our orchestra became one finely honed, marvelous instrument, responding to every nuance and shading of his sensitive, inspiring direction. For the forthcoming charter subscription season in our wonderful new home, he has chosen a carefully designed balance of repertoire and he has convinced us to "splurge" in the soloist-star department. So we take great pride in inviting both renewing and new series subscribers to share in the musical entertainment pleasures and satisfactions of the season to come.

If the new conductor is not of the calibre that has been indicated above, you must, of course, adjust your copy to the circumstances.

A continuing music director should always be given a place of importance in the brochure, for he, in the public's mind, is the symbol of the artistic character of our orchestra. In some situations he can be pictured in action (with baton in hand), alongside his message to the subscribers about the plans for the coming season. In other cases the panel can be *about* him. For instance, it may be his fifth, tenth, fifteenth or twentieth anniversary as leader of our orchestra. I once used a maestro's *sixteenth* anniversary as an occasion for a beautiful panel about him, written and signed by the board president. Why the sixteenth anniversary? Because that was the year in which that particular organization decided to begin a major subscription campaign. Thus, the "Welcome to Greatness!" for a new music director can become, "We Salute 20 Years of Greatness!" for a music director staying on, with appropriate copy to follow. Although I am very much the press agent, prone to the exaggerations and excesses of my professional tribe, I am again assuming that the conductor we are speaking of *does* possess attributes of this "greatness."

Guest conductors, by the way, deserve strong billing in symphony brochures, too. Usually, not the same size pictures as the resident conductor-music director rates, but perhaps larger than the soloists get, as there are usually so many more soloists. If there are, as is often the case, four, five, or more guest conductors, they can form a little section of their own in the brochure, with their pictures. The blurbs should be written, so as to establish, in straight, brief statements, their prestigious affiliations and credits, their status. Here is such a brochure paragraph about the conductor, Georg

Semkow, now music director of the Saint Louis Symphony Orchestra, when he "guested" with the Houston Symphony Orchestra several years ago:

**The world-renowned symphony and opera orchestras of Vienna, Berlin, Paris, Rome, Milan, London, Copenhagen and Moscow are the "beat" of this crack Polish-born conductor. His stunning American debut with the Boston Symphony, followed by his triumphant New York Philharmonic appearances, have skyrocketed his American career.**

The artistic director of a resident theatre company who is receiving wide recognition makes a good subject for special treatment in the brochure. For instance, the Long Wharf Theatre of New Haven, Connecticut, has just such an important asset in Arvin Brown. So, an entire panel was given over to him, with its bold caption reading:

**The Hottest Director in the Country**
**—and Long Wharf's Got Him!**

And then there's a big photograph of him, with the following statement:

**In the *Variety*-style parlance of the theatrical trade, Arvin Brown is "the hottest director in the country." His major New York success with Eugene O'Neill's *Long Day's Journey into Night*, his West Coast triumph with *Forget-Me-Not Lane*, and his acclaim at the international Edinburgh Festival, plus his almost uncanny judgment on plays and overall artistic savvy here on his home grounds, have rocketed him to international recognition. We who work with him have long known that we harbored a "house genius" and are more than happy that despite occasional, highly prestigious "moonlighting" assignments (with our blessings), he remains our artistic leader, providing that inspiration and high level of professionalism that has made Long Wharf the envy of the entire resident professional theatre on this continent.**

Then, the signature (a real signature, plus the name in type below) of M. Edgar Rosenblum, the theatre's administrative head—and beneath that, a caption, reading:

**A Few Choice Words from Our Executive Director**
**on the Subject of Our Artistic Director**

The artistic director of any performing arts organization is somehow even more important than his title indicates. He is in a true sense the moral and morale leader of his project. It is not only the staff and board members who look to him, but the public, too. And it is he who presumably has up his sleeve the ideas, the plans, and even the miracles we hope for. So, I have always felt that a statement from "Our Leader" has value in our brochures, and I have always sought to include such messages. They should ring with promise and optimism and contribute, in every way possible, to the overall effect of the brochure in its purpose of getting the reader to fill out the order form and send it back with his check. Let us say that an artistic director of a resident theatre is speaking his piece in our brochure. Perhaps it will be run under a caption, with quotation marks around it:

### Our Credo: "A Theatre of Excitement...Loving Care and Uncompromising Professionalism!"

With the message below reading:

**As we look ahead to what we believe will be our most successful season yet, we would wish to reiterate, for our renewing subscribers and for the thousands of new ones we expect to join us, our credo, our producing policy—which is to present the superior plays of New York, London and the Continent and the gifted new playwrights now emergent in America's burgeoning resident professional theatres. We'll bring you the most beloved of world classics, the cream of contemporary repertoire and a piquant dash of the avant-garde, too. We aim to create a "theatre of excitement," offering high quality productions, mounted with loving care, the best of taste and uncompromising professionalism from our top-drawer casts of fine performers—and all this for an intelligent, knowledgeable audience, our own, cherished season subscriber family!**

*Digby Dalton*

**Digby Dalton**
**Artistic Director**

Again, use the actual signature, as it adds much character.

### *Getting Some Mileage out of Your Building—Old or New*

Many symphony orchestras perform their concerts in fine old halls, while others perform theirs in the most contemporary of settings. In either case, there are statements that can be made in the brochure to take advantage of the special atmosphere provided by the auditorium. For instance, one orchestra which plays in a beloved, venerable structure can speak of its "lovely wood paneling seasoned by time" being "a sounding board for the mellow acoustics of this most hallowed and historic hall of music." In another case, the brochure writer for an orchestra about to move into a brand new building can really go all-out about its wonders, saying:

> **Become a charter subscriber and obtain your own regular choice seats for the first season—and countless seasons to come—in our new, magnificent, modern and luxurious home—one of the most imaginatively designed, tastefully appointed concert halls ever dreamed of—truly an architectural triumph—a splendid affirmation of our community's unbounded ambition for an ever-higher quality of life. Here, ensconced in your deep-cushioned continental seat, with fabulous legroom for your extra comfort, you will enjoy the perfect audibility and visibility which this unique auditorium will offer. Here, you will find surcease from the tensions and abrasions of daily life. Here, you will thrill to the majestic surge of our mighty orchestra, as it reveals the full beauty and grandeur of immortal masterpieces. Here you will be enchanted by the virtuoso talents of our overflowing cornucopia of world-famed guest soloists—all under the musical leadership of our distinguished, widely admired music director.**

Promotional flexibility to meet changing circumstances is an advantage that our performing arts organizations always possess. We are not locked permanently into a "party line" and can adapt to new conditions as they develop. I am thinking of the situation of a theatre company which has been performing in an old-fashioned playhouse with a lot of mileage on it. Often those who run such a theatre lament to themselves and others concerning what they regard as a handicap, when so many other producers have sleek, contemporary buildings, stuffed with every sort of modern staging facility. Our artistic director, stuck with his aging and often ill-equipped house, feels deprived and dreams of the day when he, too, will get a more up-to-date plant. But when his brochure comes out for the season, and he must still produce at the same old stand, there should be no hint of any dissatisfaction with it, nor any apology for it. On the contrary, he must make his surroundings sound as attractive as possible. His attitude must be, "If it's our playhouse, it's a wonderful place in which to enjoy plays." Conceivably, the brochure might convince us that he wouldn't take one of those antiseptic new theatre buildings for a gift. It might say something like this:

**From the moment you walk into our historic, gold-leafed lobby, with the great oil painting of that prince of actors, David Garrick, dominating the first landing of our spiraling marble staircase, you are aware that you have entered a real, professional legitimate theatre, possessing the atmosphere which you, your parents and your grandparents have always associated with the locale for enjoyment of good, solid theatrical entertainment. From every one of its 577 comfortable seats, you can see and hear perfectly. Here, you do not get theatre in the round, in the square, on the side, in the corners or in your lap. Here, our superb actors perform right up there on the stage, in front of you, where they ought to be—just as you've always loved to see them when you've come to our superior productions over the years.**

Now, let us suppose that there has recently come about a new emphasis on audience building via subscription campaigning in this theatre company. The audience has now become so much bigger than in all those past years, and so many people are now being turned away despite lengthening of seasons, that, at long last, a new, larger capacity building must be constructed. Finally, our artistic director is going to get that new home for the company. At this point, he has a completely different story to tell, and it could be along these lines:

**Now, fast-rising at the busy intersection of Main and Broad Streets is our striking new, neo-Bauhaus playhouse. It will be the epitome of modernity, so much verging on the futuristic that this structure promises to become an architect's as well as a theatre-lover's mecca. It will be a playhouse for today and tomorrow, boasting spinning rotor turntable stages and a lighting system so advanced that only technicians with masters degrees in electronics will operate it. It will offer a revolutionary concept in staging**

possibilities, made possible by a unique, vast hexagonal performing platform, thrusting boldly through the center of the audience, which will find itself raised, lowered, tilted or whirled according to the director's requirements. Yet, be assured, that there will be no compromise of your comfort permitted—and you will be happily surprised to find that this will not be one of those soulless contemporary auditoriums. Into it has been built elements of elegance which this community has long associated with theatre going. Here, under ideal conditions, you will be offered not only stimulation and a vision of the living stage's as yet unrealized potential—but good entertainment, too—along with old friends and new friends. So, we invite you now to become a charter subscriber in our new theatre— to obtain your permanent, choice regular seats, automatically renewable for all the seasons to come!

## Other Promotional Elements

Let us assume that there are some people who will receive our brochure who will need no further assurances before sending in their order than the established reputation of our company (an asset, remember, which does not exist for new projects) and the repertoire which we are announcing. Our brochure, though, may be reaching hundreds of thousands of different people, most of whom may or may not be as ready to buy what we have to offer on those basic grounds.

All of the people to whom we send our brochures, being just as human as we are, are capable of being moved to action by various stimuli. The same person who is responsive to idealistic approaches may also be susceptible to a bargain. His neighbor who really does appreciate artistic excellence in the performing arts may also have a weakness for rubbing elbows with celebrities or for having certain privileges which others are denied. Both of these people may have the need for reassurance as to their good judgment by the knowledge that thousands of other people have already found it a good idea to subscribe to our project. If our bandwagon is rolling fast enough, they simply will be unable to resist jumping on.

Still another brochure recipient requires reading the judgment of the experts—the critics. We must assume that in most cases it will require more than one of these reasons or arguments to influence the potential subscriber's to-buy-or-not-to-buy decision. It might even take a combination of five, or more, different points before the prospect collapses in our favor. Thus, we invest our brochure with in-depth strength, utilizing every element that might have convincing power for our purpose.

A staple section of countless brochures has been the "as a subscriber you will join, have, enjoy, develop, participate and take advantage" approach, adapted for different performing arts and varying circumstances. Here is an example of how this approach would be utilized for a resident theatre company:

### As a Subscriber You Will...

*...Join*

*Our great city's theatregoing elite.* **The most sophisticated, theatre-wise and discriminating audience in the Middle West of the United States.**

*...Have*

*Your own regular seat.* **Under our season-ticket plan, you are awarded the best available seats—and you may retain them for as many seasons as you choose. Thus, your foresight in subscribing now is your guarantee of good seats in future years, too.**

*...Enjoy*

*A new dimension* **of consistency and dignity in your theatre going by making this charming, unique and centrally located, intimate (no seat is more than 40 feet from the stage) playhouse and its provocative program a regular part of your entertainment and cultural way of life.**

*...Develop*

*The theatre taste and discernment* **which comes with attending these fine plays right through the season—year after year—the kind of regular exposure to the best in professional stage entertainment that only subscribers are likely to achieve.**

*...Participate*

*Directly and personally* **in this fascinating project—our city's own, first-rate, nationally recognized resident professional theatre company. Your subscription bespeaks your civic pride in it—and assures your involvement.**

> *...Take Advantage*
> *Of this biggest, best bargain* in the history of entertainment in this
> area. You not only get seating priority over the general public,
> but you pay much less than box office prices. In fact, you attend
> two wonderful shows *free!*

More often than not, we theatre people are unhappy with the critics, but
when they say something good about our productions, we quote them in our
brochures, and rightly so, as this represents a positive element for our
purpose. Critics' quotes should be placed in their own panel or position in the
brochure, with a simple caption like:

## Sweet Praise from the Press!

Then, below, we must be careful to use the slot we have allotted for this
purpose effectively, which means that we ought not to fill the space with a lot
of tiny type, trying to quote every critic who ever said anything good about us.
It is better to pick several of the best quotes and run them in easy-to-read type
with a bit of space between the lines. If there is one especially smashing
statement, by a particularly prestigious member of the critical fraternity, we
might do well to use the entire space for it. For instance:

**The Bellows Falls Repertory Theatre has achieved true greatness
in its production of *Hamlet*. In fact, it has pushed the Moscow Art
Theatre, the Comédie-Française, the British National Theatre and
Joe Papp off the theatrical map!**

And then the name of the critic:

### Jive Larnes, *New York Lines*

A few years ago I composed a similar simulated critic's statement, and
wrote it into a brochure for use by a resident company in a very big city,
merely to suggest to them that in that particular space they should put in a real
critic's quote (I didn't have their quotes on hand at my office in Chicago, or I
would have used one of those). They sent it to the printer by mistake, just like
that, including the name of "Jive Larnes," and vast quantities of those
brochures were circulated—with good results.

When our situation permits the happy, celebratory announcement of major
gains in subscription during the season just past, or the reminder of the extent

of our performing arts organization's cumulative gains in this important area over a number of seasons, it provides a valuable picture of our success. All the world still loves a lover, but it also loves a winner. A bigger subscribership, if exploited, begets a still bigger one. So you couldn't have a better, more promotionally sound panel included in your brochure than one like this:

### Thank You, Vancouver
### for the Phenomenal $981\%$ Gain
### in Subscription during Recent Seasons—

All the way from 3,515 to 38,000 series-ticket holders—making us the envy of every symphony orchestra on the North American continent. This unprecedented growth in our committed audience has made possible constant expansions, thus creating additional opportunities for still more music lovers to join our subscriber family. Ever since the first announcements of the wonderful forth-coming season with its great soloist stars, our phone has not stopped ringing, and advance subscription mail orders have never been bigger—with more and more people accurately estimating that there will simply be no single (nonsubscription) tickets left. *They* have wisely sent in their orders in time. May we suggest that *you* act now—using the official order form in this brochure.

Or a similar approach would be something like this:

### We Must Be Doing Something Right!

(Use a photograph of the box office with a long line of people trying to buy tickets, or a photograph of the box office window with a big sign across it, saying "Sold Out.")

These smirking, smiling New Haveners will be licking their chops in pure pleasure and satisfaction all season!

These grim, tight-lipped crying New Haveners are doomed to a season of depression, deprivation, disappointment!

*Versions of this cartoon depicting happy subscribers vs. depressed single-ticket buyers have been used in hundreds of brochures throughout the U.S. and Canada.*

In just these past two seasons, we've gone all the way from 2,800 to 18,400 subscriptions—a smashing rise of. . .

# 557.1%!

Please pardon us if we are in a euphoric mood, but we think that these incredible figures make us the biggest growth situation in all of America's resident theatres. Obviously San Diego loves its Old Globe Theatre—and it might be because we put on very good shows at a very good price—3 plays free to subscribers who order the 10-play series! Subscribe *now,* as seat locations for new subscribers are assigned according to the date when their orders are received.

Or how about this approach:

### We're the Hottest Ticket in Town!

We never thought we'd be fighting off scalpers for the Oregon Symphony Orchestra. But that's just the way it was, all last season, for our concerts. Why? Well, some say it's because of the Maestro Lawrence Smith Sound and who can argue about our dynamic music director's enormous success here. Others credit our orchestra musicians who must think they're the Boston Symphony, the way they've been playing lately. . . brilliantly, blazingly! Still others claim it's our guest soloist star strength. However, it has come about, it's a happy fact—we're "the hottest ticket in town"—and you'd better subscribe now if you want to get in during the season to come. We invite you to join our subscriber family—now 22,000 strong!

The attraction of "For Subscribers Only" special privileges, benefits, bonuses and dividends to which the general public has no access, is a strong one, and wise promoters of the performing arts field have tried all sorts of ways to provide these goodies to their people and to promote them strongly in the brochure. Of course, the discount factor is a prime one in most situations. However, when the subscribership has grown so large that further expansion cannot be undertaken (at least for the moment) the discount offer may shrink as the need for it diminishes, or may be abandoned entirely. Priority in seating and the retaining of seats from season to season is certainly an enticement factor. Yet, in certain cases, this benefit might not be offered either. However, there are a number of other kinds of advantages which subscribers can obtain from us, according to our willingness and ability to supply them, and on how much more we feel we need to do in our various situations. Some organizations provide bar privileges exclusively for their subscribers in a special room in the hall or playhouse. There are publications, often offering news, photographs, designers' drawings and feature material about the company's plans and, sometimes, study guides concerned with the repertoire. Some resident theatres, for this purpose, set publication dates shortly in advance of each of their productions. Subscribers are offered discounts, and sometimes free admission, to symposiums about the work being presented. A theatre may sponsor a visiting attraction of great drawing power, for a limited engagement, either in its own playhouse or in another auditorium, with its subscribership getting seating priority and discounts on ticket purchases. An opera or symphony organization may offer to its subscribers special prices on certain recordings and books. A theatre may have a children's theatre school, and subscribers who are parents may obtain a discount on tuition for their children—or if there are performances given for children by the adult actors, the theatre's regular subscribers may get discounts on tickets. Arrangements are often made with excellent restaurants in the neighborhood, so that subscribers may dine at a discount on the evenings when they attend their series performances.

Many subscribers are made happy by various social events which are planned to bring them into closer contact with the management and artists, thus to further their sense of being insiders, having a greater personal interest and identification with the company. This atmosphere is more easily created when the subscribership is smaller than when it is greater. Arrangements are made with local commercial impresarios to give seating priorities to a non-profit arts company's subscribers, who receive advance mailings for certain major attractions which come to that community. Subscribers are sometimes given special discounts on any available single tickets for out-of-town visitors or friends whom they may wish to bring with them on their series nights. In those cases where the theatre company has enjoyed persistent and widely known ticket shortages, just getting a priority on *any* seats which may become available through the illness of a subscriber or for any other reason, can be a highly prized subscriber privilege.

It is now quite common for subscribers to be able to charge their subscriptions to their department store charge accounts. Many theatre companies have, in addition to the subscription season on their main stage, a second, smaller theatre, often devoted to a more experimental repertoire. Subscribers are frequently given discounts or free tickets for these performances. Free champagne has been given to subscribers on opening nights, and free commemorative medallions have been presented to subscribers who sign up in an anniversary season. Some theatres, operating their seasons from fall to summer's beginning, have used their buildings to house profitable film festivals during the entire summer and have given their subscribers lower prices than the general public for these events. Many new subscribers for the theatre season have also been enrolled from among the motion picture enthusiasts who can be given brochures, can be spoken to and propagandized about our "living stage" offer, via film trailers on the screen.

The brochure which is published in the spring, but deals with a season beginning the following fall, might do well to feature an offer of:

**Pay Only ⅓ Down Now—the remainder not due 'til September 15.**

A symphony or opera subscription for both husband and wife might run into a financial outlay that could be discouraging if it all had to be paid for at once, six months in advance of the season. However, with the option available of making a partial payment of a third or a half down, many sales are made that otherwise would be lost. For we should begin to campaign in most situations a half-year or more before the season begins. In some places, subscription orders are accepted on the basis of:

**Just phone in your request and we will bill you.**

The brochure might also invite the public to:

**Just charge it to your account at any of the following stores....**

Then ask the subscriber to check which of the department store accounts he wants his order charged to and provide a place to fill in the account number. A similar deferred-payment offer is made in connection with the established credit cards. In the cases of the department stores, whose mailing lists are often pressed into service in our large-scale mailing campaigns, we not only sometimes arrange for the charge account convenience factor but often, with their permission, put out special editions of our brochures, in which the store itself invites its customers to subscribe to our performing arts enterprise. We have obtained excellent results with such mailings.

A resident theatre's brochure would do well to flash its exchange offer, under a bold caption reading:

**Your Exchange Privilege!**

With the explanation:

**Should you find yourself unable to attend one of your scheduled performances, our box office will gladly exchange your tickets for any other performance of the same play, according to availabilities. Such exchanges may be made up to 24 hours before curtain time.**

A brochure would be remiss if it did not point out, presuming that we had it: "Plenty of free parking space in the lots immediately adjoining our building." Or the same statement, eliminating the word "free" if we have the parking lots, but there is a charge. If a special subscriber parking privilege is offered, it should also be mentioned.

The great amount of attention I have given to the preparation of the subscription brochure, is an indication of the importance I attach to it in our overall considerations for subscription campaigns on behalf of all of the performing arts. By giving so much specific wording to cover the various elements I believe our brochures should contain in order to achieve maximum impact and results, I have not meant to say that there is no other way of saying these things. I am always pleased when organizations for which I have written the initial brochures begin to write their own, often very effective ones. I admit that I feel complimented when many organizations in the arts with which I have not worked, adopt these approaches as their standard practice, although they are often unaware of the source.

I would point out that the desire to be original on the part of writers and designers, while understandable, often presents a problem in the producing of effective subscription-selling brochures. Actually, I submit that originality in this case is irrelevant. I would view the contents of the brochure as a tool for a certain purpose, and if somebody else has developed materials which are especially effective in other communities, I would not hesitate to adapt these for my purposes. Artistic directors are often particularly insistent on *original,* highly individual mailing pieces, occasionally being more zealous about the originality and individuality of their brochure than they are about their art. If Doctors Salk and Sabin have found successful antitoxins for polio, I cannot imagine other doctors refusing to use them on the grounds that they must be original and individual. I might well understand this point of view in the realm of art, but not concerning a method for promoting the sale of subscriptions, particularly in the cases of organizations which reach only a limited, specific geographic area. It is highly unlikely that any subscriber to the Pittsburgh Symphony Orchestra will ever glimpse the brochure of the Seattle Symphony Orchestra and vice versa or that the New York City Ballet subscribers will see the brochures of Ballet West in Salt Lake City. In some respects, each brochure must indeed be custom-made, according to the special situation and circumstances of the individual arts company. In other ways, several companies may have so much in common that a particularly apt statement in the selling copy which has been created for one will be right for others, too.

Nevertheless, I hope that the readers of this chapter will not assume from some of my prescriptions and proscriptions, that I am too didactic in my approach or that I am advocating a strict uniformity which would result in all of our materials throughout the country coming out like identical peas in a pod. I believe that my concept does allow for considerable diversity in copy, format, typography and overall design. In this regard, I heartily concur with Mao's maxim, "Let a thousand flowers bloom." I think that an objective appraisal of the many excellent brochures now being issued by a wide range of performing arts organizations, all of which "subscribe" to the subscription-selling approaches which I am writing about, will bear out this point. Actually, I take a craftsman's pleasure in seeing good work, whether it is my own or somebody else's. And I much enjoy seeing the unfolding of the infinite variations on the basic theme which have resulted from the efforts of our growing body of fine promotional practitioners. It has been with special satisfaction that I have observed, season after season, how the distinguished artistic director of one of America's crack resident theatres has used my play descriptions for his repertoire selections, not to reprint, but as a challenge to write still better ones of his own for use in that company's brochures. Even in those cases where I thought we were at a standoff—our respective blurbs being "separate but equal"—I have recommended some of his to other theatres.

When a play opens, its artistic success is often inconclusive. One critic will hail it while another critic will damn it, and there may be widely disparate reactions from the audience in general. However, whether or not a subscription campaign is successful is immediately apparent, readily measurable, in terms of exactly how many season or series tickets were sold. Even when the application of such simple criteria tells the story for us plainly, people in and around the performing arts often continue to delude themselves.

Once some years ago, I encountered a seemingly and undoubtedly sincere, intelligent young man at an arts conference, who assured me that he was a masterful promoter of subscription audiences. He said he had achieved his successes on behalf of the orchestra he represented, not only by avoiding all the promotional excesses of which he had heard I was guilty, but by a sort of reverse, understated approach, at once subtle and subliminal, and particularly by using sophisticated graphics in his brochures and advertising matter. I could not help but be impressed by the impassioned, highly articulate declaration of his credo, though I was certainly in basic disagreement with almost all he was saying. Suddenly, while he was still talking, I realized that I had only recently had occasion to peruse the subscription sales figures for his recent season; they were incredibly low. In a city where the population numbered in the millions, his project had a pitifully small subscribership, despite its unquestionably distinguished status, and of all the considerable number of subscription-oriented groups present at that conference, his subscription was perhaps the smallest. I hope that by this time that tense young man has become less intolerant of the modus operandi I favor, not just because *I* favor it, but because it is demonstrably successful.

However, I fear that, no matter how intensive my missionary efforts or how many subscription-selling successes are achieved thereby, there will always be aesthetic holdouts who will never commit the ultimate gaucherie of using large, readable type in their brochures, with captions and occasional exclamation points where the message justifies; who will shrink from actually telling the person they are addressing what it is they want of him (which, I assume, is that they want him to buy the subscription); who will cringe at the thought of making so imperative a request in their mailing piece as "Subscribe Now!"; who will never, ever agree to any but the most anemic descriptions of the season's programming; who will recoil at any suggestion that a discount be mentioned or even offered; who will insist on listing discreetly, or not at all, the names of any celebrated artists who may have been signed to appear as guest artists; who will certainly veto the use of any pictures of and statements about those artists' past achievements; who will tell you that they'd rather not have subscribers who require convincing about the merits of the company and its repertoire. I am, with the passage of time, becoming reluctantly reconciled to the fact that not every practitioner in our various performing arts fields is likely to come 'round to my point of view.

## 16

### The Development
### and Use
### of Mailing Lists

Like so many other newspaper readers, I often find myself drawn to the daily astrological forecast column. Recently, just as if the forecaster had one specific Aquarius, namely myself, in mind, he ordered, "Go all out! Accent glamor! Utilize sense of showmanship!" And then, he concluded with the best advice of all, "Get direct-mail program under way!" I naturally chose to perceive in this command not only a favorable omen for my manifold consultations, but a mandate for us all.

One of the compelling reasons at the back of our minds when we put such stress on reaching out to potential subscribers through the mail is the nagging suspicion that, despite all our efforts to obtain volunteer assistance in the carrying out of the various other campaign components recommended and described in this book, and despite the original good intentions of our board and guild members, the management may suddenly find itself having to fight the battle alone with its back against the wall, with great numbers of subscriptions to be sold if the organization is to thrive. We always hope for, and we always strive to do, the right things to encourage volunteer participation in our season-ticket drives, but should the general chairman of the overall effort, an important businessman, run into some major problem in the operation of his company's affairs, he may evaporate, as far as *our* needs are concerned, and it may then be too late in the game for us to find a worthy successor. And have we not all had our problems with new, eager volunteers who, it turns out, simply do not have the competence we mistakenly thought they possessed? We, who are in the professional management end, all bear our scars of this type, and it is at such times that we take comfort in the knowledge that should all else fail, we can still do a great deal of the job through our direct-mail program, if it is planned soundly, carried out thoroughly—and if it is on a scale which is related to our need.

### *The House List*

If the use of brochures sent by direct mail is a prime instrument of subscription campaigning, it follows that the organization of the mailing lists used in our campaigns and the complexion of those lists are of vital importance. First of all, what about our own "house list"? Every performing arts group should meticulously gather the names of the most likely prospects to become subscribers. Ideally, we would want to speak to each one personally at his or her home or office. However, when we deal with many, many thousands of such prospects the personal approach might not prove practical. So, the next best thing is to send them our brochure. Every single-ticket buyer who comes to our box office should be asked for his name and address for our mailing list. I have been disappointed many times in the lack of initiative on the part of arts managements in this regard. Box office personnel can ask patrons to fill out mailing list cards. Volunteers or staff members can ask patrons, either approaching or leaving box offices, to give their names and addresses. We should also ask for telephone numbers. There can be tables at strategic places in the lobby, containing cards, pencils and boxes with signs on them reading, "Please leave your name and address here so we can send you advance notification of our future performances." Ushers can hand out such cards and pencils to patrons. At each performance which features a widely famed guest artist (thus setting off a stampede to the box office by otherwise rarely seen single-ticket buyers), we could raffle off record albums during the final intermission. All those present have to fill out (if they want a chance to win the prize) their names and addresses on the raffle tickets either before the performance or during the first intermission. The next morning, the management should check those names and addresses against the organization's mailing list. Duplications should be discarded and new names integrated into the list.

I have been shocked to find that box office employees of many performing arts groups immediately discard the envelopes containing the individual ticket mail orders they receive, as well as their notations of similar telephone inquiries and orders, without keeping permanent records of the names and addresses involved. No respectable spider would permit a fly, once having entered his parlor, to just flit back out of it. And no respectable arts management should permit this miscarriage of audience development opportunities. Every person who voluntarily makes himself known to us by ordering individual tickets to one of our performances is a prime prospect for subscribership, but only *if* we know who he is and can go after him.

## Use of Computers

Computers can be used for the maintenance of mailing lists, for the billing of subscribers and as an aid in fund-raising and development projects. However, computerization should be approached with caution in the area of assigning reserved subscription seat locations, because of the tremendous number of individual problems involved. A former official of a large performing arts center which has had years of experience with electronic programming in all its dealings with subscribers has told me that he considers the specific system in use there to be inefficient, wasteful and much too costly. On the other hand, I have spoken to an official of another large arts project who is wildly enthusiastic about the very sophisticated system which has recently been put into operation at her organization's offices. She finds computerization efficient, economical and anything but wasteful. However, while she uses her computer aid for a wide range of services, she has reserved for old-fashioned control the handling of seat allocations to subscribers. She points out that, when computerization is instituted, a careful and painstaking study by a computer specialist of the organization's special requirements must be conducted, so that the system can be tailor-made. Whether it is by any manual system or by a computerized one, the best possible, most up-to-date, in-house records must be kept.

## Selectivity of Mailing Lists

After compiling our in-house mailing list, we should consider what would most likely be the other selective lists for our purpose. If we were a resident theatre, the best possible list for our use (next to our own subscribers of the current season, our dropout subscribers of previous seasons and those of our single-ticket buyers of record) would be one belonging to a sister resident theatre company or that of a touring commercial play series which was performed in our city. Also, the lists of all summer stock companies, little theatre groups and drama schools in the area would have special value. Then, we should also seek to obtain the lists of all other culturally oriented organizations in the community: those of the opera company, the symphony orchestra, chamber music societies, summer music festivals, public art museums, private art galleries, F. M. radio stations and public television stations. Also in the category of most-likely-to-give-us-good-returns would be the lists of teachers of elementary schools, junior high schools, high schools (both public and private) and the faculty members of all the colleges and universities in the area. And, not to be overlooked are graduate students, students enrolled in university extension courses and members of various alumni associations. Librarians also make sense for us, as do subscribers to art film series which may be operating under various auspices. In addition, subscribers to certain quality publications are promising prospects.

Much of the pioneer work involved in convincing our sister performing arts organizations to share their lists with us (we do, of course, always offer to provide our own lists in exchange) has already been accomplished. This form of logical cooperation, whereby we all stand to gain in the process of audience cross-fertilization, is now widely accepted on the North American continent. This was not always so. Not many years ago, each organization hugged its mailing list to its breast, protesting, "We've worked all these years to build this up and nobody, *nobody,* is going to benefit from it but ourselves!" This selfish, shortsighted viewpoint has now been generally discredited. For, not only is it obviously hypocritical on the part of people who claim that their lives are devoted to art (Do they mean that they are devoted to art only as long as it is purchased at their store?), but it has clearly proved to be in their own best interests to enter into these sharing arrangements. Experience has shown that all organizations in the performing arts community have built larger audiences since they began to work together in this respect.

Actually, for those who have reservations about "full disclosure," it should be pointed out that we do not wish to obtain and keep their lists, but that we seek only to *use* them in our mailing efforts. So, we will deliver our brochures to *their* mail rooms, or letter services, where they can be addressed and then delivered to the post office, where we already have the third class, nonprofit postage money on deposit. We will then reimburse them for their labor costs in the addressing process. Then we will, of course, reciprocate when *they* are in need of *our* lists.

We all owe it to our own efficient operation—and to each other—to keep our respective mailing lists up-to-the-minute, by constantly combing and pruning them so that there is the absolute minimum of waste through wrong addresses, etc. By guaranteeing, in our own mailings, the return postage for all brochures that cannot be delivered for whatever the reason, we are then able to clean our lists regularly. Each season, as our campaign brings in new subscribers—and individual ticket buyers—their names must be integrated into our permanent mailing list. Any neglect or sloppiness in this regard diminishes the pace of our audience-building efforts and costs us future revenue.

Other selective lists for our purposes would be those of all the professionals in our area, including doctors, lawyers, dentists and accountants, as well as practitioners in public relations and advertising. Members of such organizations as councils on foreign relations have relevance, too, as do public welfare caseworkers. I am not attempting to list all of the possibilities here, but enough of them to suggest that our best chances lie with those members of our society who are most logically ready for us now.

Now, assuming that we do a good job of reaching those prospects and that we sign many of them up but still have a lot more seats to sell, we must push beyond the immediate periphery of our best possibilities by mailing to lists which are lower in their selectivity, but which have the advantage of offering large numbers of names (in the hundreds of thousands in good-size cities), such as those of the department store charge accounts which are efficiently organized for mailing. In city after city, the managements of such stores, as a demonstration of community service, have given the use of their lists to nonprofit performing arts groups. However, mini-brochures, "piggybacked" onto the monthly billing to the store's charge account customers, have almost always brought infinitesimal returns, although we didn't have to pay the postage. The best sales have been achieved when the full brochures were sent out separately to those lists, with us paying the postage.

In some cases the brochures suggest that the subscription be charged to the department store charge account, an arrangement which usually, but not always, costs the performing arts group a small percentage for the service. The store managements do not necessarily insist upon this as quid pro quo for the use of their lists. The stores almost always have very low-cost methods of addressing and sending out their mailings, and they usually only charge us their out-of-pocket expenses for this operation. Perhaps it is because department store owners or officials are often active on the boards of arts organizations that they have so often been helpful to us. They have performed a very great service for our organizations and for their communities by providing a consistent means to effectively reach a very large number of "middle selective" people, many of whom become our subscribers. Some of the stores have even cooperated to the extent of sending their own messages to their charge account holders, asking them to subscribe to our seasons. In some cases, we have put out special printings of our brochures, with the address side containing such messages from the stores. I know of many groups in all performing arts disciplines which have good reason to be grateful to their local department stores.

Again, for the purpose of reaching admittedly less selective groups, but in considerable numbers (though not just sending to everybody in the phonebook), major credit card lists have been employed, as have voter precinct lists and demographic ones based on specific neighborhoods. Occupant mailing, whereby the postman simply delivers a brochure which has been addressed not to a name but to an occupant at the address, has also been widely used in many subscription drives, although returns are usually lower than when the brochures are sent to specific names. However, if these demographic lists are purchased from mailing houses, the costs for occupant addresses are considerably less than for names, and this initial cost advantage could at least partially make up for the smaller returns. I am not against the use of occupant lists, if they are used *in addition to* rather than *instead of* large-scale mailings to names. As long as there are still seats left to sell, there is room for—and there is need for—diversity in our mailing methods.

Some arts administrators tend to become hung up on their own scientific analysis of the returns from lists of varying levels of selectivity. When they find certain lists producing a higher percentage of returns for the dollars spent than lists of lesser strength, they will simply eliminate the latter lists from their next season's campaign—and remain with a large number of unsold subscriptions that could have been sold at a higher, but still very tolerable, selling cost. When confronted with that old question of, "How much can we afford to spend to make the sale?" they will too frequently (and mistakenly) decide that they cannot afford to make certain lower-level distributions, and will remain with tickets that turn out to be a 100% loss for many of their attractions. What difference does it really make if a $40 subscription on the higher selectivity level costs us $6 to sell and on the lower level costs $16 to sell, if we are otherwise going to be stuck with thousands of $40 subscriptions when we don't sell enough of them and single sales do not develop? And then, we must always remember the much more favorable economics we will enjoy when we enter that happy hunting ground of renewal—which we can't experience unless we make the original sale. So, while I am certainly not opposed to obtaining the best analysis of our sales costs that we can get, with all of the aid of contemporary computerization and the consultation of business administration school graduates, I would urge that such information be interpreted and acted upon with a sense of the larger picture.

### Package Mailings vs. Self-Mailers

I have often been asked if it might not be a better investment for us to put out elaborate package mailings—in envelopes containing a letter, brochure, special order form (not built into the brochure as in our self-mailers) and other enclosures such as photocopies of reviews and news stories about our project —than to rely on the simple, much less expensive self-mailer brochure. Would not the higher percentage of returns, which the package might well bring, more than make up for the higher cost involved? The answer is, not necessarily. In fact, we have cases where the self-mailer produced more than the package in direct percentage results, plus the obvious great savings in all the costs involved. In those cases where the packages do bring in a higher percentage, the returns are too often not high enough to justify the additional costs. There is also tne danger of reacting to the natural inhibition, whenever higher costs are a factor, regarding the size of the brochure distributions. Although I generally do not think in terms of single-ticket sales, I always do keep in mind the extra advantage of larger subscription mailings; that is, in addition to subscribers, there will be many people who almost, but don't quite, buy the season ticket, but who now may be encouraged to come into the market for individual ticket sales because of our own big push. So, while I am primarily campaigning for subscribers, why not get a simultaneous, no-cost plug for single sales? The larger the number of brochures which I can cast upon the waters, the better.

Package mailings, however, may make much sense in dealing with certain highly selective lists, and personalized, individually typed and signed letters might even be included. I would advise caution with regard to this costly type of mailing (even the postage costs much more, depending upon the weight of the enclosures), though, when it comes to any large-scale demographic lists. Certainly, testing is very much in order. That is, before committing big money to such distributions, experimental mailings or tests should be made on a small scale, to sample sections of the lists we are considering for all-out utilization.

### The Economics of Direct Mail

How many brochures should we put out? In the larger cities a major resident theatre, opera company, orchestra or ballet company, with subscriptions in the many thousands to sell, could well use a million brochures in its annual series-ticket drive. I have known the figure to run well over a million. This large quantity may mean at least two different editions of the brochure: one for the spring–early summer phase of the drive and another for the late summer–early fall portion. There may be a certain amount of remailing, depending upon what the coded results have told us about the strength of the various lists used in the first half of the campaign. Medium-size and smaller cities would determine the size of their mailings according to their respective situations.

One of our great economic advantages in trading our selective lists with other performing arts producers, by the way, is that we have no cost for list rentals. Also, the use of the other lists I mentioned earlier in this chapter can often be obtained by cajoling the organizations which have compiled them. It is up to us to do that job. We should never assume that we cannot obtain the use of a certain list. If we, the staff members, cannot find the combination to the lock, maybe a member of our board will have the leverage that we do not. Even in those cases where a list eluded us last year, we must not assume that it cannot be obtained this year. Circumstances may have changed in our favor. And, in the case of a demographic list, when we have decided to pay rental, we should take the trouble to find the best possible buys. Keeping the costs as low as possible enables us to conduct large-scale mailing efforts which are economically sound. For example, take a contemplated half-million piece mailing where we have not had to pay for the lists, since they were given in exchange for ours or donated by department stores. If the brochures cost us 2¢ apiece, the postage 2¢ and the addressing cost (including delivery to the post office) a penny, we have a total cost of $25,000. Then, if we get a .5% overall return in subscriptions (that is, a .25% return in terms of envelopes with an average of 2 subscriptions in each envelope), at a $35 per subscription rate, we will be selling 2,500 subscriptions for a gross of $87,500. We would be getting our money back, plus 250% profit. If the printing were to cost us double—that is, 4¢ per brochure instead of 2¢—with the postage rate and processing costs remaining the same, our money profit would only be 150%, which would still be great.

By the way, when I use the term "money profit," I mean that there is another and more primary profit for performing arts groups than in money terms, and that is the 2,500 subscribers who would thus be brought to regular attendance at our performances. While I have used the $35 per subscription figure in the example, it is actually a very modest amount, particularly for opera and symphony subscriptions, where in so many cases, the average series-ticket price would be much higher.

Postage charges given above are based on third class nonprofit rates which prevail in the United States at the time of this writing. The general mailing costs as outlined in the preceding paragraph assume that we do not pay rentals for the lists used. Once we do pay rentals, the economics are, of course, altered.

While resident professional theatres have been distributing brochures on a large scale for a long time now, it is only in recent years that symphony orchestras have been following suit; the results have, over and over again, been consistently excellent. In fact, the costs of such promotion have regularly been proving to be not only bearable, but highly profitable. For instance, the Pittsburgh Symphony Orchestra spent $35,000 for all promotion (no big brochure distributions involved) in order to obtain a total of $200,000 worth of new sales and renewals in the season *prior* to beginning Dynamic Subscription Promotion. In the season that followed, for an expenditure of $51,748, the total of new sales and renewals went up to $573,000. By four years later, they were grossing $918,000 for a promotional cost of $76,000. Obviously, with hundreds of percent better results than in the past for each promotional dollar now spent, this orchestra's management knows it is now on the right track.

The Cleveland Orchestra, at the time of this writing, has just completed its first brief experiment with large-scale mailings of brochures which conform to the general principles and recommendations made in this handbook. Their figures show that 2,500 new subscriptions have been sold, bringing in $114,642, for a total promotional cost of $23,000, of which $20,000 came through a special promotional grant from the Cleveland Foundation. (I have long been urging performing arts groups everywhere to seek this type of earmarked grant for subscription development, a concept which is being given increasing credence by foundations, arts councils and other granting bodies.) The orchestra got its money back immediately, plus a 400% profit, for seats that went unsold last year, *and they now have the renewal rights to 2,500 more series subscriptions.*

The New York Philharmonic has also recently made its first large mailings — 830,600 brochures—resulting in the sale by direct mail of 7,035 new subscriptions (there was a total of 10,300 new subscriptions sold through all sources), grossing $398,900 at a promotional cost of $88,900. So, they got their money back plus a 350% profit (*and,* once again, the continuing income increments for years to come from all those potential renewals).

### The Purchase of Mailing Lists

Every performing arts organization is presumably out beating the bushes, flushing out new audience members, either as single-ticket buyers or subscribers. Each group has its own mailing efforts, its advertising, its volunteer activities, its specific promotional approach in audience development. Each finds and enrolls certain people that other organizations have not yet found. All of those names, addresses and telephone numbers enter each organization's list, so that, when we use each other's lists, we each get the benefits of all the promotional work that has been done by all the organizations.

There are always considerable possibilities for obtaining productive mailing lists on a trade or accommodation basis. However, I would not rule out paying for the use of mailing lists when there is good reason to believe that they will deliver subscribers in sufficient quantities to make the transaction profitable for us. There should be careful inquiry and shopping around before such decisions are made, as rental fees can considerably increase the costs of our mailings. Sometimes, by several performing arts organizations in the same community making joint purchases of large-scale mailing lists and services, enormous savings can be achieved. In one instance I recall, through such a combined transaction, three performing arts organizations (one of them the opera company with which I am associated) were able to obtain the use of several hundred thousand names, have the labels made and affixed to brochures, arranged according to zip codes, bundled and delivered to the post office—all for a $6 per thousand charge to each participant. Such a buy was only possible because of the sharing arrangement.

We must always be careful to deal with reliable mailing houses and list brokers, and check the freshness of their lists. Since it is axiomatic in the mailing field that 25% to 35% of addresses change each year, we can suffer badly if any of the lists we use turn out to be a couple of years old. Whenever in doubt about the potential power of a list to produce results, a test mailing in the tens of thousands should be sent out before committing ourselves to the hundreds of thousands. We can test not only various lists for selling strength but, at the same time, the power of different mailing instruments to draw sales from basically the same types of lists. In some situations, such tests may also be necessary to convince doubting board members and artistic directors that vibrant brochures, invested with selling thrust on multiple levels, will bring far better results than the dull-as-ditchwater, understated pieces that they sometimes favor. Although the principles of testing are simple and understandable, there is more complexity involved in the processes of it than meets the eye, and I would recommend bringing in professional consulting aid when entering this area for the first time. Here is another reason we ought to do our mailing campaigns over periods of many months, rather than compressing our efforts into a matter of weeks. We then have the time to make our experiments, learn from them, and still have the possibility of succeeding before the next season begins. Having sufficient time to do the job well requires advance planning and a sense of urgency on the part of the entire organization, from board and artistic director on down. A battle-scarred veteran of many mailing campaigns once said to me, "It *always* takes longer than you think." The best-laid plans go awry when repertoire is suddenly switched, artists' contracts are held up, last-minute changes in ticket prices are decided upon, and so on. Enough time must be allowed to permit the flexibility that will accommodate all such contingencies.

### Analyzing Our Potential Returns

From how far away do our subscribers come? In one large city, fanning out into a densely populated area, our research showed that 53% of them lived within 12 miles of the playhouse; 60% lived within 20 miles; and 80% lived within 30 miles. This same profile of distance varies only by about 1% to 2% in several other cities. If these statistics were to apply to all of our cities, it would negate the idea that we have a great subscriber potential "out there" beyond a 30-mile radius of our buildings. If what you are presenting has no competition within a large area (let us say that your project is a major grand opera company), you could think in terms of drawing subscription patronage 70 to 80 miles away, but you would be wise to use carefully structured lists, certain to reach the special prospects in those places. At shorter range, you can more safely mail with a broader sweep. It has been noted that subscribers who do come from a considerable distance, even though there may not be very many, are more faithful in their annual renewal. Should you find a community 40 miles away which produces a high rate of subscription sales, this factor must be noted for the next campaign, when those zip codes should be sent repetitive brochure mailings, even though adjacent communities might only be given a light treatment. Although I have written about duplications separately in the next chapter, I wish to emphasize that they help us to get the results we need. There are an endless number of reasons a person may not respond to our initial overture, so a succession of mailings is necessary, if we are to get the order. The most skilled salesman cannot always make the sale on his first call; why expect a brochure to do it? The higher the ratio of response of a given list or locale, the more intentional duplication or use of cross-fertilized lists which make for duplication is justified.

In going back season after season to the same lists, we might have the feeling that we have taken all the cream out. However, assuming that the lists are live and being weeded, that new people moving into the community are added, and that some who weren't ready to buy last year *are* ready this year, those lists can continue to provide us with subscription sales. I am assuming, too, that all good campaigners will be freshening the mailing stream with lists we haven't used before, whether of the various levels of selectivity for our purpose or of a demographic mix based on zip codes.

Zip code maps for every community are available at local post offices. Distance data for your area can often be obtained from automobile clubs. Commercial mailing list compilers have at their fingertips information on the number of names in each zip zone, median income breaks for residents in each zone, the number of addresses in each break, etc.

Mike Kanter, the man who has achieved the greatest direct-mail results ever recorded for the performing arts (he has been my friend and colleague for more than 40 years), recommends careful research and preparation for all mailing campaigns. He would as soon leave out the order form in his brochure as leave out the codes which will tell him where his results are coming from. In all of his campaigns he has kept meticulous records of the results of all lists used, so that he has dependable guidelines for the next time around. On the basis of analysis made from these data, he structures his next season's mailing plans, always seeking to get the maximum sales for the amount of money expended. Because lower costs enable him to increase brochure circulation, he goes to the mat with paper suppliers and printing houses for the financial edge he seeks. He understands the power of duplication, applies it regularly and has the records to prove its efficacy. Even his demographic mailings are selective on various levels and he would use unselective saturation only if his project were located in so thinly populated an area that selectivity's higher returns would certainly have to fall far short of the number of subscription sales he needed to produce. He rails against the constantly recurring procrastination of performing arts groups in settling on their artistic plans in time so that tests, if necessary, can be made, and so that promotional activities are not entered into hastily, rashly and with unnecessary expense. Like all of us in the field, he has found the use of names rather than occupant addresses to be advantageous. However, he also utilizes occupant mailings for the additional sales they bring (even at a lower return). These mailings can reach the transient 25% to 35% of the population, whose names might not yet have gotten onto our lists, while the lower cost of occupant list rentals, may, in certain circumstances, make up for the lower return.

He constructs a mailing manual for his campaigns, with each zip zone having its own page containing the following data: number of miles from the theatre; median income of the zone; census figures; number of subscribers now enrolled within the zone; number of subscribers previously enrolled in the zone (going back, up to four seasons, if information is retrievable); number of brochures sent to the zone last season and each previous season the same list was used; percentage of the list represented by subscriptions; number of subscriptions sold through newspaper coupons within the zone (there should be a parallel between single-ticket sale densities and subscription sale densities, unless a special test mailing has already been released to the zone); all test counts, character of test, code, kind of instrument mailed, date, etc.

By the way, there is now a new dimension for list selection in the demographic category. In addition to the zip code method, there is the finer pinpointing which is now possible by use of the enormous data bank of information from the 1970 census.

The superficially sound logic of sticking to the most highly selective, biggest return kinds of mailing lists, led one major commercial theatrical enterprise in a very large western city to limit its annual subscription mailings to 200,000 pieces, for which it did indeed get good returns and did build up, over a period of some years, a season-ticket audience of close to 10,000. However, the annual play series involved was presented in a huge capacity playhouse, and there was still an enormous gap between this subscribership and what the real needs were. When the management belatedly increased its mailings (and improved the selling content of its brochure) to the level of 800,000 pieces, the subscription jumped immediately to 19,000 and, with the aid of continued heavy mailings, then shot all the way up to 29,000! Since that project is a commercial enterprise and had to pay much higher postal rates than our nonprofit organizations do, one can well understand its original conservatism with regard to large-scale mailing campaigns. Yet the loss from previously unsold seats, thrown onto the other side of the scale, undoubtedly outweighed the high postal costs. All the more reason our nonprofit groups would be well advised to take full advantage of their favored postal status.

I wish to particularly underscore the perfect logic of accepting, under certain circumstances, what seem to be very low mail returns for the money committed. Take, for instance, the circumstance of a theatre which had been selling an overall 50% of its capacity, including subscription and single-ticket sales. As a result of beginning much larger promotional efforts, including the use of every mailing list it could lay its hands on, it has raised this figure to

70% for the season about to end. To achieve this, the management used many different lists and, through coding, has learned which types of lists get the best returns. In its new mailing campaign, aimed at the next season, the company now uses only the lists which had previously proved most profitable, eliminating many lists which had brought less profit and those which only broke even. I submit that, under its circumstances, this theatre was definitely wrong in eliminating these lists. If it were to again come in with 70%, its management might well feel that it had consolidated its gain. But what about the unsold 30%? In such a spot, it makes sense to trade dollar for dollar, breaking even, but getting as far up toward the 100% mark as possible. For, as I pointed out elsewhere, it still doesn't cost us any money (if we sell a dollar's worth of tickets for every dollar spent in mailing costs), and our money profit would begin the next season, when 50%, 60%, 70% or more of those people, whom we wouldn't have gotten if we had disdained the use of the lower return lists, renew their subscriptions. And, going further, would it be so bad to even take a loss—maybe just a small one—in our push to bring 30% more people to our performances — not sometime in the future when the world will be more perfect and more people will show up by themselves at our box office, but right now or by the beginning of next season? Which leads me to the following point: While we generally seek to avoid the use of any list which has obsolete characteristics, primarily the one of being too old, which would necessarily mean that too many of the addresses would no longer be valid, there *are* exceptions. If a list has otherwise valuable characteristics, such as its original, intrinsically high selectivity potential, we might find that it still has sufficient life to make it economically feasible for us to use. In such cases, tests have sometimes provided us with the green light. Behind all of our thinking in this connection must be the guiding principle that *if we still have unsold seats, we will accept lists which are of lesser strength and simply pay more to make the sale—with our spur being the certain knowledge, in some instances, and the reasonable presumption in others, that if we don't sell that seat, we will sustain a 100% loss on it.*

Lists are obtainable which are based upon people's annual income, how much the house they live in costs, whether they live "on the right side of the tracks," and so on. We must not make the assumption that we should send our brochures only to the higher income groups (ideology aside) simply because our test might show a greater response from them than from lower income people. There might not be enough people in our area who earned $20,000 a year to satisfy the number of subscriptions we need to sell, even if a reason-able percentage of them respond. Maybe there are five times as many people around, whose annual income is $15,000, and who could supply us with a greater volume of subscribers, even though the *percentage* of return is less than that of the higher income group. Once again, our main consideration should always be the knowledge that *an unsold ticket is totally uneconomical.* And then, when we think of the potential renewal income (not only for next season, but stretching out over the years); when we remember that unspoken but important consideration of more people being brought to our perform-ances—and perhaps *introducing new people* to our art form—we might well decide to make that mailing to the lower return list. I know that I have made this point a number of times in this book, and I am not being repetitive without reason. Despite my seeming youth, I belong to a generation which remembers plays that had a beginning, a middle and an end, and when a playwright wanted to be sure that the audience understood a point that was vital to the plot, he reiterated that point at least three times during the first act. My teaching method in consultations over many years with performing arts groups has undoubtedly been influenced by that old theatre wisdom, and since so many of the resulting subscription campaigns have succeeded, I am not deserting it now that I am putting it all down on paper.

What is a "good" return in large-scale direct-mail subscription selling? This is a very difficult question to reply to, because of the many variables involved, according to the many different circumstances. Is it a brand new project offering the excitement factor of a luxurious new building? Or is it an established project with not only a good reputation, but a new crescendo of artistic success and recognition? Or is it a newer project with a poor reputation and a recent record of artistic failures? Is it a project which has just a fair-to-middling artistic reputation? What about the strength of the offer itself? Is there a discount factor, and how large is it? Is the nature of the repertoire such that it appeals to the largest number of that minority which will go to the performing arts at all, or does it appeal only to the smallest fraction of that grouping? Are there "big-name stars" involved? What is the mix of the mailing lists being used? How many of the names on the lists are highly selective? How many are less selective? Once down in the lower and lowest selective ranges, are we now addressing our brochures to names or to "occu-pant"? (In Canada, occupant mailing is called the "postal walk.") For the more highly selective lists, which can only be large-scale in the larger cities where it is possible to obtain such lists into the many hundreds of thousands, we sometimes obtain astonishingly high returns — even up to 2% and 3%, particularly in the first year of such campaigning in a given area. However, it is unrealistic to think that such results will occur all the time or even most of the time.

What would be a good return for *me* in my opera company's very large-scale, annual subscription campaign? Well, with my average series-ticket price of $100, a .3% return might be just dandy, while for you, if you're promoting a resident theatre's $35 average season ticket, it would be a poor result. Given the costs of printing, postage and addressing, as they are at this writing, it would be a highly profitable transaction for me, but one in which you might just exchange dollars. Now, in certain circumstances, like your having a record of a tremendous number of unsold seats, this seemingly poor result could turn out to be a good one a year hence, when you successfully renew 78% of those new subscribers for peanuts in terms of cost. If you get the results that most of the resident theatres, opera companies, ballet companies and symphony orchestras have been getting for their ongoing season-after-season mailing campaigns, it will come out somewhere between .5% and 1.5%, according to all sorts of varying conditions and contexts.

Incidentally, when I speak here of percentages of return, I do not mean the number of envelopes that come back, but the number of *subscriptions* contained therein. You have a blessing in the government's subsidizing the third class, nonprofit mailing rate, and you are advised to avail yourself of it while you still can. For, we must not forget that we almost lost this great privilege in the early 1970's when postal officials came very close to eliminating all performing arts entities from the list of nonprofit organizations entitled to receive it. Only the most intensive and concerted counterattack on the part of those of us who most fully understood what we were in danger of losing, the avalanche of letters from our constituents (read "subscribers") which hit Washington, and the resulting careful reconsideration of the issue by high-level functionaries of the U.S. Postal Service averted what would have been a crippling blow to our audience development hopes throughout the country. While we know that our government, since then, has become increasingly sympathetic to the arts, we have no guarantee that a postal system, financially pressed as ours is by continuing inflationary costs, will not again move in the direction of our disenfranchisement from this blessed form of subsidy, nor can we be certain that our desperate pleas and arguments will once more prevail.

The questions may be asked: "Since we get such widespread circulation of our brochures in large-scale demographic mailings to high-yield areas of heavily populated major cities, must we also continue to mail to selective lists based on demonstrated cultural affiliation? Wouldn't we reach all of those special prospects anyway?" The answer to both questions is that there are many thousands of excellent prospects who do not live in the places we are reaching through our overall area coverage, and without the selective lists, we could miss thousands of our best possibilities. And besides, using both the selective and the demographic approaches gives us more duplications—which lead to more sales!

Another question inevitably arises: "When is the best time to mail?" For the majority of us, operating on fall-winter-spring season cycles, it has proved best to distribute our brochures in both spring–early summer and late summer–early fall waves, with a midsummer hiatus in order to retool—that is, to evaluate results, adjust the upcoming mailing plan and prepare the updated edition of the brochure, which will now be able to chronicle the early success of the campaign and perhaps give the latest repertoire and artist roster changes or additions. However, in situations where there have been no spring mailings, for whatever the reason, no summer pause can be taken. Even though in many places results may be less in the latter part of July and during a good part of August, the project which has had a very late spring start or has not begun until early summer must wage the battle *all* summer. There are a great many subscriber prospects who will cheerfully sign up and send in their money during March, April or May for a season that does not begin until mid-October, while there are others who will never make that move until September or early October, when the proximity of the season's beginning presses them to take affirmative action.

Finally: "When do we *stop* mailing?" We never stop, as long as there is still time until the season begins, as long as we are getting an acceptable return and as long as there are still seats to fill.

# 17

# *"Once More unto the Breach..."*
# *Duplications in Mailing*

During the past decade, we have seen a growth of subscription audiences for all the performing arts disciplines on this continent on a scale that no one had previously thought possible — not in terms of 5%, 10%, 15% or 20% increases, but in the hundreds and even thousands of percent, depending upon the base from which the gains began in each organization's case. And new arts institutions have sprung into existence with instant subscription audiences that formerly would have taken generations to build. Any examination of the reasons for this amazing metamorphosis in the subscription area would reveal that a major element in this change for the better has been the introduction of the large-scale mailing of brochures, with duplication as an important connected factor.

Although it is a fact that duplications are the yeast which makes the cake of the subscription sales rise, this concept is not understood by many people, both in and out of the arts. There is much opposition to duplicated mailings of brochures in our campaigns, often from our own board members who are especially vocal in their criticism. I think because they, personally, are usually on all of the selective lists and on some of the lists of less selectivity, they see the duplications as waste. They are not only concerned with duplications as a loss, but they fear that the image of waste on the part of our nonprofit organization will lose us the support of contributors and the sympathy of the general public.

What they forget is that duplication is a sound and basic principle of advertising, a technique by which many businesses have made fortunes in promoting their own products. Why doesn't Chevrolet have just one TV program a year to proclaim the virtues of its new model car? Why do they come at us every week with a big show, plus daily spot announcements and regular exposure in newspapers and magazines? One tycoon I know of, retired from a merchandising operation that made him a multimillionaire, approached all the performing arts boards in his city with one mission in mind—to stop all duplications of mailed brochures. Once a year was enough, he contended. In his own business, he had been a heavy, repetitive advertiser, and I think it would not be unfair to say that it wasn't just the quality of his product that made it sell so well, but the volume of his promotion. Yet, he would deny the performing arts the very tool that brought him his success.

The move in some communities to establish joint arts mailing lists has usually been brought about by pressure from board members to eliminate duplications, an act which I believe is penny-wise and pound-foolish. However, I have recommended that where these joint lists exist, they should be utilized for *controlled* duplication, which is not exactly what their sponsors originally had in mind. One of the negative factors inherent in the use of joint arts lists is that it tends to create too inbred a situation, too great a dependence on just that one combed list, and it inhibits the constant introduction of "new blood" lists into our campaigns. The seemingly wasteful method of separately utilizing every selective list and then turning to less and still less selective lists as our need to sell more subscriptions may dictate, can be done in a manner which controls the duplications in its own way — that is, by careful spacing of the mailing of the lists so that no person who may be on a number of them will receive more than one brochure on the same day or in the same week.

Let us say that we have planned a six-month direct-mail campaign in which we will use two different brochures. We will use 18 different lists of varying sizes and types, ranging from highly selective ones (obtained on a trade basis from sister performing arts organizations) to mass lists contributed by department stores, and even demographic lists of all the residents of certain neighborhoods. During the first three months of the campaign, we will mail out one of the first nine lists every 10th day. Thus, if a person is on five of those lists, we let the chips of duplication fall where they may. We do not seek to avoid the duplications because we know that they help us make the sales. Assuming that the person is a prospect on any level for what we are offering, we can afford to keep going at him. If he receives only one or two brochures, it is likely that he may just throw them away and our chances with him have ended. It might be the third brochure that he keeps on his desk and then begins to consider. Maybe it is the fourth or fifth brochure that will bring in his check and order. In some cases, we have printed the brochure in various colors, so that there is the sense of seeing something different as the various mailings are received.

Then, for the next three months, we mail to the other nine lists which we have assembled for the purpose, using a new edition of the brochure—one that looks quite different from the first one, perhaps trumpeting the success we have already had on the front or back of the piece:

Since the initial announcements of our exciting forthcoming season, 7,200 music lovers have enrolled as season subscribers. As we enter the final phase of our drive, there are only 2,712 seat locations left. When they are gone, we will have a total sellout for the entire season, and those who mistakenly think they will be able to pick up tickets to individual concerts will find the cupboard bare. So, subscribe now—and be assured of seats for every thrilling evening of musical entertainment offered!

Again, we go after our prospects in the same relentless way that our board members used in their respective drives to success in their own private enterprises.

*We*, however, have that economic advantage they did not have; that is, the nonprofit postal privilege, enabling us to mail, as this is written, at a special low bulk rate of 2¢ per brochure, while profit-making companies must pay 7.7¢ for bulk mailing of a similar piece. While government subsidy for the arts has long been retarded in the U.S., this is one form of subsidy we do enjoy. Not to use it to the full, is to neglect a real advantage when we have so many disadvantages. In Canada, where a similar special rate currently does not exist, mass distribution of brochures is accomplished by door-to-door delivery services. Results are not as good, however, as when subsidized low mailing rates allowed Canadian nonprofit organizations to distribute brochures, bearing specific names and addresses, on a much larger scale.

It is advisable to place a request in the brochure, asking that any extra brochures received be given to friends who may share the recipient's interest in what we are offering. Is there not an annoyance factor in our sending out such a volume of mail which certainly includes duplications? Yes, but the amount of annoyance in relation to the benefits we derive is minor. I know of many campaigns in which a million or more brochures have been sent out, with no more, on the average, than a dozen letters and another dozen phone calls commenting upon the duplication. We answer each letter and telephone call fully and with courtesy, explaining our position and needs. I have, myself, over the years, answered a number of such complaints and have yet to receive a second letter saying, "Despite your explanation, we do not forgive you." I do not recall a single telephone call on this subject that did not end in the complainant being mollified.

I remember, in one of my own subscription campaigns, a telephone call from a $500 contributor, implying that he would withdraw his annual contribution if this "wasteful duplication of mailings" was not stopped immediately. We had already sold $1.5 million worth of subscriptions in that drive. Do you think I would kill the goose of duplication that had laid that golden subscription egg for this man's $500? However, I didn't say that to him, as I am, after all, supposed to be a public relations man. I told him what was indeed true in his case, that because he was one of the most culturally connected persons in the community, he was on just about every selective list that we used, but that most of the people we were seeking to reach were not. Thus, they did not receive as many as he had. I also explained the theory behind the duplications and told him of the practical results we were experiencing at that very time. He was satisfied, and he thanked me for the explanation. He subsequently increased his annual contribution substantially.

One of the most experienced and knowledgeable persons I know of in the direct-mail sales field says, "Duplications work *for* us, not against us, despite criticism from those who view what we do superficially. Based on the experience of hundreds of mail campaigns, I assure you that in every case where an attempt was made to eliminate duplications, sales went down sharply."

Today, many large mailing lists which are used in our various drives are computerized, and the computer produces labels, which are affixed to the address side of the brochures by machines at great speed. Should the computer slip and print out that man's name and address four times instead of once, we and he are in danger that he will go to his mailbox and find four brochures in one delivery. That is not good, but there isn't much we can do about it. Then, we may be victimized by the same person being on another organization's mailing list we may be using, in a number of ways. For instance, Mr. Dwight Jones may be there also as Mr. Dwight Jeffrey Jones and Mr. D. J. Jones—and his wife may have entered the lists separately, as Mrs. Philomena Jones, Mrs. Dwight Jones, Mrs. Dwight Jeffrey Jones and Mrs.

D. J. Jones. Now, all organizations do seek to root out these kinds of internal list duplications, but some organizations are more zealous than others in this respect. All of us owe, to our own cause and to others, the most conscientious maintenance of our mailing lists, so that these dangers will be minimal.

And now for some figures which will graphically illustrate the power of repetitive, duplicative mailing of brochures: The response tabulations of one of the most consistently successful resident theatres show that an August 21 mailing of 36,000 coded brochures to its own house list produced .58% sales returns. On August 28, only a week later, 27,660 additional brochures were repeat-mailed to a portion of the same list, with a .59% result, slightly larger than the first time around. Then, still from the same list, 20 days later (on September 17), 17,600 names were selected for a follow-up which pulled a percentage of 1.1—*almost double the percentage response of the first two releases!* Now, to another of the same campaign's mailing components: On August 14, 84,800 brochures went out to resident addresses in the metropolitan area (no names), obtaining a response of .68%. Three weeks later, a local bank's list of 82,300 names brought in .91%. It is certain that the bank's list covered virtually 100% of the same people who had been reached through the occupant mailing of August 14, as such lists cover every address within the area, except for some newcomers whose names conceivably could have been on the bank's addressograph plates without yet being on the resident list. These figures are conclusive and incontrovertible, yet by no means unique. There is little room for doubt that the continued response in rising crescendo was brought about by the cumulative effect of the repeat mailings—*the duplications.*

Sometimes, a performing arts company's management, after some seasons of very successful promotion of new subscription sales during which time a certain scale and schedule of brochure distributions has been established, will suddenly eliminate some very important part of that promotional routine. This deviation virtually always results in a detrimental, and sometimes drastic, effect on the sales pattern. Often this omission is done in an attempt to kill two birds with one stone; that is, to presumably save money and, at the same time, to lessen the incidence of duplications which are allegedly a negative factor. Time and time again, when such action has been taken (or perhaps we might say when such *inaction* has been taken), there is a much larger immediate loss in subscription sales monies than the savings in printing, handling and postage. And, cutting down the original print orders actually raises the unit cost of smaller-size mailings, since unit printing costs decrease in direct ratio to the increase in the number of brochures we buy. Then, there is an incremental loss on all the renewals for years to come, on the subscriptions that aren't sold. Thus, these "economy" measures often turn out to be very expensive. As far as the benefits we are supposed to derive from fewer duplications, we have no evidence at all of any increase in subscription sales thereby. A related case in point would be that of a public television station which had sedately and only very occasionally mentioned its need for subscribers (contributing members) over its own broadcasting facilities. When it made a radical departure from this policy, embarking on an aggressive campaign of greatly increased, regular, repetitive appeals to the public, there was a soaring from its previous subscribership of 22,000 to its present one of 123,000. Recently, a staff member of this television station asked me if I approved of the aggressive promotional policy which has brought about this sensational increase, even though some people have been critical of the station's bringing its selling message to listeners so forthrightly and so frequently (you might call this their form of duplication) on the 60 to 70 "pledge nights" which have annually been set aside for this purpose—as well as through large-scale mailings. Well, if he was expecting me to agree with the criticism, he asked the wrong man. My answer to him was in the form of a simple question: "Why," I asked, "didn't the more than 100,000 subscribers who have joined you since the switch to Dynamic Subscription Promotion join you before?"

If there is indeed an annoyance factor in duplications, particularly because one's own subscribers are getting additional brochures even after they've renewed, it can be much mitigated through employment of wit and tact, and by simply informing people of the reasons we are doing what we're doing. One theatre which had for the first time sent out large-scale mailings in the full awareness that many people would be receiving several copies of their brochure, dealt with the issue in their subscriber newsletter:

*If you didn't get 27 of our brochures this spring, you didn't win this year's popularity contest. Here's the explanation: In order to grow and reach new people (and to remind our regular patrons), we must send thousands of our brochures. We use many different mailing lists. We send these brochures under a bulk mail permit which puts a brochure in your mailbox for less than 2¢. Thus, if you received 5 brochures, our total mailing cost was only 9¢. Since eliminating duplications from 27 different lists would cost much more than postage, we risk your ire to bring summer thought and entertainment to a larger audience.*

*P.S. It works! We have found thousands of new subscribers this year!*

# 18

# *Casting Our Bread*
## *upon the Waters —*
### *Other Ways to Distribute Brochures*

We use the mails as a primary means for large-scale distribution of brochures bearing order forms simply because this method has proved an efficient way to reach a large number of people to whom we feel we have a chance of selling our subscriptions, and the cost of carrying out these mailings is feasible within the economies of nonprofit performing arts groups. However, any way in which we can get our brochures into the hands of people is a good way, and some of those ways cost even less than mailings, which compensates in part for the fact that the percentage of returns might be less than we achieve by mail distribution.

Brochures, reduced somewhat in size and printed on lighter weight paper to hold down the cost, can be inserted in all of the programs which are distributed each night in our own auditorium, and exchange arrangements can be made with other theatres and concert halls in the area, enabling us to get our brochures inserted in the programs of many other places where patrons of the performing arts are present in large numbers. One theatre company distributed 140,000 inserts in this manner, which yielded 922 subscriptions at $35 apiece—for a cost of only $1.08 each. This is just about as good economics as you can get, except for the usually even lower cost of obtaining renewals!

Brochures inserted into the full circulation of newspapers and periodicals have sometimes proved to be very successful. The San Francisco Opera received excellent returns in the use of a very attractive, jumbo version of its brochure inserted in the *San Francisco Sunday Examiner & Chronicle*. Another opera company bound its brochure into the program guide center spread of a leading FM classical music radio station, obtaining very good results. Some of the best returns have come from the tipping in of brochures in neighborhood weekly publications.

In some cases, it has been found that newspaper insertions are better made on weekdays than on weekends, when the papers are often already stuffed with many other supplements. The charge made by the publication for the insertion usually has come to less than the cost of postage and addressing and has often proved more effective than an ad run in the same paper. Not in all cases have the insertions been successful, but it is a method which deserves consideration and experimentation. A full-size supplement in the newspaper can also be used instead of the inserted brochure. I do not mean the type of rotogravure supplement which has many pages, is filled with institutional articles and photographs and which only incidentally contains subscription information and an order form. In such instruments, the subscription-selling aspect is too minor an element and too diffuse for successful selling. However, when the supplement is subscription oriented only, primed and aimed at getting the order, good results can often occur. Arena Stage has recently reported excellent sales, at a cost which made sense, through such a supplement in Washington, D.C. However, another arts organization in the same city, trying to emulate that example, reported that its 750,000 distribution through a newspaper insert (at a cost of $10,000) drew only 800 subscriptions, though its follow-up mailing of only 200,000 pieces (at a cost of $10,000) brought in 2,000 sales. I would suggest that the soundest approach is not to use the insert distribution *instead of,* but rather *in addition to,* the conventional mailings.

The Toronto Symphony Orchestra, like all other Canadian performing arts institutions, must run its promotional campaigns under the handicap of having to pay regular postage rates. The symphony distributes 850,000 brochures prior to each season, with 600,000 of them delivered to certain areas via the Canadian "postal walk," which operates in the following manner: The brochures are delivered in bulk to the post office and the postmen, on their rounds, simply put them into all the mailboxes in the areas which have been designated. How is it different from our occupant mailings? There are no addresses. Under our occupant mailing plan, there may be no names but there are addresses on each brochure. How does the Toronto Symphony Orchestra account for the other quarter-million brochures? Sixty thousand of them are distributed at subscription booths which are maintained on the grounds of Ontario Place, where the orchestra plays its summer season; 40,000 are used in three mailings to the orchestra's house list during the life of the campaign; 30,000 are sent to the Coordinated Arts Services subscription list, covering the combined subscribership of the major arts groups in the city;

and another 100,000 to those postal walk areas or zones which have shown, via their coded return order forms, that they are the most productive, following the earlier 600,000 distribution. Another 15,000 are inserted in an issue of the Canadian *Jewish News,* and 5,000 are stuffed in the programs at performances of the Canadian Opera Company. What are the results? The percentages are not as good as when the old postal rates operated in Canada, when arts groups were able to send brochures which had both names and addresses. However, despite this handicap, the orchestra has built up a 23,000-strong subscribership. It remains my hope that the Canadian government, which so generously supports the arts in the most direct way (it gives them money, much larger amounts of it than their counterpart organizations in the U.S. receive from government sources), will eventually relent on its present policy of parity in bulk mail postal charges for its nonprofit and profit customers.

Another way of distributing brochures is to write to every firm in the area which has more than a certain number of employees, asking the president how many brochures he might wish to have for the use of his staff. The letter contains an order form for him to fill out and send back in an enclosed postage-paid envelope. It is amazing to see the large number of order forms come in. This company can use 50, another 500, and so on. The brochures are sent out in packets at the lowest postage. And subscriptions come back. The cost is much less than distribution by mailing directly to individuals, which helps make up for the lesser returns—but there *are* returns.

An aggressive audience developer of my acquaintance saturated his area with an autotyped letter (names and addresses filled in) mailed first class to heads of retail, wholesale and manufacturing firms, college presidents, school principals, office heads in all levels of government, hospital superintendents, heads of social service agencies and directors of chambers of commerce. The letter generated a 2% response to his offer to supply brochures in bulk. The heaviest response came from schools and colleges. One large university requested 13,000 brochures. The packages were sent variously by parcel post, regular mail, United Parcel Service, motor freight or special messenger. The promotion was profitable. The overall costs of brochure distribution were much less than if they had been conventionally sent out to individuals, and the subscribers obtained, of course, became eligible for renewing in the seasons that followed.

In some communities, brochures have been distributed by hand to residences by companies which do similar chores for shopping publications and other commercial enterprises. In other cases, arts groups have organized their own forces of youngsters to carry out this task. This process eliminates the costs of postage, addressing, and bundling, and costs only the distributors' fees. The main drawback is the sometimes lack of dependability on the part of the distributors.

In one project I worked with, brochures were inserted in pouches attached to posters which were placed on bulletin boards in stores and in many public places. Dedicated volunteer workers divided the neighborhoods of the city among them and, all during the life of the campaign, made daily visits to the poster locations, to replace the brochures which people had taken the day before. I was happily surprised by the steady number of sales which came in on those coded order forms.

If we really have something worthwhile to offer, and our brochure tells our story well, we must have the confidence in its power to convince the people who receive it and read it. Thus, our rationale must be to keep casting our bread (read *brochures*) upon the waters.

# 19

# The "Xmas Card List" Component: Private Mailing Lists

All of us know many people who might well be subscribers to our performing arts companies. They possess the educational and cultural backgrounds which make them prime candidates to attend our performances regularly but, for the simple reason that they have never taken the step, the connection has not been made. That is, they have not, on their own, ever come to the decision to commit themselves to attend on a series or seasonal basis. Many years ago, in trying to find more ways such connections *could* be made, I worked out an approach which has since been responsible for the sale of countless thousands of subscriptions on several continents.

Looking at a dog-eared address book on my desk, I suddenly realized that it contained a treasure trove of potential subscribers. For many years I had been putting names, addresses and telephone numbers into it of those people whom I would need to reach by mail or telephone at various times. They were people with whom I had professional and personal contacts on a wide variety of levels. Suppose I wanted to send out a holiday greeting card or notification of a change of my office location? Would I sit down and begin to address the envelopes out of my head? No, I might well forget some people who ought to receive it. So, I would turn to that book and make my selections from it. I said to myself, "I'll bet there must be 300 people in that book by now, of whom a certain number would subscribe to my project if *I* asked them." Then I started to count the names. I was astonished to find that I had written into that book, over all those years, almost *800* names, addresses and telephone numbers. Of these, some 200 had moved to other cities or were deceased. And, in almost 100 cases, I couldn't remember who the people were or why I had written them into the book. However, there were some 500 whom I still knew very well and who might be potential subscribers to the project at hand. I then remembered that I had another, similar book on the telephone table at home with many more names than I had in the book at the office.

I selected 100 names of the people with whom I felt I had the best chance because of all the various bonds between us. I wrote a beautiful letter, had my secretarial service autotype it on my personal stationery, personalized to each of my hundred prospects, asking them to subscribe for season tickets to the new performing arts project. I then signed all of the letters and enclosed each in an envelope along with the brochure and a return envelope, *addressed not to the new arts company, but to me, at my home address.* This last touch gave power to the ploy. These people, whose names I had so carefully selected out of my address books, would know that I would know whether or not they complied with the request; it was not just a case where I had supplied their names to an organization and might never learn who had or had not subscribed.

It worked beautifully, and I received, in the weeks that followed, a 40% overall subscription return for my pains. About 18% of my friends, associates and relatives had sent back the return envelopes to my home. Each envelope contained an average of slightly more than two subscriptions. A man replying usually ordered for his wife, and sometimes he sent in three subscriptions, including an additional family member. Occasionally, the envelope contained a check for four subscriptions: for the man, his wife and the couple next door. The average number of subscriptions sent in by mail order in the U.S. and Canada is somewhere between 2 and 2.5 subscriptions in each envelope received. Certainly, we can deduce that the basic unit of subscription sale is at least two. Thus, this happy two-by-two-they-go-marching-through advantage makes every subscription campaign only half as hard as it sounds. If you need to sell 15,000 subscriptions to be entirely sold out, you need find only 7,500 points of sale to achieve full success.

I was, of course, very pleased with the results I had obtained, and I felt very good about those 40 people who were now going to be enjoying regular exposure to the wonderful season which our organization was in the throes of producing. I felt that, had I not taken the initiative, they might have had to watch television or play bingo on what would now be their series nights. Now, conscious of having promoted the cultural and social good, I began to seek 100 other people to supply me with the 100 most selective names from *their* books (dog-eared or in perfect condition) that were on their office desks and home telephone tables. For now I had a vision, a sort of montage in my mind's eye, of almost 10,000 names come to vibrant, pulsating life as wonderful subscribers, jamming our lobbies, applauding our performances and renewing joyfully for the next season, too. As names in the address books, they had just been suppliers of various kinds of merchandise, members of civic, philanthropic, political and religious committees, doctors, lawyers, fraternity brothers, sorority sisters, nephews, nieces, bankers, bakers and candlestick-makers. Now they would be transformed into something better; as subscribers to our performing arts company, they could realize their highest human potential!

In that frame of mind, I began to visit board members of our project, certain members of our women's association, cultural and political leaders, everybody who figured to have address books filled with many people who might find it hard to refuse the request to subscribe. I had to visit and talk to more than double the 100 list sponsors I sought before I reached my goal. Understandably, not everyone approached was willing to supply his or her list. I showed each of them three fine letters from which to choose; or they could write their own, using the salient points of the sample letters I had prepared. Most of them chose one of the suggested letters. I asked each list sponsor, when he made his 100 selections from his hundreds of names, to also make note of how each person was to be addressed. If he were writing to his fraternity brother from college days, it would be something like "Dear Eddie." If he were writing to his aunt, it would certainly not be "Mrs. Lewis," but "Dear Aunt Geraldine." If he were writing to last year's community fund chairman, with whom he had a formal relationship (but for whom he had knocked himself out when called on to work for that cause), the greeting might be "Dear Mr. Willoughby." I asked each of my list sponsors to supply me with 110 sheets of his stationery (10 for possible spoilage) and 200-odd envelopes (100 for mailing the requests for subscription and 100 to be enclosed for return). I then had a letter service complete the typing and addressing and brought each letter back for personal signature. I never left the letters with the list sponsor, for I would then not be certain that he mailed them. I took them back to my office, where I put into each envelope the letter, the brochure with its built-in order form and the return envelope addressed back to the list sponsor and, as I completed each set of 100 letters, mailed them. Now I had, in effect, 100 separate extension subscription box offices to check with. When all the returns were finally in, 15% of those written to replied—for an average of a little over 2.1 subscriptions in each envelope—a total of 3,200 subscriptions—an overall 32% response in terms of season-ticket sales!

Because this procedure has become a consistently valuable campaign component, I have taken the trouble to describe it here in considerable detail. Obviously, its success for me at that time was bound up not only with its basic efficacy but with the scale on which it was carried out. Had I organized only 10 lists of 100 names each and received the same rate of return, I would have sold only 320 subscriptions. Since my campaign's goal was 10,000 (I succeeded in selling 13,000 by the time that season began), it was obviously necessary to plan and carry out all the components in the campaign on a scale that made sense in relation to the need. This point cannot be emphasized too much. More than once I have been told by officials of performing arts groups, "The private mailing lists worked beautifully for us, but we made one mistake—we didn't go out to get enough of them."

Performing arts groups have usually been able to bring in from 7% to 20% in overall subscription returns through this method, depending upon the quality of the lists used and the care with which the procedure is carried out. Shortcuts like nonpersonalized letters which are mimeographed or plano-graphed; "Dear Friend" form letters with handwritten notes at the bottom; and return envelopes addressed back to the arts organization's office rather than to the home or office of the list sponsor; might bring some results, but not much better ones than do standard large-scale brochure mailings.

In the event that there may be duplications of names among those presented by your various list sponsors, just vary the letters that are sent out, which you will be able to do if you gather all the lists to be used before beginning the mailings. The same man getting several of our letters will make his own decision as to which of his friends who are soliciting him will receive his order; then, he will likely phone the others to tell them something like, "It isn't that I didn't do what you asked. I bought the subscriptions for Marian and myself, but Joe's letter got here first, so I sent my check to him."

New Haven's Long Wharf Theatre sent out 1,400 of the "Xmas Card List" letters (I have so designated them because it is from those same address books at office and home that people select the names to which they send holiday greeting cards) and got back a 42.9% subscription return. That is, 300 of the people written to replied for two each, resulting in the sale of 600 season tickets. Recently, I received a happy telephone call from the board president of a small symphony orchestra which had just finished selling out its season entirely on subscription before the first concert took place. He reported that he had achieved a 60% overall return on his personal mailing list! His orchestra, incidentally, has just announced that it will double the number of its concerts for the coming season. In an excellent subscription effort, which resulted in a major gain in audience for the Cincinnati Symphony Orchestra, its women's association obtained a consistent 15% return for the large number of such lists which were used. In all of these cases, as in so many others, new subscribers would not have been acquired were it not for the extra thrust which this campaign component provided. The proof? They had not subscribed in the past.

Why has this approach been so consistently valuable for us? Undoubtedly, because each time we aim at a very specific target, we have an excellent chance to score a bull's-eye. Where, in our conventional, large-scale mailings, we depend only on the convincing elements in our brochures, here we have the powerful extra advantage of the personal relationship between the signatory and the person to whom the letter is sent. The only variation on this method which can produce even larger returns is having each of our list sponsors make follow-up telephone calls or personal visits to those of their prospects who, after a reasonable time, have not yet responded. However, I will admit that such volunteer zeal, while extant, is hard to come by.

# 20

## *The Boon of Radio and Television Public Service Time*

Performing arts groups have a built-in boon via the Federal Communications Commission licensing practices, which encourage radio and TV stations to devote airtime to public service announcements on behalf of nonprofit organizations. Thus, our most alert and more aggressive publicists are often able to obtain considerable free benefits from the radio and television stations in their communities, in connection with our subscription drives.

I would recommend that publicists take the time and make the effort to visit the public service directors, program directors, traffic managers, or whichever officials of the stations may be in charge of the allocation of these free announcements. As of 1976, there were more than 8,000 radio stations in the U.S., of which 181 were public radio stations, and there were 962 television stations, of which 257 were public. There are also a number of commercially operated classical music stations. Unquestionably, these stations represent a tremendous promotional potential for our subscription campaigning, especially the public stations, which often tend to focus more heavily on arts programming.

It behooves us to make it as easy as possible for the officials of these stations to help us and we should consult them concerning their requirements. It might be advisable to have prepared radio announcements containing our message in 25 words for a 10-second announcement, 75 words for a 30-second announcement and 150 words for a full-minute announcement. For television, we may need to produce, with professional assistance, the slides or film we would want telecast. Many stations have segments of time devoted to a "community bulletin board," during which they give reports on philanthropic, religious, civic and cultural activities. We should regularly send news bulletins concerning events connected with our subscription drives to such programs, addressed to the person in charge. Our knowledge of "who's who" at the various stations should be on an up-to-date basis. Contact, by phone and in person, will bring better results.

Under certain circumstances, we might wish to augment this public service largesse with paid announcements over commercial stations at preferential rates since some stations give such special consideration to nonprofit organizations. Subscriptions have been sold, too, with the station providing the announcements on a commission arrangement. Purchasers phone in or mail in their orders to the station, which receives its commission on the gross subscription sales it is directly responsible for obtaining.

I recall a subscription campaign in which I participated, where a powerful radio station carried out a remarkable saturation spot-announcement effort over a period of several months, in conjunction with concurrent volunteer efforts in other subscription components. This effort not only boosted a theatre company's subscribership from 5,000 to 10,000, but resulted in a significant increase in single-ticket sales, in a situation where such sales had been extraordinarily poor. The radio station owner did not take on the promotion for the very modest commission involved, but because of the tremendous argument he could make to potential commercial sponsors if he could prove his station's sales power on behalf of something as hard to sell as subscriptions to a theatre which had always had a very hard time in successfully marketing its "product." I think he loved the idea of being able to say to prospective airtime buyers, "If I could sell *that,* can you imagine what I could do for your beer, or your automobiles, or your cosmetics—things that people *want?*"

Another type of arrangement which can sometimes be made is to trade so many subscription tickets for so many announcements. The station may then use these tickets as prizes in contests they are sponsoring or as gifts to the advertisers. A performing arts group with a previous record of considerable unsold seating capacity is in a good position to enter into all kinds of special deals of this type. It has nothing to lose since the seats would otherwise go unsold. And, by entering into enough promotional activities on many levels, it might well fight its way through to success.

A theatre company I worked with, when it had only a summer season which was mainly attended by tourists, increased its attendance by offering a coupon-book subscription to the local population, via a special all-evening radio program in which it supplied entertainment and took orders by telephone. As each order was taken at the radio station, it was turned over to a taxicab dispatcher who immediately sent a driver over to the purchaser's home to pick up the check or cash. This was a voluntary effort on the part of the cab people. Two thousand coupon books were sold in this way. That "aces wild" coupon book was later jettisoned for a conventional subscription, where the subscriber goes to all plays of the season, on specific dates and in certain seats. The company has been so successful in its promotion that it was able to launch a winter season and has remained a year-round theatre ever since.

Major symphony orchestras now annually raise huge sums of money through "symphony marathons," whereby an FM classical music radio station gives over an entire weekend to the playing of request symphonic recordings, with contributions accompanying each request. An adaptation of this method for the sale of subscription tickets can also be made. The New York City Opera, for example, in its recent initial effort along these lines, sold 2,500 new subscriptions via a weekend appeal over radio station WNCN. The $55,000-worth of sales was achieved at a promotional cost of only $1,200. The second year the results increased to 4,000 subscriptions. The opera company intends to make radio promotion a regular component of its annual subscription drives.

The Oakland Symphony Orchestra has proved that its "Series-Ticket Telethon" can be a viable annual event. Through its most recent effort, 1,780 series-ticket subscription sales have been generated in this way, with the cooperation of KRON, a leading television station which donates 90 minutes of prime viewing time, as well as the services of its production staff and advance advertising for the show. The station also prepares and mails a brochure about the telethon to the symphony's mailing list and to its own viewer lists and arranges for its two top newscaster personalities to be the program's hosts. The symphony provides the services of the orchestra and of soloists for the live pops concert, which is the centerpiece of the show. The symphony management further supports the telethon with four large advance newspaper ads, including a half-page one which appears on the day of the show, in which the details of series and seating availabilities are given. The large ad does double duty in that it contains a coupon for ordering. A local record retailer supplies free classical LP's for all who phone in their subscription orders during the telethon. Fifty phones are installed in the studio and are answered by celebrity volunteers who personally take and record the orders as they come in. The symphony management is convinced that, in addition to the direct sales it obtains from the telethon, it later receives many more orders than it would have in the absence of such an event, and that even single-ticket business is stirred up by the momentum generated through such a powerful force as television certainly is. And what about the benefits of permeating public consciousness for fund-raising efforts?

The Oakland Symphony Orchestra, in commenting upon the success of its telethon component says, "Television is a powerful and persuasive medium that has not previously been tapped by arts organizations in this area. We feel confident that we are reaching and selling to people who would not otherwise buy subscriptions to our series. We would recommend to other performing arts organizations that they pursue such a program in their respective communities." I think that this recommendation is a sound one, and when I recently passed it on to the Buffalo Philharmonic Orchestra, its management immediately stirred this component into the promotional mix of the audience development drive which it was then launching and which, when completed, resulted in a gain of 150%—from 3,000 to 7,500 subscribers. Their 90-minute series-ticket telethon, titled "Super Band," on WBEN-TV, involving the participation of the orchestra's musicians, music director Michael Tilson-Thomas, guest conductor Mitch Miller and board president–general manager Harold Lawrence, netted 1,287 new subscribers. The 16 telephones (not enough, they learned), manned by a team of local celebrities, kept ringing for an hour and a half after the program ended. The proceedings, except for a filmed section, *A Man and His Music* narrated by Maestro Tilson-Thomas, was presented "live." The records indicate that most of those who subscribed through the telethon had never before done so—and among the new enrollees were some who said they had never before attended any Philharmonic concert. At an average series-ticket price of $50, the income derived was about $65,000. However, more important than the money, is the fact that 1,287 new subscribers will be going regularly to the concerts and, hopefully, a considerable percentage of them will be renewing for many seasons to come.

Almost at the same time I advised the Buffalo people to utilize this fruitful component, I made the same suggestion to the Denver Symphony Orchestra's management staff, who were then preparing for what became a most successful subscription drive. They used it not only for its direct-sales value via a one-hour show on KOA-TV, but made it the kickoff for an intensive 11-day-long effort, which involved a ticket center in the window of a major, centrally located department store and the cooperation of other local television and radio stations (and the press, too). During those 11 days that shook Denver, 2,267 new subscriptions were registered.

Obviously, the power of radio and television to reach people effectively is great. Seemingly, a tremendous number of people in their incredibly large audiences are subject to headaches and indigestion, and are thus in the market (a truly vast market) for the commercial remedies offered so unremittingly on the airwaves. However, *our* situation is different, and mere announcements of what we have to offer are most often not enough to achieve the results we seek. For our market is, at present, a much more limited one. So, in order to obtain a significant number of series-ticket sales for the performing arts, we must employ these media aids—which are often so helpful to us— imaginatively and strongly, as the organizations I have been writing about in this chapter have been doing.

I want to advise avoidance of the institutional approach, when we get on television and radio. If we hope to sell subscription tickets (or get contributions), we should not waste our precious radio and TV promotional opportunities with announcements and slides which say only something as vague as "Support the Performing Arts." We should always be specific as to which arts organization is to be supported (ours, of course) and as to how it is to be supported (by telephoning in an order, or by sending a check to a certain address, of course).

While I have utilized the examples of several symphony orchestras, the TV telethon for subscription sales is a component which can make sense to all kinds of performing arts groups, and I am constantly urging more of them to take action along those lines. Certainly there are problems, starting with getting the television station to do it, to say nothing of the myriad, complicated arrangements which must be made in order to produce the show successfully. However, once you begin to think promotionally, your capacity to bestir yourself keeps increasing.

## 21

# Subscription Parties:
## Make the Sale
## While They're There

Bringing people together in homes for the purpose of getting them to subscribe to the performing arts has been a respectable means of accomplishing
that purpose for longer than anybody can remember. These gatherings are
variously called coffees, teas, brunches, parlor meetings, cocktail parties,
wine-and-cheese parties, according to the customs and mores of the sponsors.
(In the American Southwest, they are often designated as "patio parties.")
They all have in common that they take place at the homes of our performing
arts organizations board members, guild members, friends, subscribers and
other enthusiasts for what we have to offer. Their specific locales within the
homes which have been generously opened for such occasions range from the
living room–dining room area to the basement playroom or family room, the
front porch, the front lawn, the backyard, alongside a swimming pool and
even in the built-in meeting room facilities of modern apartment buildings,
which are available for the social events of their tenants.

Some people blanch at the idea of inviting their relatives, friends,
neighbors and business associates over with the idea of selling them anything,
which can certainly be understood if it is Tupperware, insurance or real estate
that is being sold. However, when the beneficiary of the effort is a fine, civic,
nonprofit institution such as ours, and when we are trying to convince those
who attend to subscribe to something we believe they will find much pleasure
in, the suggestion appears to be much more reasonable and acceptable.
Indeed, the thousands of subscriptions which are currently being sold by this
method testify to that fact.

However, if a man who is asked to open his home for a coffee party appears
to have a strongly negative feeling about it, experience has shown that it is
almost impossible to persuade him. It is more constructive and productive to
ask instead for his participation in one of our other components. For example,

in a recent resident theatre's subscription campaign, a board member who demurred at holding a coffee party substituted another personal effort that resulted in the sale of 70 season tickets.

There is no single formula for the running of successful coffee parties. There is no special time. Some are in the morning, others in the afternoon, at cocktail time and in the evening. Because the cocktail parties and the later evening ones are usually for couples and because a wife cannot then say, as she might at a morning or afternoon affair attended by ladies only, "I want to take it up with my husband and then I'll let you know," the number of immediate sales is greater in the evenings. Some of the best sales results are obtained at meetings with 10 to 15 couples present, rather than with 50 couples, for the reason that in the more intimate-size groups, more personal attention can be given. We do not expect to sell subscriptions to everybody who comes to our party. If we average four pairs of immediate sales at each party, and we organize 100 such gatherings, there will be 800 subscriptions sold; for many of our organizations, this is a more than sizable result. However, the sales can be higher than an average of four pairs per party, depending on such factors as the selectivity of the prospects, how well we have run the meeting, and to what extent the host and hostess have prepared their guests at the time of inviting them. In a most competently managed series of coffee parties held recently, an average direct-sales result of 7½ pairs of subscriptions was realized each time—that is, 705 subscriptions sold at the 47 parties held by the orchestra women's committee responsible for this component of the campaign.

An indispensable ingredient for a coffee party is the speaker, who may be the artistic director, the general manager or any staff member, a board member or any other volunteer who is capable of making a convincing talk about the ideology of the project, the concept of subscribing, what it means to the organization, and what it can mean to them if they subscribe (benefits, bonuses, discounts, etc.). If the party is being given on behalf of a theatre company, then the event can be much enriched by having two actors perform a short scene. If it is a musical organization, then artists of that genre should perform, if possible. Sometimes, carefully prepared slides or films can be used to great effect at such parties. And when the coffee and cake are being served, the speaker should announce that he is ready to take orders. Brochures, order forms, seating charts, pens and pencils should be passed out. An all-out effort must be made to pin down the subscription sale *while the people are there* (although subscriptions can and do come in, in some instances, at a later date) on order forms, which indicate by their codes that they were distributed at that particular coffee party.

One of the problems that can develop is that of "flinching at the crunch," which happens when those responsible for running the coffee party subconsciously begin to sublimate the real purpose of the party, turning it into a basically informational session rather than a sales-oriented one. One organization with which I was working for the first time, drew goose eggs in sales for its first three coffee parties. A meeting was held of all staff and volunteers who were involved, and in an illuminating moment of self-analysis, they all agreed that they had been "flinching." They resolved that they would not fall into this error again and, indeed, they did not. That meeting was a turning point for them. Despite that inauspicious beginning, they made their goal and, as the other components also produced good sales, the full campaign was successful.

It happens that there are many important concomitant gains from the coffee parties, although we are primarily seeking direct, immediate sales. When a coffee party is in the process of being organized, a tremendous number of telephone calls must be made and countless conversations take place before we even get to the date. All of this word-of-mouth activity about our project redounds to its benefit. Some of those who don't buy at the party may send for subscriptions later. Others enter our market for single-ticket sales (should there be any available after we have sold the subscriptions). All who attend the coffee parties leave there with much more information about us and, hopefully, a better impression of us than they had before, which they presumably communicate to others who were not present themselves.

"Booking" the coffee parties is an important task and must begin many months in advance of the season, as must the entire drive. For most organizations, best results are obtained by a chairman or by cochairmen of the volunteer corps especially assigned to this area. Logically, they should be people with wide personal connections, with prominence and prestige in the community so that they are not easily turned down in their request. However, this is not the only way in which such "bookings" are arranged. In the case of Actors Theatre of Louisville, which has managed some 200 such parties annually for the past half-dozen years (and which has one of the largest subscription audiences in the country for the size of the local population), flyers are sent out to its 18,000-plus subscribers and its 250-member women's volunteer group, asking them to hold the parties. During the theatre season, at least one member of the administrative staff is assigned each night to "mix" with audience members during intermissions looking for possible party hosts for the annual subscription drive. At each party, the speaker asks people who attend to hold their own parties—with good results. All board members are expected to hold parties. Either a staff member or a volunteer, or both, are assigned to solicit party dates via telephoning people who have shown any special interest in the theatre's activities that year. For instance, every person who attended the organization's annual fund-raising auction is telephoned, and many dates are arranged as a result.

Coffee parties are a truly grass-roots kind of subscription promotion—very community and people oriented. Although based on a sales motive, they can be pleasant social occasions, too. Their success depends very much on the wills and skills of the people who are running them for us and, above all, on the hosts and hostesses whose own enthusiasm on our behalf is of the essence. To performing arts organizations, always hard pressed for funds and usually loath to expend monies for promotional purposes, this component is ideal. Its out-of-pocket cost to the organization is, in almost all situations, minimal.

The Detroit Symphony Orchestra recently arranged for an interesting adaptation of the coffee party component. Two hundred coffees were scheduled on the same day, with a leading TV station supplying its facilities for a half-hour telecast which was the central feature for the parties being held. The symphony's music director and other luminaries were featured on the television special. Not only did the orchestra stand to benefit by the direct subscription sales made at the coffees, but it had an additional benefit, in that the telecast reached the vast general viewing public at the same time and provided the information and inspiration that will, hopefully, result in considerable additional sales. Such intensive activities, requiring much preliminary planning and organizational work, pay off not only in direct sales, but in creating a better overall context for the entire drive. This orchestra ended the campaign with the biggest subscribership in its history.

# 22

## *Bloc Sales:*
## *A New Market*
## *for Many Arts Groups*

Just as each sales transaction of a season- or series-ticket subscription fills a seat for a succession of our productions, a bloc subscription sale fills, as its designation suggests, a bloc of seats to those same offerings. In the latter multiple sales area, lies a considerable potential in relation to our overall possibilities which is often overlooked entirely, or realized only minimally, by performing arts groups. While many organizations have long utilized this sales component as a regular part of their annual subscription campaigns, others have neglected it even when similar arts groups in the same communities have succeeded in obtaining excellent results thereby. As in the cases of other logical and useful selling components, it usually turns out that the main reason this component is not being exploited is just that nobody has seriously developed it.

A logical sector for development of bloc sales of subscriptions is the commercial and industrial one. All manner of wholesale, retail, manufacturing and service enterprises are our targets. Any company which transacts any kind of business and which has people working for it and buying from it, could well become the purchaser of a bloc of subscription tickets. Companies can use these season or series tickets in a number of ways—all of which make sense to them, when they are effectively reached by us. These tickets can be used by the executives and their wives and the members of employee clubs. Subscriptions can be given as prizes to members of the firm's sales force for outstanding achievement. For example, a gifted vacuum cleaner salesman in a downtown department store racks up a new record, having sold 32 machines in one day. He is not only given that fat commission check, but at a meeting of the entire staff, the company's president presents him with a pair of subscription tickets to the entire seven-play season of the city's professional stage company. Another business organization might send annual gifts to certain important customers or clients. The selection of these presents is always a difficult decision. Why not send certain of these people, whose tastes may run to theatre, symphony, opera or ballet, subscription tickets to one of those arts institutions? It is a gift which will be gratefully remembered at each of a number of high-level entertainment occasions. Remember, too, that purchase of subscription tickets by companies for all of the purposes listed here are tax deductible as part of their costs of doing business.

Sometimes companies are not approached for purchase of these blocs of subscription tickets for fear that sales might interfere with fund-raising efforts, the idea being that you cannot ask them to contribute, as well as purchase subscriptions. The answer to that objection is that there are usually many more companies that don't contribute than do. If all the companies solicited gave us contributions, fund-raising would be a pleasure instead of the chore it is. So, there should be no inhibition on our part in going after noncontributing companies to buy subscriptions. Probably the reason they *don't* contribute is they need more incentive than just supporting a good cause. Now we come to them, not asking for a contribution, but *offering* them tickets which, we point out, they can use in any of several ways which are in their own interests. Now, they hear us. We're talking their language. We can do business. For those companies which *do* contribute to our fund-raising campaigns, it has often been found that they will, in addition, buy the blocs of subscription tickets when called upon, as the monies come from a different budget. The contribution is charged to the philanthropic budget, while the bloc of subscription tickets is charged to employees' incentives, customer relations or some other expense of doing business.

Merely circularizing prospective companies by letter is not likely to obtain the results we seek. There is nothing wrong with sending letters introducing the idea, but unless there is a follow-up drive on a personal level, this component will not get off the ground. Committees of businessmen, under the chairmanship of one of their own, are especially effective in carrying out this component, ideally with the president of one company calling upon the president of another company, a man with whom he is personally acquainted and with whom he may be doing business. I think that the Minnesota Orchestra's special effort on bloc sales to companies when it was still performing in the huge Northrop Auditorium (before Orchestra Hall was built), is a dramatic example of how excellent results can be achieved when careful planning and vital leadership are major ingredients of the promotional mix. In this effort, bloc sales were enlarged from 50 companies to 250 companies (an additional $62,000 worth of subscription tickets) in what was called "Operation Sound Decision" by the dynamic chairman of the businessmen's committee that put it all together. He gave leadership to a committee which brought 48 businessmen to a luncheon, convinced them to pledge their own companies' participation and to go after other companies, too. They worked from the lists of firms which had been purchasing season tickets to the football, baseball and hockey teams, and they succeeded in convincing the responsible officials that the orchestra was also worthy of their support. What is most significant about the successful implementation of this campaign component was that over 90% of the companies which became bloc buyers for the first time *renewed* a year later, thus indicating that they had found good use for the subscription tickets and that their season-ticket patronage could be regarded as a permanent asset to the orchestra. One year later, a separate campaign along similar lines "discovered" 50 additional companies in neighboring Saint Paul to patronize the orchestra's series at the I. A. O'Shaughnessy Auditorium there.

The names of all of the companies which purchase season-ticket subscriptions are listed in the printed programs for the concert, and they have also been prominently displayed in an impressive double-page layout in the Minnesota Orchestra's magazine *Showcase*. Such recognition not only properly expresses thanks to these companies for their enlightened participation in our important audience-building effort, but serves, too, to remind officials of business organizations which have not yet signed up on our dotted line that many of the area's most prestigious firms have already done so.

This experience underscores how such an opportunity can be exploited according to the amount of effort expended. Although the orchestra had been performing in that community for almost three-quarters of a century, no one had ever made the match between it and the some 200 local businesses. Had not the "matchmaker" entered the picture, perhaps another 75 years might have been lost.

Other performing arts organizations, inspired by the success of "Operation Sound Decision," have launched their own versions of that subscription-selling component. The Saint Louis Symphony Orchestra, for instance, has recently managed to enroll 189 companies in 856 full-series tickets (at an average of $73 per subscription), for a total of $62,441 in sales. This effort, now in its fourth season, has already been responsible, cumulatively, for $181,113 and 2,297 subscriptions—a lot of money and a lot of audience which the orchestra would not have had were this rewarding work not begun.

We have learned by experience that our overall success in this component will be the greater when we concentrate on selling a small number of subscriptions, but to a large number of companies. I have worked with organizations that have one big corporate customer for, say, 50 subscriptions, but that is all they sell. On the other hand, the organization that sells 50 companies an average of 5 pairs each has 500 to show in the final count. In this component, as in all the others we use, the scale of the effort—the number of companies upon which calls are made—is of the essence. I recall a campaign in which a theatre company offering subscriptions at very attractive, highly discounted prices, achieved most of the goals which had been set for it. However, in reporting to me, the manager spoke of the bloc-sales effort as having been a failure. "We sold only 50 subscriptions that way," he lamented. When I asked him how many companies his people had seen, he admitted that they had seen only 10, of which 5 had purchased an average of five pairs. I pointed out that the component was really highly successful. One out of every two companies contacted had bought subscriptions (an astonishing percentage of success). The "failure" was only in the fact that he carried out the effort on such a small scale, not at all in relation to the number of subscriptions needed, nor in relation to the component goal of 350 subscriptions which we had originally put into the plan. Using the same percentages of return as they had received for the minuscule commitment of effort, had 70 companies been called on, with 35 purchasing that average of 5 pairs each, the full goal of 350 subscriptions for bloc sales to companies would have been attained.

The number of subscriptions a company will buy bears relationship, of course, to the price per subscription, which varies according to the situation. As ticket prices run, a major symphony orchestra offering a main series of 24 concerts might have a top price per subscription ticket of $150; a major opera company, with its incredible costs of operation, might charge that much for one-third as many performances. In general, ballet and theatre companies usually offer subscription packagings at much lower prices, such as $37 maximum. In the case of the Minnesota Orchestra's first big push for industrial bloc sales, the series tickets sold (for 20 concerts) averaged about $100 apiece, with each of the 200 new corporate customers purchasing an average of a little more than three subscriptions. Had the committee in charge opted to sell the orchestra's series of 10 concerts rather than 20, the number of subscriptions sold to each purchaser might have been more, but the results in money terms would have remained the same.

Not in every situation does the company pay the entire cost of the subscriptions it buys for the use of its personnel. In some instances, the company resells the subscriptions directly to its employees or to its employee club at a lower price than it has paid for them, absorbing the cost differential. Whether the company makes an outright gift of the season or series tickets or gets some of its outlay back from the recipients, it should be pointed out that this offer can be looked on as an attractive fringe benefit which will foster goodwill between the employer and the employed. Posters for company bulletin boards, and stories and photographs relevant to the productions offered on the subscription series should be provided for the internal publications which all company personnel receive. One theatre offers a free subscription if the company buys as many as 25. Whether an additional discount, beyond the regular schedule of subscriber discounts, should be offered for industrial bloc sales is a matter of local option. In many cases, because of the civic pride aspect and the leverage of the blue-ribbon businessman sales force we are able to command, the regular price prevails.

Other fine bloc-sale possibilities are in the areas of finding earmarked contributions with which to purchase subscriptions as "scholarships" for needy students in the local universities; economically hard-pressed senior citizens who may be participating in Golden Age programs at community centers; and disadvantaged persons in the community.

Attending our universities are many fine young people who would not be there were it not for their having achieved brilliant scholastic records. They may be working in the school dining hall for their meals and in the library for their pocket money. They are unlikely to be able to purchase tickets for the performing arts on their own. So, we organize a special committee to find bloc sponsors from among members of our board, our women's association, our present subscribers, affluent members of the community, service clubs, and everywhere else we can. We convince them to buy blocs of subscriptions— three, four or five apiece—so that these college students can be invited to attend the entire season of theatre, symphony, ballet or opera in full dignity, sitting in their own regular seats, and not given a once-over-lightly treatment on the basis of a cut-rate "student rush" ticket for which they have had to stand in line at the last moment, not knowing whether or not they would be able to get in. Given the opportunity to attend a full season of one of these arts organizations, it is far more likely that they will be won for life and that we will have made a gain on more than one level for our cause. Many potential sponsors of such blocs might turn a deaf ear to a conventional appeal for contributions, but when they are told that we will earmark their money for this specific purpose, they will regard the request with much more sympathy. And when they receive letters at the season's end from the young people who benefited by their generosity, you can count on a favorable reaction concerning renewal of their bloc for the next season, so that other worthy students might be given the same opportunity.

One medium-size symphony orchestra has developed a list of 100 sponsors, designated as "Angels," whose generosity enables a large number of musically talented young people recommended by their music teachers to attend a series of 12 concerts annually. Unless they demur, the Angels are listed in the printed program at all concerts. It is expected that this component will be regularly expanded.

It is quite common for those who run performing arts groups to receive telephone calls and letters from community centers, requesting donations of unsold tickets to our performances for use by their elderly clients (who are often living on tiny retirement incomes). There may be times when we haven't sold enough subscriptions or our attractions have failed to draw the single-ticket buyers, when we would welcome such "free" guests. However, is it not much better to have sponsorship for senior citizens to occupy those unused seats for the entire season or series? The community center would know in advance when buses would be needed, and the recipients of the gift subscriptions would be able to plan ahead of time. We would also have some income for those seats throughout the season. Similar arrangements can be made for the attendance of others in the community who are unable to afford tickets on their own, by working through community centers and social welfare agencies.

These types of sponsored bloc-sales components are in constantly wider use in our campaigns, and they provide a perfect constructive outlet for those of our workers who think more in terms of fund-raising than of subscription, as well as those inclined toward social service. For, this is a sort of hybrid component, containing elements of all three of these necessary activities. There is no one way in which this component must be carried out; it lends itself to many individual interpretations and styles. Some organizations have poached entirely in their own already large subscriber preserves, asking their series-ticket holders to contribute to a special fund for the purpose of buying subscriptions for those who cannot afford to attend on their own. Others have added this concept on to the options for subscription use suggested to corporations and companies which are being asked to buy blocs.

In one case that I most happily recall, a board member of a ballet company, when he heard me discussing the sponsored subscription component, volunteered to do a one-man campaign. A gifted salesman (his field was real estate), he took the trouble to find out details about some of the students and disadvantaged youngsters for whom he was setting out to obtain subscriptions. Let us say he was speaking about a college student who would be one of the recipients of the gift subscriptions he was soliciting. He was able to say that Elizabeth Smith was 18 years old, came from a farm family in modest circumstances, had a straight-A scholastic record all through high school, was seeking to be a home economics teacher, had never seen a professional ballet performance but had a desire to do so, and so on. By the time our salesman finished, he usually scored. He was not talking amorphously about "students," he was talking about specific personalities. The long and short of it is that he sold 500 subscriptions for our company, and he was shortly thereafter elected its board president.

Unquestionably, for professional performing arts organizations the area of bloc sales represents an ever-present opportunity for expansion of subscription audiences and for bringing in many new people who could not be won to us by brochure distributions or by newspaper advertising.

# 23

# Get By
## with a Little Help
## from Our Friends—
### Other Organizations Sell Our
### Subscriptions on Commission

It is commonplace in communities everywhere in America for all sorts of organizations to run benefits in order to raise funds for the implementation of their various programs. Very often, a given organization takes over an entire evening or a bloc of tickets for a performance of, say, a touring play which has come to the local booking house. Then, the organization's members all buy tickets and get their friends to buy tickets, for which a surcharge is added— that is, the donation portion which is the organization's profit for having undertaken the benefit. While the benefit has been a major prop of the commercial legitimate stage in New York City and elsewhere, it is also in use in connection with other kinds of professional performances. I am unenthusiastic about this kind of ticket selling for subscription-oriented theatres, for the main reason that the conventional benefit is connected with single tickets. I would much rather have my seats filled with subscribers who attend regularly than with benefit-ticket buyers whose primary loyalty is to *their* organization, who may well be indifferent audience members, and who most likely will not return to our theatre unless that organization sponsors another benefit. Also, when we sell that benefit to one of our plays on, say, the third Thursday night of the run, that kills for subscription the third Thursdays of all the other plays of the season, and tickets must be sold singly to the general public (which might not cooperate) or to other benefits (which might not materialize).

I much prefer to retain the basic concept of the benefit—*but apply it to subscription*. That is, the sponsoring organization instead of selling tickets to an individual attraction, sells *subscriptions* to our season, and we pay a commission on the gross receipts brought in by the sponsoring organization. Once out selling, it is not that much harder to sell the subscription than it is the individual ticket. Instead of having to pay a *higher* than box office price, as he does for the conventional benefit tickets, the purchaser usually pays *less* than the box office price for the tickets he buys in the subscription form. He may get one or two plays free, in relation to the ticket prices if he had purchased them individually. He may also get other bonuses and advantages which the subscription plan may offer, and he will have his own, regular seat. He will, just like the single-ticket, benefit buyer, still have the good feeling of having assisted a charity, except that he will have it not once, but at every performance he attends for the entire subscription season. And instead of the once-over-lightly theatregoer conditioning he would have gotten on one occasion, he will undergo in-depth exposure by attending all the plays of the series. And then, our own in-depth benefit begins to manifest itself, when the vaccination takes and he renews for the season that follows.

We should be diligent in our search for organizations to carry out this important task for their (and our) advantage. How many times do local philanthropic, civic, cultural, religious and fraternal organizations buy blocs of tickets for commercial bus-and-truck touring performances, with the promoter leaving town on Saturday night with the loot? How much better, more logical, that these same organizations ally themselves, for their fundraising projects, with a resident arts company right in their own community. Is it not likely that sitting on the boards and the women's guilds of our performing arts groups we have members who are also active in the kinds of organizations named earlier in this paragraph? How right to bring together two organizations they are enthusiastic about—their favorite charity or social organization and us. How fitting that those other nonprofit entities should raise funds by working with a sister nonprofit group in the community—our performing arts company.

What kind of commission can we afford to offer such organizations? Often, a lot more than we think we can. When we pay for printing, postage and addressing of large-scale brochure mailings, we may be paying considerably larger "commissions" than we realize. Sometimes, we can buy an ad in the paper and not get back more than half the cost of the ad. It happens all too often in the nonprofit performing arts field. Then, we have actually paid a 100% commission! Thus, I am never able to understand when board members go into a state of shock at the idea of paying 10%, 15%, or 20% commissions to an organization for sales which, in so many cases, fill previously *unsold* seats where we were *losing the entire 100%*. We should offer a commission sufficient to give the organization the incentive to do a great selling job. It may be advisable to create a sliding scale, giving larger commissions for larger sales. For example, a 10% commission for 500 pairs of subscriptions sold, 15% for 750 pairs, 20% for 1,000 pairs. Of course, the amount of money we will take in and the amount of money the selling organization will earn, also depends upon the price of our subscriptions. And the paying of commissions, just as the giving of discounts, must be decided upon in relation to the number of unsold seats and our ambitions or needs for increasing the number of performances presented.

Some years ago, the manager of a struggling new resident professional theatre company in Fredericton, New Brunswick, came to see me in Halifax, Nova Scotia. He related the following tale of woe:

Lord Beaverbrook, the great British press tycoon and a native of New Brunswick, had generously built a magnificent playhouse on the main street of Fredericton, splendidly located right across the street from the Lord Beaverbrook Hotel and less than half a block away from the Beaverbrook Art Museum. It then turned out that there was little use for this fine building. Fredericton was off the beaten path, so that few touring attractions came there and there were no local professional performing arts companies. So, it was decided to begin a theatre company. Actors were brought in from Toronto, scenery was built, costumes were made, 300 subscriptions were sold and a series of plays was presented. However, there were 1,000 seats in the theatre, and single-ticket buyers, not surprisingly, were few and far between. Thus, the new company was able to play each production for only one performance, with the 300 subscribers plus the handful of single-ticket patrons rattling around in the capacious auditorium. I still recall being touched when the manager said, as if he were speaking of some unattainable dream, "Ah, Mr. Newman, if only we could play a second night," and then he said that going on to another season appeared impossible. Of course the project was an economic monstrosity, with so few performances over which to amortize the costs of producing. And undoubtedly, the people who attended, even if the shows were reasonably good, were discouraged by the huge number of empty seats they saw, which would undoubtedly affect the rate of their renewal.

Here was a project in need of immediate promotional input if there ever was one. I suggested that there might be an established organization in the community, with a large membership, which might well be grateful for Lord Beaverbrook's generous act. Perhaps such an organization might need money to carry out its own program of activities and, for a commission of 10%, 15%, or 20%, it might undertake a major effort to convince its own members and their friends to become subscribers to the next season. Suddenly, there was a gleam in the manager's eye, followed by his exclamation in a sort of Eureka-I-found-it manner, "I–O–D–E!" Now, I did not know what he meant, and I was not to find out for several months, since at that very moment another visitor (the theatre manager from Charlottetown, Prince Edward Island) knocked at my door. As I was greeting him and ushering him into the hotel suite where this meeting was taking place, the Fredericton man simply bolted, disappearing while my back was turned, without explanation. I realized that he must have looked at his watch and found that he had overstayed and was in danger of missing the last plane home. Some months later I learned that the acronym IODE stood for the Independent Order, Daughters of the Empire; those wonderful ladies had by then sold 1,500 subscriptions for the theatre, receiving a 10% commission for their own organization. This instant audience boom not only made an important contribution to the theatre's survival and immediately realized the manager's dream of a second night for each play, but it created the atmosphere and the basis upon which a fine and successful company, now subsidized by the government, could be built in a very few seasons.

In a city of only 27,000 people, the company now gives a *week* of performances for each of the plays produced and then tours all of them to nine other cities in the area, where nine other subscription audiences await it.

Today, when officials of the Canada Council speak with justifiable pride in their country's excellent, various professional theatres, Fredericton's Theatre New Brunswick is most honorably mentioned, and so should be the simple idea of inviting outside organizations to sell performing arts subscriptions on commission. Although I cannot recall exactly how much the subscription-ticket price of that theatre was at the time, let us arbitrarily say that each subscription cost $20. That means the manager gave the good ladies their organization's 10% commission, or $3,000 out of the $30,000, which would have resulted from the 1,500 sales. But, it is really only an illusion that he gave them anything at all. What he gave them was *$3,000 of their own money,* right off the $30,000 "roll" that they had just given him for what would otherwise have been empty seats. *That* is promotion! Yet it is beneficial for both sides—the performing arts group and the organization which goes out to sell the tickets for us and for its own income.

As I started to write this chapter, I received word from one of the theatre companies I advise, that the professional women's division of its local Junior League chapter has already sold approximately 500 subscriptions in a campaign not yet finished. I would hope that such an arrangement could become an annual one, with continuing benefits to both the theatre and the organization which is out selling the season tickets.

For an explanation of this method as it was carried out by a symphony orchestra in its subscription campaign, I will quote from a letter which was sent out by the Indianapolis Symphony Orchestra Society to a large number of nonprofit organizations to take part in the symphony's season-ticket campaign:

"The groups that participated were paid a 15% commission on each new subscription sold through their efforts. The clubs made money and the ISO is playing to record-breaking subscription audiences. The procedure was very simple. Clubs were provided with copies of a sales brochure that could be enclosed with a covering letter in a mailing to their membership. Orders were returned to a representative of the club, who recorded them before forwarding them to a representative of the ISO's club benefit committee, who also made a record of them before turning them over to the symphony box office for processing. Commission checks were issued from these duplicate records at the close of the subscription campaign in October. This fund-raising opportunity will be repeated in the ISO's upcoming campaign for the next season. We encourage you to discuss this project with your members at your next meeting, and if they are interested in participating, please complete and return the enclosed reply card so that a representative of your group can be provided with full details as soon as we are able to announce next season's series attractions. Thank you."

I do not want readers to get the impression that sending out letters is the only way or the best way to successfully implement this approach to obtaining subscription sales. Often the letters, as in bloc sales to companies, are only an opening approach, which must be followed up by telephone calls and by personal visits. Having somebody you know on the board or an active member of the target group is also an invaluable leg up in getting results.

I want to emphasize that there is a wide range of possibilities for us in this kind of promotional effort, and that we should look for this kind of sales assistance in many directions—from sororities to ski clubs. I believe that there is a great, largely untapped potential of subscription sales which we can develop via imaginative arrangements of this kind between cooperating nonprofit organizations, and the conduits for such contacts are primarily ourselves, our staff people, members of our boards and auxiliaries.

# 24

## Sales by
## "Ma Bell":
## Telephone Solicitation

The use of the telephone to sell subscriptions for the performing arts is widespread. In some organizations, a very large number of sales is transacted through this means—not only for renewal but for new subscriptions, too. And occasionally the customers call *us*. For, in some places, it is almost the norm for a person who has been convinced to order a subscription by the brochure he has received, to pick up the phone and call in his order, asking to be billed, rather than filling out the form and sending it in by mail. It is, however, development of new sales by telephone promotion on our part that I wish to discuss now.

Whom do we ask to do this job for us, volunteers or paid professionals? The answer would have to be both, depending upon the individual organization and a number of different circumstances. We have had a number of successful volunteer telephone efforts for the procurement of new subscribers. In one recent case, an opera company which produces mainly avant-garde works had previously performed to painfully small audiences. When it entered into its first serious subscription drive, the telephone, used by volunteers under the hard-driving direction of a dedicated chairman, turned out to be the star vehicle, bringing in more sales than any other ingredient in the campaign. Suddenly there were packed houses for all of the performances.

It has proved to be a good idea, when utilizing the services of volunteers, to arrange for them to work, under supervision, in a telephone center set up for the purpose, rather than from their own homes. Without the central telephoning office we have no way of knowing the number of calls really made. Furthermore, people are usually spurred on by elements of camaraderie and competition. However, there are certain cases where solitary telephoners, working from their homes, have functioned successfully.

Many of the volunteer complements of performing arts organizations which have provided willing and successful telephoners for annual renewal efforts have been reluctant when asked to take on the harder job of selling new subscriptions by phone. Obviously, many of them find it a difficult, even ignoble, task, often unbearably discouraging at first in the face of negative responses.

For these reasons, in many of the cases where telephoning is an important factor in our campaigns, paid (on commission) personnel are used. One of the currently most successful theatres in the U.S., in its first big push for subscription, organized a group of paid telephoners under the direction of a professional sales manager and sold more subscriptions through that one component of its campaign than it had sold in any of its 15 previous seasons.

Undoubtedly, there are certain individuals who are especially gifted in their ability to win the confidence of a person they are talking to for the first time (not face-to-face, but by telephone) and to sell them something—in our case, a subscription to both a series of performances and to a certain kind of institution. This "instinct for the jugular" can manifest itself in volunteers, as well as professionals, especially when the volunteer is a business person with a background of sales experience.

One of the finest practitioners I have seen and heard in action is just such a man. Now retired and in his 70's, he has had astonishing telephone selling success on behalf of a midwestern opera company for which he volunteers his services. I confess that he could sell me anything! On the other hand, in a southwestern American city, a young administrative staff member whose background is surprisingly that of a schoolteacher, single-handedly sold 2,000 new subscriptions by phone for a recent opera season there!

It is not entirely a coincidence that the year the American Place Theatre, located in New York City, carried out a direct telephone selling effort, with the assistance of a sales instructor and sales instructional materials (both provided by the telephone company under its "phone power" program), the organization went over the 10,000-subscriber mark for the first time in its history. I suggest that other performing arts groups contemplating telephone campaigns check with their phone companies about obtaining similar, specialized professional aid.

At summer's end, shortly before its season began, the Cleveland Orchestra recently decided to enter into areas and scales of promotional activities which it had never before espoused. It enjoyed immediate success in obtaining a significant increase in subscribership over the previous season—a gain of

20% accomplished in what was really only a brief, pilot effort. One of the experiments it made was assigning a man to full-time telephoning for the one-month period left before the season began. They supplied him with the names and telephone numbers of dropout subscribers of past seasons, single-ticket buyers of record, nonsubscriber members of the orchestra's support auxiliaries, and business firms which had not replied to mailed solicitations for small bloc-subscription purchases. He proceeded, within the limited time span, to single-handedly produce $19,047 worth of new series-ticket sales. Undoubtedly, this component will figure importantly in that orchestra's future promotional plans (probably with more telephone personnel assigned), as will other components which proved themselves beautifully in that mini-campaign.

A widely respected dance company with which I have been working for some years has fought its way up from a few hundred subscribers to almost 10,000, has raised its box office income more than 850% and has increased its annual hometown seasons all the way from 8 to 40 performances, by its aggressive leadership's willingness to undertake the implementation of a wide range of subscription campaign components. One of these methods, consistently, conscientiously and competently carried to success each year has been the telephone method, with the pattern showing that each successive year of such efforts brought better overall subscription sales. Last season, 1,717 new season tickets were sold via the telephone.

The company's report showed that it achieved the best results by bringing in a professional manager for telephone sales and giving him an attractive percentage, out of which he paid all expenses directly concerned with the execution of the effort. The largest item of expense, of course, was the commission paid to telephoners. The cost for securing each new subscription sold was 33¢ of each dollar earned. Since their renewal costs proved to be only 3¢ per dollar taken in, one can see how favorably the economics work. Even on the level of the new sale, there was a "profit" of 67%, and after each new subscriber is aged in the brine of regular attendance for one season, his renewal will bring 97% of the price he pays.

A careful search for the sales manager must be made. He or she might be found through a local newspaper or any other stable, local enterprise which normally carries on sales work by telephone. Their people are likely to be honest and dependable, because they work for companies which must retain the goodwill of their home community. Needless to emphasize, even then, the sales manager and his telephoners must be indoctrinated concerning the speciality of our product, the details of our offer and the characteristics and background of our kind of organization. Most of the telephoners can be found through standard advertisements in newspaper classified sections, followed by interviews to determine whether they have an effective telephone personality. Naturally, past experience is in their favor, although it should not necessarily be the sole determinant of their employment. There is turnover, according to the results achieved by the individual telephoner. Sometimes, the best of the telephoners have graduated to the manager or supervisor job. New telephoners who have previously worked for commercial products have tended to like their new assignment better, soon discovering that, because of our organization's prestige in the community, the people they call are friendlier and more respectful than those they had been used to. They soon have reason to believe what we told them: that they are engaged in an honorable public service. A minimum wage, or a bit more than that should be paid to new telephoners, but as soon as they show a capacity to make sales, that wage should be raised immediately; this raise plus the commission incentive should work well for both the employee and the organization. It must be pointed out that we can hardly expect to operate this kind of sales component with maximum efficiency and results without a certain amount of trial and error. Even the companies with the most success in this area are still perfecting their approaches and techniques.

For obvious reasons, it is necessary to provide new telephoners with a sales talk, but eventually, results will be improved by their beginning to improvise from the supplied standard version. This more natural approach will engender a greater conviction on the part of the caller, and even if the improvisation strays somewhat from the self-image of the organization, it may result in more sales—which, after all, meets our primary need. In the last and best analysis, our arts company's perfect image will be seen by the new subscribers when they attend the performances, which they would not have done had our telephone representative failed to convince them. Still, telephoners must be supervised and monitored to a reasonable degree, and they must be urged to make the maximum number of calls during the hours they are working. For, given that they are able and skilled, they can make more sales only if they make more calls.

Two shifts are required, one for the late morning and afternoon calls to reach people at home (doctors and businessmen at their offices), and another for the evenings, in order to reach all those people who are not reachable by day. Each shift must double back on those people who were called but who could not be reached during either the daytime or evening periods.

There may be those dreary days or evenings when sales seem to be bogging down, and incentives may be helpful in maintaining morale and regaining momentum: "First one to get an order in the next half-hour wins a free lunch on me!" Or, "Telephoner with the highest sales record today gets a new fountain pen!" Prizes can work as incentives and should be presented as an honor and with affection for that wonderful person who has, by making an effort above and beyond the usual, not only earned extra commissions and the premium, but has helped make our forthcoming season a greater success! The sales force will know if we really feel that way, and we must communicate to them that their work is terribly important to us and is appreciated. There is nothing that can help telephone sales for our kind of project more than the sound of genuine pride in the seller's voice. We should inculcate this feeling of pride in different ways. For instance, the artistic director and leading artists of the company might be introduced to the telephoners and tell them what it means to play to full houses for more performances than would be possible without this great advance subscription promotion. Now, when the telephoners talk about the artists to potential subscribers, their enthusiasm will be all the greater. These points would also apply in those cases where volunteers are involved.

Almost a quarter of the telephone sales can evaporate when payment for the subscription is due; thus, the goal for this component should be about 125% of what you put down on your quota sheet. Commissions to telephoners should also be based on cash receipts rather than credit orders. While most telephone orders during the main part of the drive are followed up by a bill mailed to the customer, we might, in the closing days of the campaign, send over a messenger to pick up the check. It has been found that even when verbal telephone orders are not fulfilled, they are still retrievable in some cases, if they are followed up by phone or in person before the season's beginning. In fact, approximately 10% of such cases have finally subscribed.

What lists to use? Exactly the same kinds of lists mentioned in the chapter on mailing lists, ranging from the highest selection down through the lowest, depending upon how much more effort we need to achieve our goal. "Eager beaver" telephoners have even used the city telephone book with surprisingly good results, aiming at telephone exchanges which indicate certain high-response neighborhoods or areas. By the way, it has been found that it is extremely helpful to the telephoner's chances for making the sale, to start the conversation with the name of the prospect and his or her own name. Like this: "Good afternoon, Mrs. Wilkins. This is Mrs. Ellwood of the Pirouette Ballet Company." In that way, even an unknown telephoner seems to be able to change an uninvited solicitation into a more personal invitation.

The modus operandi I have described here is not the only way in which telephone selling for the performing arts can be approached. It is entirely possible to work out, according to individual promotional styles and taking into account various strengths and weaknesses, variations in the methodology. If your telephone selling works for you, then that is what is important.

# 25

# The Public Service Offer:

### Subscriptions for Students, Senior Citizens, et al.

Obviously, there is a sizable potential for specially discounted performing arts subscription sale to students in all communities, particularly at the university level. In fact, much of this potential has been realized according to the intensity of promotional efforts directed at those sources, in many places. Yet it is not unusual to find a resident theatre in one city with a very large student subscribership and, in a neighboring city, a similar theatre company with hardly any students holding season tickets. And the same applies to the other arts companies, too. One symphony orchestra with which I work has several thousand such subscribers, who at one time comprised almost half its total audience. When a major subscription drive was, at long last, initiated and successfully carried through, so many thousands of new regular buyers were found at the full subscription price that there developed the temporary embarrassment of not having any room for the students, who had been given a 50% discount, and without whom there would have been virtually no symphony audience for many past years in that city. This predicament precipitated the move to create an additional series of performances and, not only were the students accommodated, but many more regular subscribers were found, setting off an entire chain of expansions, from 5,000 to 20,000 subscribers in all series within several seasons.

In another case, that of a theatre company, a different situation prevailed. Very few students were on the subscriber rolls. A spectacularly successful promotional effort, in which extraordinary cooperation of university officials was achieved, brought a huge infusion of student subscribers. The financially troubled company was able to much more than pay for the difference between its special discount price and what the general public paid for season tickets, via various grants and subsidies based on this special service to youth. In effect, for many of our arts companies, the idea that they are doing something especially altruistic in providing 50% subscription discounts for students is a self-serving illusion. In so many cases, the seats thus filled would be empty otherwise, a grievous loss considering our reason for existence (and the 100% loss in money). It has often been maddening for me to hear from an orchestra manager, season after season, that he is *limiting* the number of student subscriptions to, say, 300 tickets, when for five years in a row, he has had at least 900 seats unsold at the average concert! Some managers, artistic directors and board leaders refuse to face the reality of their ticket sales situations. They offer all sorts of wishful interpretations of their box office reports.

In one instance, I took all the box office reports of the season and simply added up their bottom line figures to find that 52% of the seats had gone unsold for the very limited number of performances that made up the season. I was told by a top official of this organization that it couldn't be so because he was there personally at every performance, and he saw that the house was at least three-quarters full. Upon careful inquiry, it turned out that he was right, if you consider the main floor level to be the sole component of the "house." He had never once gone into the mezzanine, the balcony or the gallery (in all of which you could have shot deer), which represented about 70% of that auditorium's capacity. Perhaps he was subconsciously avoiding ever going upstairs?

Student subscription sales are sometimes de-emphasized by performing arts groups where the "student rush" ticket plan may already be in operation. Under this arrangement, as each event of the season takes place, students line up at the box office at performance time to buy any unsold tickets for discounts often as great as, or greater than, those offered for student series or season subscription. Unquestionably, if one must choose between the rush system and the subscription system, the weight of all logic lies with the subscription system for the same reasons that apply to a choice between dependence upon regular single-ticket sales and subscription. Under the rush system, students tend to ignore all the events except those which have sufficient basic box office drawing power and, thus, are of little help to us for the season's long haul. Under the subscription system, they are in attendance throughout, and the aggregate amount of money derived from ticket sales is also much greater. The effect on the students of the exposure to a much wider repertoire is an important, if not always a tangible and immediate, benefit to them and to us. However, choosing subscription over rush as the main vehicle for audience development in the student area presumes that there will be a truly major promotional effort to sell so many season or series tickets that there will be little or no need for rush sales. Rush selling of tickets to individual performances does have appeal for many performing arts managements, because it fits their line-of-least-resistance habits. It is easy to do. It also doesn't do very much for our greatest needs. Subscription selling is hard to do. But, if accomplished on a scale sufficiently meaningful within our number-of-seats-to-be-filled economy, it does a great deal for us.

Student subscriptions are sold in a number of different ways. A starting point is to create and pinpoint the distribution of a special brochure, or to adapt our regular brochure for the purpose. The 50% student discount (which is often 50% off the already discounted regular subscription price), must be strongly featured throughout the piece. Thus, the incentive to subscribe is terrific.

The incentive to subscribe can be made even greater by something that is not often articulated; that is, by pointing out that this phenomenal bargain is made possible by generous gifts from whatever our sources of subsidy happen to be, whether they are from board members, other individual donors, corporate contributors, foundations, arts councils, the National Endowment for the Arts—or any combination of such donors. The idea that *somebody else* is paying a large part of the cost of one's subscription is something that will appeal to students and, for that matter, to almost anybody.

It is not always easy or even possible to obtain the home addresses of students, but they should be gone after with much perseverance. In the case of one theatre which managed to obtain this information from universities in its area, a major breakthrough was accomplished, virtually entirely by mail. Selling subscriptions to students has a built-in complication, because the school year often begins just a short time before our fall seasons start. We must work in advance, in the spring, and then again in the fall with great speed. Home addresses, therefore, enable us to reach them earlier in the fall than we might otherwise. In some cases, we are able to have brochures distributed through the college registrars, so that our offer gets to the students along with vital information concerning educational activities. Brochures should be distributed to activities offices, dormitories, student unions, coffee houses, and student ticket centers. Sometimes, faculty members in the humanities and arts fields can be helpful. It is not unusual to have the head of a drama or music department contact the professional performing arts company directly, with a multiple order (a bloc sale) of a number of subscriptions for which he has already collected the money. In the case of Lyric Opera of Chicago, there are a number of such annually renewed orders, and in this case there are no discounts offered, either to regular or student subscribers.

It behooves us, as the ones who require tapping the special audience which their student bodies represent, to make special efforts to develop and maintain good relationships with the professors at local academic institutions. With this in mind, I wish to suggest that there are often many university-sponsored performances taking place in campus auditoriums, and permission to insert brochures in the programs they distribute could be a valuable privilege. We might reciprocate by inserting information in our own programs about university events of particular interest to our audiences.

I also wish to suggest that the regular brochure, which may receive enormous circulation in the overall community, should contain the student subscription offer, although subordinate to the one being made for the general public. Many sales are made in this way. Parents receive the brochure, become aware of the special student offer and point it out to the younger members of their families.

Should a college offer courses in arts administration, the professor in charge might make the promotion of our subscription a class project. As this is written, that concept is in the experimental stage on behalf of the Pennsylvania Ballet, with graduate students of the Wharton School of Finance and Commerce involved. Thirteen hundred subscriptions were sold in the initial effort, and the sales manager believes that this number will be doubled the next time around.

We have often achieved excellent returns in student sales through ads placed in university newspapers—much better results than we sometimes obtain for our regular offerings through ads in the metropolitan press. Student subscriptions can be sold either by volunteer or commissioned student sales forces on the campuses. Commissions can begin with payment in free subscriptions for so many sales and then be continued in cash for additional sales. One symphony orchestra I assist has an excellent group of sales volunteers, who appear at on-campus locations on dates publicized in advance, and students in considerable numbers come forward to place subscription orders.

Some years ago, I found an excellent student sales-force, organized as a sort of club, working at all the campuses of the area on behalf of a theatre company, selling on an individual or single-ticket basis. Because this theatre was launching a subscription drive, the "college reps" (representatives), as they were called, decided to switch over entirely to promoting subscriptions. They helped enormously by selling 1,800 season tickets and I was happy to accept the honorary presidency of their organization.

The Indianapolis Symphony Orchestra, in special on-campus offers which resulted in 2,000 subscription sales, utilized some 2,500 frisbees marked, "Go Symphony!" as a showmanshiplike promotional aid to create a warmer selling context. However, make no mistake, the mere distribution of the frisbees and the use of the slogan were not the determining facts in the sales made. They were peripheral elements in a fully organized, efficiently functioning selling process.

Sometimes educators are offered the same discounted rates as their students. If this offer is made, it should be promoted with great vigor, as there may already be a number of teachers who are subscribers and they would then have a right to apply for the educators' discount. Thus, we would have to sell enough additional subscriptions through this special offer to more than compensate for that problem. Mailings to all educators of the area making them aware of the offer usually bring good results, as does advertising in professional publications received by teachers.

There is always much talk in the arts world about the need to bring younger elements into the audiences. An artistic director friend of mine, whose theatre company has enjoyed a spectacular subscription audience-building success, believes that playgoers over the age of 30 are no longer capable of the proper response. ("Are they likely to leave the theater," he asked, "and rush to the barricades as a result of having just experienced a play urging social action?") He was genuinely troubled about this problem, even feeling that audience members in their middle or late twenties (many of whom were among his subscribers) were "over the hill" for his purposes. He really wanted more in the 18- to 22-year-old range. I suggested that if the board of directors agreed, more of the seating capacity for the next season could be reserved for students. Since the theatre was selling out all performances of its seasons, the larger student discounts would mean loss of income. However, the altruistic board president gave the go-ahead, and the youth quotient in the audience became much greater. Now there will be room for many more young people and even for some beyond-the-pale oldsters like myself, for this theatre has just moved into a new, much larger building. Most performing arts companies are not usually sold-out, like the theatre group mentioned above, so they do not have to sacrifice any immediate income in order to sell more student subscriptions. On the contrary, it is to their financial, as well as ideological, advantage to sell as many student subscriptions as they can. And I think it is entirely safe to say that there is still room for considerable growth of sales in this component for a large number of companies.

Although I have dwelt upon the university level of student sales, many of the same approaches are successfully applied to selling subscriptions in the high schools. Discounts larger than those given to the general public are sometimes offered to teachers; the clergy; military personnel; nurses; senior citizens; city, county, state and federal employees. These offers are all similar to those made to students, although not always at such a high percentage off the regular subscription prices. We call these "public service offers."

The immediate objection which comes to mind is that a large number of these people would have bought the subscription at the regular amount, so that sales made via this method are illusory. However, in one of the most successful of such experiments—in Los Angeles—the facts proved otherwise. The offer was not made until the main campaign was virtually at an end, and 2,000 additional subscriptions suddenly materialized, coming in on the special order forms taken out of the 120,000 brochures which had been distributed, not by mail, but in bulk packages to the officials of agencies that had agreed to make the offer known to their people. Although the regular subscriptions already sold were in the many, many thousands in that campaign, only a dozen letters were received from buyers, stating that they had already purchased subscriptions at the higher general public price and requesting refunds, to which they felt entitled as members of groups to which this special offer had been made. In each of these cases, a refund was promptly sent, accompanied by a letter. Another factor which diminished static from subscribers was the fact that the public service offer was restricted to matinees and specific nights of the week, with Saturday nights, needless to say, not offered at all. All the special order forms requested the buyer to state his occupation, thus "officializing" the extra discount privilege.

The promotional cost was minimal, because of the way in which the brochures were distributed. One organization took 13,000 brochures. A teachers' association sent 30,000 brochures out enclosed in the mailing of its monthly periodical. Whether these brochures were effective can be judged by the excellent sales figures quoted in the preceding paragraph. What the performing arts project "gave away" in larger discounts was more than compensated for in dollars and cents by the savings in mailing costs. In some cases, there were no mailing lists available for people eligible under the public service offer, and they might not have been reached otherwise. Because of mailing cost savings, the public service offer produced a net return in dollars equal to the regular price subscription, and thousands of seats were filled, mostly by people who would not otherwise have attended. Considering the limited size of our "natural" audience, this audience gain is not a small consideration.

In Washington, D.C., taking advantage of the enormous concentration of federal government employees there, a performing group offered them a small additional discount and, through a special arrangement, got the brochures delivered directly to the desks of the target personnel. Results were excellent, and the effort was not only immediately profitable, but we were able to renew a considerable number of those new subscribers for the seasons that followed.

Senior citizens are ideal participants when this offer is extended to them, either singly or in groups. Matinees are particularly desirable for them, and since it is so often our afternoon performances which need special help, we have here the basis for a natural partnership between the "golden agers" and the performing arts. For all the economic reasons we know so well, necessarily budget-minded older people having the time and inclination to attend our performances can better be brought to subscription involvement by an extra discount. Brochures can be distributed through community and recreation centers with programs for senior citizens. These brochures should contain information about bus schedules and restaurants nearby which might welcome luncheon groups by offering special price inducements.

A highly successful theatre, now in a period of considerable expansion, has made a special effort, including a newspaper, radio and TV publicity campaign, to develop direct sales for its matinee performances by arranging a large number of speaking engagements for members of its staff at meetings of senior citizen groups. In addition to speakers, slides are shown and actors present readings. As a result, many subscriptions have been sold to older persons of long-established playgoing predilections and to those who have never before attended "live" theatre.

# 26

## *Knock, Knock;*
## *Who's There?*
## *Door-to-Door Selling*
## *of Subscriptions*

Forty-two years ago, I had my first exposure to selling subscriptions door-to-door for a performing arts project. Perhaps it was because the people I called on were unusually kind, or maybe it was because I was offering a very good bargain in those economically depressed times, but I did sell quite a number of those season tickets despite my inexperience. Then again, perhaps it was because of that very inexperience and even naiveté. I really thought the people whose doorbells I rang would be receptive to the idea of coming regularly to the wonderful shows for which I was the press agent. At any rate, up through the mid-1930's a great deal of door-to-door solicitation occurred for a wide range of products, and it was an almost daily event for an eager young man to come to one's door with any of a number of weekly or monthly magazines and a sheaf of order forms in hand. He would begin his pitch, saying, "You see, I'm working my way through college...." I, myself, have always been receptive to the direct approach and recall buying a very expensive set of books I really had no interest in, because I felt the salesman who had hesitatingly knocked at my door was so hapless that, unless I bought, nobody else would. In retrospect, I suspect that seeming ineffectuality was his highly personal and (I can testify) very successful sales technique.

Some years ago, while attending some high-minded cultural seminar, I found myself seated next to a charming gentleman who, it turned out, was the founder-director of a little theatre group in a medium-size city. I was astounded to learn from him that his group had 10,000 season subscribers. Even granting that there was an attractive discount offered for taking the entire season of so many plays, it was the largest committed little theatre audience I had ever heard of. When I asked him the secret of his selling success, he said that he had long developed a system of canvassers, who went door-to-door covering every household, office, factory and shop in the town, and who were mainly responsible for the impressive size of the loyal subscribership.

On another occasion, when meeting with the board of directors of a symphony orchestra, I learned that a locally sponsored musical recital series, which had once flourished but had since lapsed entirely, had been revived that very season with an entire subscription sellout of their 2,700-seat auditorium via a door-to-door selling effort carried out by a large volunteer women's committee. On still another occasion, I met a man who was planning to open a new arts company and had arranged with the local chapter of a national philanthropic organization to have its large membership canvass the entire community for season tickets, on a door-to-door basis, one Sunday that was to be selected far in advance. Much fanfare was planned so that the citizenry would be expectantly waiting for their doorbells to ring. Unfortunately the opening of the project had to be postponed a year, and the philanthropic organization, which was to get a commission on the sales, found a conventional benefit project instead. However, the concept is basically a good one, and I mention it in the event that a performing arts promotional person, reading this handbook, might take it from there.

In the main, it has proved most difficult to develop enthusiasm for door-to-door selling for nonprofit projects on a volunteer level. Many volunteers, as in telephone subscription solicitation, dread the possibility of being turned down. The worst possibility of being turned down *rudely* is simply not acceptable to them. Thus, in most cases where this component is employed, the sales force works on a commission basis. As a matter of fact, the experience of the university students who have been employed during their summer vacations for this purpose has often been far from unpleasant. The promotional director of the Royal Winnipeg Ballet, in speaking of his organization's experience in carrying out this recommended component, says, "It has not been found more undignified or unpleasant than any other way of selling theatre and concert subscriptions." And he adds, "The customer is usually happy because the service has been fast, efficient and personal." This company engaged the services of a person who had a background of commercial direct selling to indoctrinate and supervise the work of university students during their summer vacation. They sold approximately 800 new subscriptions in that initial door-to-door component. When I pointed this out to the promotion man of Toronto Arts Productions, a theatre company performing in that much larger city, he immediately put this component into the works, and although his campaign was only two weeks from ending he managed to come up with 500 sales. I felt that this was one of those cases where "there's gold in them thar hills" and urged that the next time around a much bigger effort be made over a longer time period, which was done the entire following summer with a stunning result of over 6,000 new subscriptions sold. Since that company had exactly 6,000 subscriptions the previous season from all of its other promotional efforts (and managed to replace its attrition mainly by its brochure distributions), it was able to go into the new season with 12,000 subscriptions (a 100% gain in its subscribership), the best position it had ever enjoyed. The success of this component was made possible because the theatre's promotion director had the good sense to follow the successful pattern already established in Winnipeg of bringing in an expert, a person experienced in door-to-door selling. In this case, it was a man who had run such campaigns for newspaper subscription. This very capable professional interviewed the university students, instructed them, replaced them when they either fell out or proved ineffective, kept the records and paid them their 20% commissions.

When working in the area during that season, I happened to chat with a couple who were dining at a table adjoining mine in a local restaurant. They mentioned that they had just moved to the city that year and had been sold subscriptions by a university student who rang their bell. They said that they undoubtedly would never have thought of attending that theatre had the solicitation not taken place the way it did. In that particular campaign, it was reported by the student salesmen that they were received with friendliness and courtesy, and I believe this reception was the result of special advance publicity and advertising which preceded their knocking on doors. In effect, they were expected.

How was the sales force recruited? Classified ads were placed in metropolitan newspapers. Interested students filled out standard employment applications at the time of their interviews. Those selected were given training sessions by the professional in charge, which included orientation on the background of the project, its repertoire and the artists involved in the season for which subscriptions were being sold. Materials provided to the sales force included brochures, separate order forms, blank checks, receipt books, a letter from the project's general manager attesting to their authorization as sales representatives, forms for daily and weekly reports, and a fine selection of photographs of outstanding productions from the previous season, organized in a binder. The students signed on for a summer assignment of eight hours a day, five days a week. Each order form contained the code number of the sales person. At least once a week, orders were turned in to the supervisor (who received a 10% commission on all sales, in addition to the 20% which the students received). After checking them for errors, he sent them to the accounting and box office departments for processing. There was considerable turnover as the less able dropped out or were weeded out, so that recruitment for replacements had to continue throughout the summer.

Best results were realized in middle-income residential areas and from businesses of all kinds. Besides achieving the record-breaking increase in subscribership, the company also realized more single-ticket sales than ever before, because of the publicity involved in the entire direct-sales effort. The thousands of calls made upon people who *didn't* buy a subscription made them aware that plays were being produced at that location. After all, the artistic direction was the same as it had been the year before, the repertoire represented the same taste, the artists were, more or less, of the same calibre. Obviously, what accounted for the enormous rise in attendance for that season was the enlarged promotion, particularly the addition of the door-to-door component.

Lest anybody think that this exercise was a flash in the pan, after several seasons' lapse in this particular kind of effort, the very same organization tried this component again. This time, the door-to-door sales began in the late spring, continued through the entire summer and into the early fall. And this time, 7,000 new subscriptions were sold (bringing in approximately $200,000), 1,000 more than the previous result over which we had so exulted. I might mention that, by this point, the costs to the management had become 40% of the gross sales, which was admittedly larger than the previous 30%, but still no greater than what many mail campaigns cost us—*and 60% cheaper than leaving the seats unsold.*

To date, most of the performing arts organizations which have utilized this component have been Canadian ones. However, a U.S. theatre company has only recently made a short-term experiment along these lines, which produced 1,200 new subscriptions, at an average of $25 apiece, racking up $30,000. This success should encourage many other groups in the U.S.; in fact, as a direct result of that brief campaign, another one of the country's oldest theatre companies has put such a component on the promotional agenda for its next subscription drive.

In the past when we have used the door-to-door method of selling subscriptions, it has been because we feared that we were going to be stuck with large numbers of seats otherwise. What I mean is that this component, unfortunately, and really unjustifiably, has a sort of "last resort" aura about it, an attitude with which I do not agree. Management and board people, incorrectly assaying the true costs of our other commercial promotional components, such as printing, distribution of brochures and newspaper advertising, are unduly concerned with the costs of the commissions for door-to-door work. With the alternative being 100% loss on any unsold seats, they would do well to opt for getting as much cash and audience as they can for the season at hand—and for the built-in renewal potential on each subscription.

An arts manager, whose company has done well selling door-to-door, tells me he is particularly pleased with the new audience element that has emerged through this special effort—those people who had been impervious to all other methods of promotion. He feels that, among them, were many who really were interested in attending the art but who simply didn't subscribe, or begin to go at all, until it was made so easy for them. They began to attend only when the application was brought directly to them by somebody who was willing to talk to them about it and convince them. He calls them the "inertia" people. At the same time, he speaks of another audience element which hadn't felt comfortable at all about the idea of attending the art—those with no previous exposure to the arts, who felt they might be "out of place" if they came. With such reservations, they had never responded to publicity, newspaper advertising or brochures. It took salesmanship on the confrontation level of the door-to-door approach to bring them into the fold. The same manager, in accounting for some excellent initial results of his new salesmen, reminded me of something that is certainly true—that they sometimes have an astonishing number of sympathetic relatives and friends who may be among the most likely people to attend the performances we offer, but who simply have not been doing so for all those reasons people just don't show up at our box office on their own steam. Now that an opportunity to oblige the son, niece, cousin, neighbor or friend is involved, the decision to subscribe is suddenly made. My informant also does not limit his sales force to students; he seeks practitioners who have previous direct-sales experience for commercial enterprises, though he takes great pains to indoctrinate them to his very different nonprofit professional arts product, instilling in them a special feeling of pride about it. He is willing to pay commissions up to *40%*, intelligently recognizing that if the seats go empty, as they may have in the previous season, he will lose the entire 100% of their value. He pays no commissions until all the money due on the order is paid by the purchaser. He publicizes the door-to-door selling plan strongly before his people move into the area and never begins until advance brochure distributions have taken place. Although his is a good-size city, he has found better average results when sending his sales personnel into suburban areas and smaller neighboring communities. He emphasizes my own leitmotif on all levels of subscription promotion: commissions paid for original sales are reasonable when viewed from the standpoint of future annual renewal income potential at minimal costs. He has relied heavily on outside professional expertise in setting up this component for his company.

   In the door-to-door campaign of a large musical organization, a photograph of its world-renowned maestro was given as a gift to each person visited. The professional expert who acts as consultant for this component in the drive is an official of a firm which has a record of consistent success in selling its products entirely by door-to-door solicitations. Because of the nonprofit status and the wide prestige of this symphony orchestra, special permission has been obtained for door-to-door selling in areas where there are specific ordinances banning it. Here one sees the special advantages which we do have because of our being what we are—and this goodwill should be utilized whenever possible.

   I have recently received in the mail a copy of a letter which the publicity director of one of my projects has just sent to a member of the door-to-door sales force. The letter says, "Dear Tom: Congratulations on the really impressive beginning of your door-to-door efforts in the Mount Lookout area. The 24 subscriptions you sold the first day and a half prove you're a top salesman right at the outset, and we now happily anticipate more and more sales in your territory. Keep up the good work, and we look forward to paying you more and more commissions." Obviously the writer of this letter well understands that recognition of work well done is important even to paid workers. Although the supervisor gives the salesman credit, along with commissions, for his good work, the arts project official should also be in immediate communication with him. This principle has been emphasized by our successful telephone campaigning organizations, where paid personnel have been utilized, too.

   I do not recommend any one specific sales talk, because I believe that our product is a very special one which has many individual nuances and possibilities, according to each situation, and thus requires careful consideration in every instance. Each approach should be tailor-made, with the aid of professional practitioners who will help our staff work out the proper adaptations of their past approaches to our needs. We must allow for periods of experimentation, too, to adjust and hone our techniques to fit the circumstances, in many ways related to the way we would develop our telephone selling components.

I recognize that many performing arts groups are especially loath to engage in door-to-door selling of subscriptions, because it is an obviously difficult component on many levels, requiring the kind of advance planning and complex arrangements which few nonprofit groups are capable of on their own. That is why I have stressed the necessity of bringing in specialized expertise. For the knowledgeable and confident professional, the problems involved are "all in a day's work." Unquestionably, there are subscription sales out there for us. In this case, the race is not to the swift but to the willing.

A significant reason for the willingness of Canadian performing arts groups to undertake such demanding components as door-to-door selling is undoubtedly the fact that, as I've mentioned, their postal system does not grant low-cost mailing rates to its nonprofit organizations. Thus, the much higher cost of large-scale mail distribution of brochures in that country has encouraged Canadian arts managements to diversify their subscription-selling methods. Conversely, many U.S. groups have tended to limit the range of their promotional repertoire, in the knowledge that they have a chance to go all the way with the heavily subsidized (by Uncle Sam) mailing instrument which is available to them. And, undoubtedly we have had many cases where the partnership of the effective brochure and the third class nonprofit mailing privilege has worked wonders for us. But there are also many other situations where this happy, comparatively easy, promotional panacea cannot accomplish the job, or at least, not all of the job. Then, we must look for more arrows in our campaign quiver. One of those which must be regarded seriously is the door-to-door component.

# 27

## Aces Wild, Anyone?
## Alternative Formats
## for Subscription

Subscription is any kind of multiple ticket sales to a series of presentations. There are several basic formats for subscription offers from which stem many variations, according to the special needs of various types of performing arts organizations. In one way or another, these several approaches can be adjusted to meet the needs of ballet companies and symphony orchestras, as well as resident theatres and opera companies.

In the most conventional subscription format—the one that seems to fit best and work best for a large number of theatre companies—all the scheduled performances of one play are presented before beginning on the next one. The subscriber attends each of the productions of the season on, say, the first Monday night of the run of each play. He has his own regular seats which are automatically renewable for the next season and, hopefully, for many seasons to follow. There are also situations, usually in small capacity theatres, where the subscribers attend on specified nights, but the seating is unreserved.

Some companies do not perform their repertoires in that consecutive sequence. These companies are the ones in the rolling-repertory category. By this term, I mean that the theatre plays *Hamlet* on Monday evening, *Uncle Vanya* on Tuesday evening, *The Birthday Party* at the Wednesday matinee, *A Delicate Balance* on Wednesday evening, and so on, throughout the season. (An opera company would perform *Aida* on Thursday evening, *Angel of Fire* on Friday evening, *Carmen* at the Saturday matinee, *Vanessa* on Saturday evening, and so on, through its season.) They will usually offer packagings by numbers, such as Series 1, 2, 3, 4, 5 and 6, or by letters, such as Series A, B, C, D and E. Each series will list the specific dates and attractions which the subscriber is contracting to attend. It is also possible, within this system, to assign regular seat locations. Either of the two basic approaches just described possesses the virtues of distributing our audiences evenly for each of the productions of our season, giving the weaker attractions the precious advantage of attendance parity with the stronger ones, and hastening the progress of the audience in developing an understanding and appreciation of the full repertoire which we offer.

However, the next type of subscription which I will describe does not realize these benefits. I am speaking of the coupon book, especially in what I have called its "aces-wild" variation. At one time it was widely utilized but has been, for some time now, on the decline. This coupon book permits the holder to apply one or more of his coupons to any performance of any production of the season. His coupons are exchanged at the box office or by mail for the reserved seats. This type of subscription has a short-range advantage in that it quickly answers a potential subscriber's fear of being "tied down" to a definite commitment to specific dates. It also has a basic and very destructive defect from the long-range standpoint in that it tends to defeat one of the most important advantages we get from having a subscription audience. And that is the defect of permitting the coupon book holder to wait through much of the season for a "convenient" time to go—and particularly for what might turn out to be the big hit of the season. Then, the coupon book holder uses all of his coupons for that one production, bringing his friends, relatives and business associates. Thus, he is permitted to lapse into the bad habits of a single-ticket buyer, with the result that some of our productions are badly attended, while one or two of the other plays cannot accommodate all who wish to attend. Some subscribers become unreasonably angry at us because they can't get in on those occasions. In some cases this problem has been mitigated by a telephone reservation arrangement. Another inherent problem in the coupon system lies in the subscribers figuring that they may as well use their coupons on Friday and Saturday nights, when they really could go on one of the weeknights and might have (had we been using a specific-night-of-the-week form of subscription) selected a Monday, Tuesday, Wednesday or Thursday evening as their regular time to attend.

I have had the experience many times of convincing performing arts organizations to entirely eliminate their aces-wild coupon books, successfully substituting an offer whereby the subscribers began to see all of the productions of the season or series on specific dates and nights of the week. The large-scale, successful promotion of the "new" offer was of the essence. For the coupon book promoters—when they saw the great increases in attendance with the new system—began to appreciate the advantage of assured seat locations and specific dates of attendance.

In other cases, we have at least achieved an important modification of the coupon book, in which each coupon is for a specific play, so that even though the subscriber still hasn't committed himself to a certain night of the week, he now attends every production. In some cases, we continued the coupon book offer for those who wanted it, while at the same time strongly promoting the new full commitment to subscription, with the result that, after a few seasons, the coupon book phased itself out and the former coupon book holders voluntarily joined in the new system in droves.

Another form of coupon book is the "student pass" or "senior citizen's pass," sold at larger discounts than the more conventional types of subscription being offered to the general public for the same season or series. These passes are often limited to use on weeknights or matinee performances. They, too, are subscription offerings. Then, we've seen a system whereby a theatre presenting, say, 10 plays per season, offers all 10, or just 5 of the plays on subscription, whichever package the purchaser chooses to take. However, the 5-play subscriber may pick which 5 he wishes to attend from among all 10. Advertised as "Pick Your Own Series," this plan is not only wrong just because it is like letting the lunatics run the asylum, but because you can be certain that the purchasers will pick the five most attractive repertoire items, leaving the plays of lesser appeal bereft of an audience. And, of course, this system encourages many of the buyers not to take all 10. This example is exactly the kind of lopsided distribution of theatregoers that subscription audience builders seek to avoid, and offering such a series sets a performing arts company back a considerable distance on the road toward the ultimate degradation of total dependence upon single-ticket buyers. On the other hand, there is nothing wrong with a theatre which produces a large number of plays each season, offering them in two distinct series—with the subscriber having the option to buy both series (at a greater discount) or either of the two series (at a lesser discount).Officials of large opera companies, in making up their often numerous short-series packagings, really sweat to balance them delicately so that their respective quotients of popular and less popular works are as equal as possible. Thus, both in renewal and new sales, certain series are not avoided like the plague and others vastly oversold.

Although I am unenthusiastic about the coupon book format for subscription in the majority of performing arts situations, there are certain, special circumstances under which I believe it to be useful and well worth promoting strongly. An example would be a summer music festival, which has not only a pavilion of large seating capacity, but huge, unreserved space on the immediately contiguous lawns and other outdoor sections of its parklike setting, and which offers programs of mainly one-night events. Here, an aces-wild book, its coupons good for so many dollars of ticket value, could be utilized by buyers of both reserved and unreserved seats, and the outsize seating capacity would create greater flexibility for dealing with rained-out nights than would a conventional subscription format. At the Meadow Brook Music Festival near Detroit, the management has been offering reserved-seat, specific-night-of-the-week subscriptions inside the pavilion, and coupon book subscriptions for the unreserved lawn space.

The rolling-repertory system, especially when combined with the aces-wild coupon book feature, has a great deal of appeal for many artistic directors of theatre companies. It affords them freedom from the necessity of advance planning of seasons, in contrast to the discipline of adhering to a specific announced schedule of performances as required under the more conventional subscription format. Managers and artistic directors of rotating-repertory theatres which offer coupons applicable to any play, or which do not have the security of any form of subscription at all (and thus depend on single-ticket sales only), prize their freedom to maneuver, their ability to schedule fewer performances for their box office "weak sister" productions and more performances for their big-draw productions. (Actually, if there are sufficient subscriptions sold under a specific-plays-on-specific-dates arrangement, there *are* no weak sisters. *Every* play is then in the sellout category.)

The rolling-repertory system has many valid artistic elements. It does, however, have certain economic drawbacks, not the least of which are its track record of being more expensive, operationally, than the consecutive manner of presentation and its special difficulty in promoting single-ticket sales because of the public's constant confusion as to which play is being performed on which night, necessitating costly daily advertising throughout the season. The basic experience of the resident professional theatres has been, overwhelmingly, that in either the case of rolling-repertory or the more widely used consecutive schedule, a large subscription audience in relation to the capacity is an asset of immeasurable value.

There are many performing arts projects which can't see subscription as suitable for them at all. I can well understand, for instance, that some experimental, improvisational and alternative theatre groups will feel that many of the recommendations in this book (and indeed the entire concept of subscription itself) are not suited to their ideologies and to their preferred life-styles as organizations. I am often told by the people running smaller performing arts organizations, ethnic theatre and dance companies, jazz groups, and organizations devoted to special policies such as avant-garde productions or the development of new playwrights or composers, that the subscription concept is fine for the "establishment" institutions or organizations with large seating capacities, but it is not for them. And I remind them that, with very few exceptions, the companies which they now consider big and established were once small, no more established than they are now, and that the vehicle of their growth—in some cases, very quickly accomplished—was the subscription dynamic.

Managers of small arts organizations sometimes see greater, more immediate relevance for themselves in voucher-ticket plans. Such programs in some half-dozen cities encourage senior citizens, students, union members and workers in clerical and service jobs, who seldom attend performing arts events, to do so via cut-rate admission prices subsidized by private and public funds. However, vouchers for a wide range of different attractions are still in the single-ticket category and are not at all the same as subscription, through which we have a commitment to attend *all* of one producing organization's events in a given season—and by renewal, a long-term commitment.

A year or so ago, a young man rang my apartment doorbell and introduced himself as an actor-director-playwright and recent graduate of a theatre school. He had leased, in an outlying city neighborhood, the second-floor premises of a building (it had previously housed a Chinese restaurant, I believe), which he proposed to convert to a 130-seat playhouse, in which he expected to produce provocative plays, including some of his own authorship. He asked for advice about getting an audience for his project. I advised him that his chances for success would be greatly increased if he were to obtain a reasonably good subscribership right from the start, and I outlined to him a number of the methods which are delineated in this handbook. Starting from absolute scratch, but with an excellent spirit of determination, he ran an intensive campaign and was able to start his first season with 1,000 subscribers in his 130-seat loft theatre. This gave him a real leg up, and an assured attendance for each play in relation to his house capacity and to his limited runs. The subscribers evidently liked what they experienced and spread the word to their friends. Single-ticket buyers showed up, too, and he had to put in extra chairs at many performances. I understand he ended his first season with an average attendance of over 75%. Had he sold about another 500 subscriptions, he would undoubtedly have played to 100% throughout.

Many other "off-off" theatre companies in many places have begun to bite the season-ticket bullet, and I have recently questioned a number of them as to the outcome of their initial campaigns. What was especially interesting to me, after they told me what their respective subscription promotion efforts had consisted of, was how well they had done in relation to their investments of time and money. I had the impression that they didn't realize how well they had done. In one case, the percentage of returns for brochure distributions was much better than those of many of the much larger theatres from which I receive regular reports. I judge that they need to increase the volume of their brochure distributions (especially to selective lists, considering the special-ness of their repertoire) and to develop more selling components, more sources of sales. In all cases, they were continuing with their subscription plans for future seasons and felt that they would do much better now that they had gotten their feet wet, so to speak. One young manager told me that "lack of capital and lack of knowledge" had handicapped her subscription cam-paign, and I would say that the same would have applied, not all that many years ago, to a good many of the now well-established larger companies—the kind that many people undoubtedly now regard as fat cats. Of course, if they really knew more about their problems, they would realize that they are not all that "fat." For all of us in the performing arts—large and small—hang by similar, fragile economic threads, and it is wise to recall that old saw (in slight paraphrase), "The bigger the budget, the harder they fall." Big or small, a sizable subscription audience in relation to capacity is the best possible crash insurance.

I assume that there will always be certain producing groups which still will not or cannot enter the subscription arena. However, I submit that on what-ever basis they operate, they could gain much advantage from adopting at least some of the effective management and promotional procedures which are currently operative in so many of the professional performing arts institu-tions. I suggest that advance planning is not only possible, but is an absolute necessity for *any kind* of arts company and that, while spontaneity undoubt-edly has its artistic value, it has no value at all in the organizing and promoting of a theatre project.

Therefore, I suggest that before dismissing out of hand the potential "subscribability" of a project, the management ought to look into the possibility thoroughly and without prejudice. To perhaps initiate second thoughts on the part of some of those who have closed their minds to this subject, I will, in the next few paragraphs, speak about several projects which might have seemed unlikely candidates to seek and find subscriberships, but which have done so—and have thereby been greatly benefited.

While the Inner City Cultural Center of Los Angeles, serving mainly blacks, Asians and Chicanos, is not an "establishment" performing arts organization by any standard, it has developed a subscription system which it has found to be of value and has, at the time of this writing, increased its committed audience almost 900% in a two-year period.

While showboats have been thought of as more connected with top-hatted, silk-waistcoated Gaylord Ravenel types than with season tickets, the Showboat Majestic, moored at an Ohio River pier opposite downtown Cincinnati, has risen in attendance from a limp 40% of its capacity to a prosperous 85% since switching to a subscription-based economy.

There are also certain nonprofit "presenter" entities, which emphasize booked-in touring attractions rather than resident productions, where it might be thought that subscription didn't quite fit the situation. Yet, these organizations have built subscriberships, offering various packagings of the performing arts disciplines represented in their bookings.

I suggest that small or unusual performing arts organizations of all kinds keep an open mind about subscription and its applicability to their situations. I think their managements should try to see those elements in what I have been discussing which make sense for them. Then, they should work out the subscription formats which fit their needs and put them into operation for their respective projects. Let the art be whatever it is intended to be by the artists. But, do not open a play or a season without the advance time and promotional preparation which are necessary to make it known to the prospective audience. If for any reason, doctrinal or otherwise, a theatre company should eschew the subscription system on any level, I will not be hurt, although I will be fearful for its future.

## 28

### *Subscription for Touring Companies and Local Sponsors*

Some years ago, an orchestra musician wrote a letter to the "Voice of the People" section of a major metropolitan newspaper to state his views on what was then a long-standing impasse in contract negotiations between the management of a great opera company and its orchestral employees. The musician may have been a fine artist, but he was obviously ignorant in practical affairs. He assured the newspaper readers that the opera company could get all the money it needed to meet its obligations, if only its executives were bright enough to take to the road—for the company to go on tour to many other cities and thus earn great profits. In fact, the opera company was then losing $30,000 a night on every sold-out house while performing on its home ground (now, some years later, this nightly loss has escalated to almost $60,000). Going on the road would only add to the costs of moving and housing the army of principal singers, choristers, conductors, orchestra personnel, stagehands, costumers, wardrobe mistresses, makeup men, dressers, armorers and so on, "ad bankruptcy." For the logistics and expense involved in taking a grand opera company on tour are hardly less than those of the Normandy Beach landings on D-Day. Furthermore, should there be less than sellout attendance away from home (where the company is not on subscription), the already staggering losses would be even greater, far more than any guarantees put up by the local sponsors. That is why touring opera companies are rapidly becoming as extinct as dinosaurs, and that is why the letter-writing musician had the opera staffers falling off their chairs with hysterical laughter at his naive recommendations.

However, not all nonprofit performing arts organizations bear the monstrous economic burdens to which opera producers are heir, and so touring is still possible for them. Some resident theatres, while rarely touring across the country like commercial theatrical enterprises, have arranged exchange productions for themselves with sister resident companies in other cities, whereby each includes the other in its annual subscription offering. This arrangement has the benefit of providing a special feature for the subscriber audiences of the respective companies involved in the exchange and gives both sets of actors the opportunity to meet new audiences and test themselves on new stages.

A resident company which truly serves a region, as its name implies, is Theatre New Brunswick. Following the run of each of its seven annual productions at the Fredericton Playhouse, it takes the plays on tour to waiting, subscribed audiences in each of eight other communities. The base for the entire operation was the original successful establishment of a subscription audience in Fredericton. Subsequently, subscription campaigns were launched in each of the other towns, with local assistance involved, but directed from the theatre company's central office in Fredericton. One brochure, containing separate lists of dates for the performance of the seven plays in each community, is utilized and is indeed the central and unifying instrument of the yearly subscription campaign.

A similar arrangement has been made for the Atlantic Symphony Orchestra which is headquartered in Halifax, but which also serves another half-dozen cities in Nova Scotia and Newfoundland. The vagaries of the road hold no terrors for either Theatre New Brunswick or the Atlantic Symphony. Their artists are not ever likely to be stranded while away from home without an audience on a cold and windy night. Their audiences, despite some difficult winter weather in their areas, are committed via subscription and are overwhelmingly present under all conditions.

The New Jersey Symphony Orchestra, at one point badly floundering for lack of audience to fill the modest-size auditoriums of the 10 communities it served, put on a strong subscription counterattack that gave it a virtually sold-out season, thus enabling it to add 5 more cities to its touring itinerary within the next two seasons. A 340% gain in subscribership (and resulting new confidence in its ability to promote its interests) has quickly catapulted this organization to a 50% increase in the number of communities it visits. An unjustified belief that patrons in considerable numbers would show up to buy single tickets at the box office had previously almost ruined this organization.

Old-line, major symphony orchestras have long offered series in cities not too far away from their home bases; for example, the Chicago Symphony Orchestra in Milwaukee, the Philadelphia Orchestra in New York City, and the Los Angeles Philharmonic Orchestra in San Diego. Subscription is the factor that makes such regularly occurring visiting concerts feasible. Such arrangements are the deluxe version of what orchestra managers call "run-out" performances, because the musicians return home after the performance.

Theatre Communications Group, at the time of this writing, has issued a listing of some 44 nonprofit professional theatre companies which are available to tour. I would recommend to these organizations that, even in those cases where they obtain full guarantees or are performing for a flat fee, they send in promotional materials as well as competent advance representatives to assist the local sponsors in every possible way, so as to assure that performances in those places are sellouts. The officials of a touring company can congratulate themselves endlessly about having come off well with their full fee, but if the local sponsorship organization has suffered a debacle because of poor attendance, you can be sure that the company will never be asked back. And such touring companies should always have in mind the possibility of establishing a subscription series for themselves in those communities, so that there can be developed a much higher level, more permanent and fruitful relationship than is afforded by an occasional one-night stand.

Professional dance companies and resident theatres, established in cities not too far away from other communities of sizable populations which do not have such performing arts groups of their own, are in a particularly advantageous position for creating satellite subscription audiences in those places.

The development of regular tours to such circuits could well become, for many organizations, a valuable extension of performance possibilities, and thus, of fuller employment for artists.

The National Theatre of the Deaf, which has achieved a unique and respected position for itself, has always been primarily a touring company. However, it lacked sufficient touring opportunities until it was joined by a new executive who had previously been the head of a resident professional theatre, for which he had employed large-scale direct-mail subscription promotion methods. Immediately upon taking over the responsibilities of his new assignment, he began to apply this approach to the solicitation of touring performance dates for the National Theatre of the Deaf with such success that he tripled its bookings, thus stampeding many performance sponsors into signing up for dates years in advance and catapulting this organization into a new era of greater success. What did he do to achieve this? He compiled lists of many thousands of potential sponsors for performances of his troupe to which he mailed excellent illustrated brochures which told his story so well that he was soon flooded with inquiries that led to a record number of new engagements. While he has had many return engagements (his renewals, so to speak) in subsequent seasons, whatever his attrition happens to be in any given year is more than compensated by the results of his annual brochure distribution, which remains his primary source of promotion.

Theatre Communications Group, which has, over the past 15 years, quietly performed a monumental task as "midwife," counselor and supplier of practical services to virtually all of the American nonprofit professional theatres, conducts a Touring Information Service. Through its widely distributed publications, possible sponsors for touring units are sought. Information on this service for sponsors and touring theatre companies is available from TCG, 355 Lexington Avenue, New York, N.Y. 10017.

My editor has suggested that I discuss a few concepts which could be useful to local arts series sponsors who might, on some occasion, be presenting some of the performing arts organizations for whose benefit this book has, in the main, been prepared. For, thus far in this chapter, we have been looking at it from the standpoint of the touring unit. Now we will look at the problems of the host or sponsoring organization. There are a number of nonprofit organizations such as the Auditorium Theater Council (Chicago), the Society for the Performing Arts (Houston) and the Music Hall Center (Detroit), which are basically bookers and promoters of events, rather than producers of them.

They serve a most important function in many communities. Sometimes they coexist with local commercial impresarios. Such sponsoring organizations usually present a diverse list of attractions, comprising the entire spectrum of the performing arts. Just like resident companies, they are usually subscription oriented and their survival, too, is most often bound up in the cycle of annual campaigns for renewal of series-ticket holders and replacement of subscriber attrition by promotion of new sales. The star system is often very important to them, and big-name, blockbuster attractions are counted on, not only for sold-out houses when they appear, but as insurance that there will be good-size audiences for the less popular elements on the subscription offering.

Their brochures must contain wide-ranging descriptions of all of the performing arts disciplines. The positive principle of such "department store" brochures is that they offer many things for many tastes, so that large-scale distributions will have maximum sales possibilities and will bring maximum returns on the investment in printing, postage and processing of brochure distributions. If the man who receives the brochure is not interested in a folksinger series, he may be just waiting for somebody to offer him an Afro-Asian dance series. If he won't buy the piano series, there may be a good chance to get his return check for the tenor series. Perhaps the market this year will favor series which contain Belgian ballet companies, Viennese operetta troupes, marionettes, baritones, violinists, avant-garde or classical theatre companies which, when made into combination packagings and offered at enticing discount prices, are as tempting as the Godfather's "offer you can't refuse!"

The appeal of the discount for nonproducing presenters is every bit as important as it is for resident producing organizations. It should be first displayed out front, on the address side of the brochure, and described not only in terms of percentage, but how many events the purchaser will get *free:*

**The Great Theatre Series offers 8 Broadway hit shows for the price of 5 = 3 plays Free; the Best of Off Broadway Series offers 6 provocative plays for the price of 4 = 2 plays Free; or the combination of our Gold Curtain Series and our Wide World Series, all 9 musical entertainment events for the price of 6 = 3 delightful divertissements Free, a smashing discount of 33$1/3$%!**

... and so on, adapting the very same bargain-pricing approaches outlined in other chapters of this book.

Without any question, the names and photographs of the star quotient in your offer should be given major placement in the brochure, and each attraction should be described attractively, so that when you send out the brochure, you have confidence in its ability to convince the reader. If you are presenting the Royal Acrobats of Persia and the Senegalese National Dance Company on their first American tours, you must not just say something academic like, "These energetic performers are well trained in acrobatics" (for the Persians) or, "A fine group of dancers to provide you with an exotic dance experience" (for the Senegalese). How about this:

**Tumblers to the Shah, these mightily muscled Iranians are direct heirs to the acrobatic genies who brought joy to the heart of Darius the Great. The members of this unique, all-male group take pardonable pride in their extraordinary, amazing physical prowess, their dazzling dexterity, descended from a tradition of a thousand years!**

Or, how about this:

**Out of the hot, tropical grasslands of Africa has come this crack troupe of folk-dancing masqueraders, celebrating their cycle of life, love, peace and war—often whirling in the ecstatic trance of men and women possessed of primal secrets. A spectacle to astonish!**

If you're talking about the Alvin Ailey American Dance Theatre, you could say (but I wouldn't recommend it for evoking sales) that it is "one of the most highly regarded dance companies of our day." I would much rather you said:

**This troupe bowled 'em over in London, captivated 'em in Paris and charmed 'em in Moscow. Its dancers possess a superelectric charge that flashes and crackles all over the stage. Wherever they are, this troupe is great!**

Should you have the popular guitarist, Chet Atkins, coming in on your folk or pops series, you would not be doing him justice to speak of his "outstanding ability as an interpreter of music for the guitar." I would suggest something like this:

**He disdains the plastic pick, preferring his own, powerful quicksilver fingers—and he bestrides the country and western musical field like a latter-day colossus, secure in the affection and adulation of his army of fans, millions strong—who call him "Mr. Guitar";**

who buy his recordings in incredible numbers; who follow him like
the Pied Piper on radio and TV; and who set attendance records for
his personal appearances, like the one we have coming up!

If one of the plays on our classic theatre series should be Rostand's *Cyrano
de Bergerac,* you would be telling it like it is if you said, "It is a classic work,
filled with romance and poetry!" However, you would be doing your ex-
chequer a favor if you tried it this way:

> **Grandiloquence and gallantry flourish in this colorful, romantic
> tapestry of a play whose hero orates like Marc Antony, pens poetry
> like Rostand and duels like D'Artagnan, yet fears to face the fair
> Roxanne 'cause his nose is like Jimmy Durante's. No protagonist in
> drama's vast repertoire is as warm and as touching as is this
> swashbuckler whose heart's as tender as his sword is sharp!**

If there's a *Merry Widow* on the series, writing about it as a superb example
of Lehar's operatic art will not accomplish much, but you could really help
sell the series ticket by describing the work thus:

> **Recipe for Delighting Audiences: Take a lovely, young, wealthy
> widow. Match her to a handsome, dashing bachelor prince in
> romantic, turn-of-the-century Paris. Then, pour on a profusion of
> beguiling and bewitching songs like "Vilia," "The Merry Widow
> Waltz" and "Meet Me at Maxim's," to the accompaniment of ex-
> quisite orchestral melody, contrasted with the vivacity of the "dar-
> ing" can-can—and you have the main ingredients for the most
> fabulously successful musical divertissement of all time!**

I could go on and on, giving all sorts of examples, since the scope of
attractions of the booking-presenting organization is very wide, but I think
I've already given my idea of the kind of copy that gives strength to such a
brochure. I would suggest, however, that the sponsors of such multi-series
not limit their promotional efforts to the distribution of brochures. Just as in
the case of the resident producers, there are a number of other ways in which
subscriptions can be sold, and many of those ways are discussed within the
pages of this manual. A nonprofit resident booker-presenter has all the same
advantages, benefits and reasons for utilizing these extra methods as do
resident producing organizations. He also has a board of directors and
identical possibilities to develop volunteer auxiliary assistance.

# 29

# Which Comes First,
# the Chicken or the Egg?
# Subscription or Fund-Raising?

I believe that the development of professional performing arts institutions in our society has been unfortunately and unnecessarily retarded because several generations of people like ourselves—those to whom these projects are important—have proceeded on the assumption that our primary obligation toward the performing arts, in addition to providing the required artistic apparatus, was to obtain financial contributions for their support. Had we, let us say, from the turn of the twentieth century onward, given anywhere the same kind of consideration and effort to audience development that we did to fund-raising, the position and the status of the performing arts in our society would have been entirely different in our time. That is, if we now had a much larger committed audience for symphony orchestras, theatres, opera and dance companies, we would have an entirely different, healthier, more successful relationship to the communities in which we operate our nonprofit arts organizations. Were we to have regularly attending audiences of, say, a quintupled size, contributions on all levels (from private individuals, companies, foundations and the three governmental levels) would, most likely, not only be five times greater, but would be extricated much more easily.

We have not understood that the cart of fund-raising has been placed before the horse of audience development. Too often we sweat and strain to obtain financial support on behalf of projects which too few people attend, thus perpetuating a vicious, frustrating circle. For, as long as a performing arts organization remains the interest of so tiny a coterie in relation to the overall population, the possibility of evoking enthusiasm for contributing monies to us from sources that have never given, and the possibility of getting those who have given in the past to give more, are very poor indeed.

I know, by experience, that achieving the turnaround by which major subscription selling efforts come to be seen as the logical prerequisite to more successful fund-raising, is not always as easy as falling off a log. It is, more often than not, very difficult to change the deeply ingrained, habitual, hallowed (but basically fallacious) concepts of those I call "nice people in and around the arts." The unnatural situation of having to continually raise considerable amounts of money in a community for an activity that is hardly visible in terms of people who are interested in it, can and does result in our often losing sight of the true purposes for which our project originally came into being. If you were to ask many of our volunteer board leaders the question, "What is the purpose of having your performing arts group in this city?" they might well reply, "Why, so that we can have our annual fund-raising drive, of course."

It has almost been automatic that whenever and wherever we have succeeded in promoting into existence large-scale audiences, subsidies have increased in ratio—from both the private sector and the government. The greatest incentive to contributors of all kinds is the joy of seeing sold-out houses, the resultant expansions of seasons, and the thrilling sight of people beating at the doors, trying to get in. In such cases, it becomes obvious that these arts producers deserve to receive increased financial support. Conversely, poorly attended performances and the atmosphere and substance of stagnation that this condition generates, are powerful deterrents to affimative contributor action. I do not mean to say that those producing organizations with minuscule audiences (lots of empty seats) and no picture of growth can't get *any* contributions. There are always some charitable folk who *will* throw a bone to the starving artists, but they are unlikely to ply them with seven-course dinners. On the other hand, the human compulsion to leap onto bandwagons can be counted on—and should be exploited. But, we must bear in mind that the prerequisite for such exploitation is the ability to create successful subscription campaigns.

Fortunately, an increasing number of organizations have seen the light on this issue. They have benefited a great deal in their fund drive efforts from the enlarged subscriberships resulting from the new priority accorded to such audience development promotion in overall planning. I recently attended an executive board committee meeting of a symphony orchestra society which, in the areas of both attendance and fund-raising had been in the dormant category from 1919 to 1970, the year in which it began what was to be its great leap forward. In every way, the management concentrated on subscription promotion, handpicking its professional personnel with that orientation in mind. An active marketing committee recruited from the board went into continuous action. The board voted promotional funds on a scale that far exceeded past budgets in this area. The results were spectacular, with an average increase of subscribership of over 140% each year, for a cumulative five-year gain of 700%.

Now, the point is that the atmosphere in which the fund-raising is now carried on has so much improved, the credibility of the organization is now so much greater, the enthusiasm of the sources from which money must be raised is so much higher, that contributions and subsidies from all sources have increased over 400% in the same period. And those in charge would be the first to admit that they have not, by any means, fully exploited all the possibilities for contribution which their new prestige has opened up for them. A worthy goal for this organization, in my judgment, would be to match the 700% gain in committed audience with a 700% rise in grants and contributions. In this situation one might really add to the contributions the ticket income for previously unsold seats. For isn't that fund-raising, too? As additional rewards for its new importance, this orchestral organization has also increased its fortunes by embarking on an exciting foreign tour and building a multimillion dollar new home. Both benefits had eluded it for the first half-century of its institutional life, during which lack of sufficient audience had, decade after decade, prevented their fulfillment.

Many performing arts organizations do not realize the potential for fund-raising that lies in the goodwill and even the love and affection which subscribers can come to feel for us. This potential may vary, of course, according to all sorts of factors which might apply to different projects at different stages of their development. However, we should not forget that our subscribers are certainly the most likely people in the community to understand and sympathize with us when we are in financial need (which is just about all the time). Who would more likely feel deprived if we were to be forced to close our doors than those who have been going regularly to our art, perhaps for a number of years?

However, we cannot expect that our subscribers will automatically send us contribution checks, themselves divining that we are in need of them. And we cannot assume that a statement or an appeal printed in our programs is sufficient. This consciousness-raising of our season or series subscribers concerning the disparity between what they pay for the tickets and what our cost of operation really is, must be a continuous educational process. Unless we do this job effectively and unremittingly, it is quite possible for a person of means who occupies the most expensive seats, on a subscribed basis, to think of himself as a "Patron of the Arts," making the assumption that his purchase of subscription tickets is "supporting" the institution, when, in fact, his ticket is actually subsidized—up to 60% or more for instance, in the case of large opera companies, even when all seats for all performances of the season are sold. If he doesn't give a contribution to at least make up for the gap between what he pays and what the cost actually is, or give some money in addition to pay the freight for a person of lesser means for whom the price of the ticket is his limit, how will we get by? Although government has begun to support the arts, its contributions, measured against our total needs, can only be regarded as a helpful, hopeful omen of future, enlarged assistance; but it is far from decisive in our current economic picture.

The idea that we need more money for our operations than we can take in at the box office, even when we pack 'em in—and that this does not mean we are inefficient, wasteful and extravagant—must be patiently explained over and over again, without assuming that everybody understands it as well as we do. Often we are surprised to find people in our community assuming that similar institutions to ours in other places have no financial problems, and that there must be something wrong with the way we operate if we are always seeking contributions. Also, there is a tendency on the part of many to confuse nonprofit groups with commercial show business where the entrepeneurs involved are known to make occasional killings with their hit productions. We must tell our story through our speakers' bureaus, through publicity in the press and other media, through our newsletters and brochures—and we must be prepared to continue this educational campaign through the years.

The mistaken idea that fund-raising and subscription promotion are, some-how, in competition with each other has done a great deal to inhibit the growth of performing arts organizations. Actually, these two activities are complementary to each other and should be closely coordinated, with the chicken of audience development preceding the egg of fund-raising as the natural order of things, if you agree with my observation that it is the subscriber who most often grows into a contributor, rather than the other way around.

Some years ago, while employed as the publicist–audience builder of an arts company, I found myself in a continuous, unhappy struggle with the fund-raiser, who seemed to regard my seemingly obsessive efforts to sell more and still more series-ticket subscriptions as some form of subversion.

After all, was I not diverting money, staff time, volunteer manpower and, indeed, the concentration of the organization from its one, great essential task—the sacred solicitation of donations? I finally realized that my argument about the absurdity of even trying to raise money, while performing without audiences, was falling on deaf ears. So, I took a different tack. I convinced my nemesis to join me in a simple study of our records, which proved conclusively that the subscribers we did have at that point were also the majority of our contributors—*and* that their subscribership had preceded their contributions. Overnight, that fund-raiser became a rabid enthusiast for increased subscription campaigning and never failed to suggest that I ought to send out another few hundred thousand brochures. He had come to understand that, if I found another few thousand subscribers in a given year, they would soon become prime prospects for his department to cultivate. I cannot emphasize too much the necessity for the promoters of audiences and fund-raisers to work in tandem, in order for the institution itself to achieve maximum success. As in so many other instances in this book, I am making the assumption that the art being offered is of high quality. However, in those cases where it is not, the good work of the subscription sales force and of the fund-raisers can, and often does, buy us the time for its improvement to the point where long-term survival becomes much more possible.

While all of us in the nonprofit performing arts have in common the need for fund-raising, opera companies' requirements are unquestionably the greatest. Well into the third decade of its life, Lyric Opera of Chicago still finds it necessary to explain why it must have the community's financial support—now more than $3,000,000 of it annually—in addition to the monies its sold-out seasons bring in at the box office. In its twentieth year, Lyric Opera took its case to its subscribers and individual ticket buyers (all of the 70,000 persons on its house mailing list) and to the community at large, with much vigor. A number of different personalized letters were sent to many thousands of potential donors. Some were sent by board officers and directors, others by the general manager and other staff members. Particular care was given to the various categories of series-ticket subscribers. I mean categories in relation to their respective records of contributing, for instance: those who had given last year but had not yet given this year; those who had not given in two or more years; those who had given up to $100 during the current year; those who had given more than $100 during the current year (special appeals were made to those who had already given in the current year to add to their contributions before the campaign's end); those who had never given at all.

Among the direct-mail instruments used was a handsome issue of *Lyric Opera News,* containing not only photographs and stories about the impressive season in prospect, but a major article on the fund drive, plus a strategically placed pledge form. Also enclosed was a large, illustrated brochure which prominently displayed the names of over 400 businesses which were already giving yearly cash gifts. Listed were all of the educational services the opera company provides to the community. There was a quote from a statement made about the company by a distinguished music critic which read, "What is an opera company, a good one, worth to a great city? . . . It is beyond price." Then, there was a quote from a speech made by one of the opera company's celebrated, international singers saying, "Chicago without Lyric Opera would be a maimed city!" The historic ticket sales achievement of the preceding season when 102.6% of the capacity was reached, was chronicled, as were the numbers of subscribers (20,820) and established contributors (10,411). Also included was a joint call for financial support (with reasons) from the board president and the fund drive chairman—and two panels which are reproduced in this chapter.

That campaign for the $2.8 million succeeded. The following year, when the combination of inflation and the costs of even more ambitious productions brought the fund-raising need to $3.2 million, the momentum held and that goal was reached, too. Many factors are involved in the success of such campaigns. In the case of that particular organization, they included strong and skilled leadership from both board and management, as well as the participation of a volunteer network embracing the efforts of a women's board, a guild board, a large number of city and suburban area chapters and a president's committee. Passing the ammunition was an in-house professional fund-raiser, and feeding the publicity fires throughout the campaign was the company's own press agent (me). When the contributions were all finally recorded and banked, it was apparent that if there was a secret weapon employed, it was to be found in the support of the series-ticket subscribers, who were—in their capacities as private individuals or as corporate officials and trustees of local foundations—clearly the single greatest source of income to the drive.

Let us underscore the point that *they were not contributors who had become series-ticket subscribers. They were series-ticket subscribers who had been the subjects of constant indoctrination concerning the organiza-*

# ONCE, A FEW TYCOONS — NOW, MANY THOUSANDS OF CONTRIBUTORS!

### The Democratization of Opera-Giving

Grand Opera is a collective art-form—the glorious confluence of *all* the performing arts—And thus, it *is* fabulously expensive. Yet, all societies and systems, Monarchies and Democracies, Capitalists and Communists, have agreed that Opera is worth the price. In most places, that price has been paid by governments.

In America, in Chicago, the price has been met overwhelmingly by the private sector. In the Old Days, a few tycoons sat around a Board table and divided up the annual deficit between them. And when the time came that they wouldn't or couldn't, the Opera curtain came crashing down in Chicago. Oversimplified? Perhaps. But that's the story behind the life and death of the half-dozen major Chicago opera companies which preceded Lyric Opera.

Lyric, however, has built on a broader base—with more than 10,000 contributors who give according to their means, from very modest amounts to munificent ones. As Lyric has grown, all the way from an initial three performances in the Spring of 1954 to 1973's 53 performance season, the costs have mounted—and they're still burgeoning. Lyric Opera needs more and more contributors, so that it will SURVIVE—and THRIVE, too!

*A panel from the Lyric Opera of Chicago fund-raising brochure explains the need for contributions.*

# WHY EVERY NON-CONTRIBUTING TICKET PURCHASER IS A "CHARITY CASE!"

Whether you pay the lowest price of $5.50 or the highest price of $17.50 for your seat this season, you are clearly *A CHARITY CASE*—unless you make a contribution in addition, commensurate with your means.

Why? Because it will cost Lyric Opera an average of $93,000 to produce each performance of the 1974 season, and each sold-out house brings in $40,000 in ticket sales. Thus, there is a deficit of $53,000 for every performance of the season—and this adds up to the need for $2,800,000 in contributions.

There are some ticket purchasers who are straining to pay just the price of their tickets. Were Lyric to double the ticket prices in an effort to raise its monies, they would be disenfranchised, unable to attend opera any more.

Others, who can afford higher prices, are urged to do so voluntarily, by contributing to the maintenance fund.

> *Ticket sales do not even cover half the performance costs. For every $17.50 ticket sold, Lyric loses more than $20.00!*

*A succeeding panel from the same Lyric Opera brochure gives the facts and figures of opera economics.*

*tion's needs and who had, through their regular attendance of that opera company's performances, come to love it, so that when called upon to contribute, they possessed the motivation to comply.* Many thousands of them have been doing so for years now. To amplify this last statement, Lyric Opera of Chicago's 1975 fund drive records show that $1,486,316 came from private individuals who were, overwhelmingly, series-ticket subscribers. A considerable number of the corporate and local foundation gifts which collectively represented the second largest source of funds (a total of $1,280,684) can be traced directly and indirectly to a subscription connection.

I have no way of knowing what the future will hold for Lyric Opera of Chicago or for any other performing arts entity. All such nonprofit, professional producing organizations—even the largest of them—suffer continuously from the same frightening gap between what tickets sales bring in, even at a total sellout, and what the real, much greater cost of producing their art may be. Inexorable inflation, which is, for an entire complex of reasons, seemingly higher in our field than in commercial enterprises, scares the daylights out of us. Government financial assistance, while it exists here (at long last), gives little promise of providing major assistance in relation to overall budgetary requirements. Thus, our situation clearly demands of us that we devise and effect more successful subscription drives, and that we lose no time in starting the effective indoctrination of the subscribers we obtain from such efforts, so that a significant number of them will also begin to support us financially, *beyond* the price of their tickets.

Although this need for the intensive development of the subscriber-contributor hybrid has been of critical importance to the performing arts groups of the U.S., the situation has been somewhat different in Canada, where nonprofit producing organizations have felt more secure because they have enjoyed a higher degree of governmental subsidy. However, because inflation crosses borders easily, and because of the enormous recent proliferation of performing arts groups in that country (sparked, in great measure, by nationwide Canadian success in subscription promotion), nonprofit producing units have begun to feel a squeeze that is inevitably changing things for them. Now they must inevitably seek more and more of their funding from the private sector, U.S.-style. And their own ticket subscribers must represent an important potential source of contributions which will undoubtedly be given increasing attention all the way from Vancouver on the west to Newfoundland on the east. By our own determination, by our own hard work, we can convert nonsubscribers into subscribers and then turn them into contributors, too, a beautiful parlay that means our salvation and our fulfillment.

# 30

## *Pirandello's Fantasy— and Mine!*

Much of this book has been given over to various methods and approaches by which we can, if we successfully employ them, bring people into the fold as regular members of our performing arts audiences.

Because I have dealt with arts people for many years, I know that some of them, despite all the arguments set forth in the foregoing pages, might be saying to themselves, "Granted these are effective means by which people can be sold subscriptions, but do we really *have* to do these things to build audiences? Is it really sporting to trap people into going?"

What can I reply to these gentlefolk other than, "Yes, our common experience teaches us that we must do some of these things, or all of these things, depending upon how resistant the individual situation is and how ambitious for expansion those in charge are." About the fairness of entrapment of unsuspecting citizens for our purpose of turning them into committed arts spectators, I would like to tell the following story:

I was once called upon to assist a theatre company which had 1,900 subscribers and performed each play for two-and-a-half weeks to half empty houses, after many years of existence. Subsequently, 20,000 subscribers were found. Each play began to run seven weeks to jammed houses, resulting in tremendous artistic growth. Now, whenever I visit this theatre, I take much pleasure in prowling the lobbies during intermissions (like the fabled Harun al-Rashid walking among the people), eavesdropping on the conversations of the fine, alert, progressive subscribers—many of them men who undoubtedly wear tweed jackets, smoke pipes and read copies of the *Saturday Review* when they are sitting at home in front of their fireplaces, while their equally accomplished, progressive wives are baking ceramics or fashioning wrought iron sculptures in their basements. I know, having identified the targets for the theatre's promotion, that many of the men and women present are young executives, schoolteachers, university faculty members, graduate students, doctors, lawyers and other professionals.

Let us say that, on one of these evenings, a drama by Pirandello is being performed, and between the acts I listen in on many intensive discussions about that gifted playwright's limning of the fine line 'twixt illusion and delusion, sanity and insanity, and so on. Suddenly, I have the fantasy that I will approach one of these little knots of subscribers, where a fine-looking chap is denying his friend's claim that Pirandello is obscure in his meaning. "Not at all," he is saying, "It's perfectly clear to me," and as he warms to his subject, I annoy him by tapping on his shoulder, thus interrupting him. "Sir," I begin, "I am conducting a survey for *Time* magazine. Would you please tell me what made you decide to attend this performance tonight?"

And, as my fantasy evolves, the man draws himself up haughtily and protests, "What kind of question is that? Can't you see that my wife, myself, and our friends are members of the cultural elite—the superior people of this area? Isn't it obvious to you that I'm the type of man who has a tweed jacket at home, and that I always wear it when smoking my pipe and reading the *Saturday Review* in front of my fireplace, while my wife bakes ceramics in the basement? Don't you know that this is *our* kind of theatre, one that produces plays by Shakespeare, Ibsen, Shaw, Edward Albee, Tom Stoppard, Eugene Ionesco, Joe Orton and Pirandello? We're season subscribers and have been for six years now. We belong here. How dare you ask such a question?" At that moment the warning chimes sound for the beginning of the second act, and he storms back into the auditorium in a huff.

Now, were I totally honest in my fantasy, I would chase after him, yelling "Why you miserable phony! Where were you and all of the others like you during all those years before we began to run those big subscription campaigns? Do you know why you're *really* here tonight? You're here because you received 11 brochures in a row—one every 10th day, six years ago, when we made the first big push—and you collapsed on the 7th brochure! And you, his friend, do you know why you're here? You were an easier mark. *You* signed up after only the 4th brochure." As the audience files past me on its way in to enjoy the second act, I tell them, one at a time, how we trapped them into becoming subscribers. "You, sir, you're here because your boss bought one of our blocs of subscriptions which were sold to industry; he gave you and your wife a pair, and that's what started *you* coming here. And you, madam, a philanthropic organization to which you belong sold subscriptions for us, receiving a commission for its earning fund, and that brought *you* here."

And I go on and on, listing all of the *unsporting* ways in which these people were *dragged* to the theatre, some of them against their will, kicking and screaming. We schemed and we worked to get them here, despite their long indifference to us. They were, indeed, the victims of Dynamic Subscription Promotion. But once they had subscription tickets, it became a part of their way of life; they renewed for the next season and they have been renewing ever since.

Will I ever really act out this fantasy in the lobby of that playhouse—or of any other one? No, of course not. Why should I? Are these people not going to the theatre regularly—to every play of the season? They are. Are they not discussing Pirandello knowledgeably, in the manner of sophisticated, dis-criminating theatregoers? They are. Are not a considerable percentage of these people renewing their subscriptions each season? They are!

So, the lesson for us is that it doesn't matter how they originally got there. All that matters is that they are there *and for all of the plays of each season!* In fact, they have forgotten how they got there, and I find no advantage in reminding them of the process. This wonderful, large audience body was indeed artificially created, but the moment it existed as an audience, there was nothing artificial about it. It had substance, reality, from the very moment that these people walked into the theatre for the first performance of the first season to which they subscribed.

# Epilogue

## *The Proof Is in the Pudding*

The old saw that the proof is in the pudding can certainly be applied to Dynamic Subscription Promotion and its efficacy. Indeed, I would be hard pressed to find a performing arts organization which has embraced even a few of its tenets without experiencing a substantial audience increase.

In trying to decide which organizations to list here, I have had to ask myself, "What size subscription gain is important enough to be highlighted?" Since I consider *any* addition to an ongoing subscribership desirable, that question becomes difficult for me to answer. However, for the purpose of underscoring a point, I have left out many groups which only gained from 50% to 99% and have decided to mention only those organizations with increases amounting to 100% or more since I first started to advise them. As you will note, some of those on my "honor roll" have seen their subscriptions rise hundreds of percent and even, in some instances, have exceeded 1,000% (depending upon the size of their subscriberships at the time they began DSP). I am also listing situations where there were no subscriptions at all prior to the introduction of DSP, since the organizations were either entirely new or had not previously offered season or series tickets. While in such cases we lack past starting points from which to make comparisons, our knowledge of subscription's snail-paced growth before DSP's appearance on the performing arts scene helps us realize how truly remarkable some of those audience-building achievements have been. Although some of the organizations listed are small, and their subscription figures modest compared with those of the larger companies, their breakthroughs in relation to their seating capacities have been occasions for pride—theirs *and* mine. Remember, too, that some of the larger organizations were, not so long ago, in the small category, and it is because of their promotional zeal that we can now speak of them as being large. Some of the companies which are included in the "100%-plus club" have worked with me only a very short time, while others have taken longer to attain their present subscription positions through steady growth. Some of the newer projects are just beginning to develop a head of steam and, I believe, now stand upon the threshold of much greater subscription gains. I have not, in each case, selected the highest point which the respective subscriberships have reached, but am using the figures of their most recent seasons, as reported at the time of this writing.

## Dynamic Subscription Promotion Results

| | Number of Subscribers | |
| Name of Organization | From: | To: |
| --- | --- | --- |
| Academy Festival Theatre<br>Lake Forest, Illinois | 1,500 | 8,500 |
| Actors Theatre of Louisville<br>Louisville, Kentucky | 0 | 18,000 |
| Alley Theatre<br>Houston, Texas | 1,200 | 19,838 |
| Alliance Theatre Company<br>Atlanta, Georgia | 0 | 4,300 |
| American Conservatory Theatre<br>San Francisco, California | 0 | 21,309 |
| Asolo State Theatre<br>Sarasota, Florida | 2,200 | 4,737 |
| Ballet West<br>Salt Lake City, Utah | 0 | 5,293 |
| Baltimore Symphony Orchestra<br>Baltimore, Maryland | 3,292 | 9,800 |
| Bastion Theatre<br>Victoria, British Columbia, Canada | 1,137 | 4,850 |
| The Boston Ballet<br>Boston, Massachusetts | 0 | 5,500 |
| Brooklyn Academy of Music<br>Brooklyn, New York | 2,000 | 20,000 |
| Buffalo Philharmonic Orchestra<br>Buffalo, New York | 3,019 | 7,500 |
| California Actors Theatre<br>Los Gatos, California | 0 | 8,100 |
| Canadian Opera Company<br>Toronto, Ontario, Canada | 0 | 10,262 |

| Name of Organization | Number of Subscribers From: | To: |
|---|---|---|
| Centaur Theatre Foundation<br>Montreal, Quebec, Canada | 0 | 13,000 |
| Center Stage<br>Baltimore, Maryland | 1,040 | 11,530 |
| Cincinnati Playhouse in the Park<br>Cincinnati, Ohio | 600 | 11,401 |
| Cincinnati Symphony Orchestra<br>Cincinnati, Ohio | 7,800 | 17,000 |
| The Citadel Theatre<br>Edmonton, Alberta, Canada | 1,300 | 15,800 |
| Cleveland Orchestra<br>Cleveland, Ohio | 6,021 | 13,000 |
| Cleveland Play House<br>Cleveland, Ohio | 3,975 | 9,226 |
| Dallas Civic Opera<br>Dallas, Texas | 843 | 7,442 |
| Dallas Theater Center<br>Dallas, Texas | 2,300 | 10,500 |
| Denver Symphony Orchestra<br>Denver, Colorado | 4,703 | 11,500 |
| Edmonton Opera Association<br>Edmonton, Alberta, Canada | 1,500 | 5,600 |
| Festival Singers of Canada<br>Toronto, Ontario, Canada | 190 | 735 |
| Folger Theatre Group<br>Washington, D.C. | 456 | 5,810 |
| Globe Theatre Productions<br>Regina, Saskatchewan, Canada | 0 | 2,384 |
| Goodman Theatre Center<br>Chicago, Illinois | 1,800 | 16,000 |
| Gryphon Theatre Company<br>Barrie, Ontario, Canada | 400 | 1,530 |
| The Guthrie Theater<br>Minneapolis, Minnesota | 0 | 19,000 |
| Hamilton Philharmonic Orchestra<br>Hamilton, Ontario, Canada | 1,710 | 6,879 |
| Hartford Stage Company<br>Hartford, Connecticut | 0 | 13,000 |
| Houston Ballet<br>Houston, Texas | 500 | 4,500 |

| Name of Organization | Number of Subscribers From: | To: |
|---|---|---|
| Houston Grand Opera Houston, Texas | 4,113 | 10,000 |
| Houston Symphony Orchestra Houston, Texas | 3,258 | 6,836 |
| Indiana Repertory Theatre Indianapolis, Indiana | 0 | 6,500 |
| Indianapolis Symphony Orchestra Indianapolis, Indiana | 2,271 | 6,055 |
| Inner City Cultural Center Los Angeles, California | 350 | 3,000 |
| The Joffrey Ballet New York, New York | 0 | 5,051 |
| Lake George Opera Glens Falls, New York | 350 | 1,050 |
| Les Grands Ballets Canadiens Montreal, Quebec, Canada | 0 | 3,040 |
| The Long Island Symphony Orchestra Long Island, New York | 1,050 | 3,500 |
| Long Wharf Theatre New Haven, Connecticut | 3,500 | 12,000 |
| Loretto-Hilton Repertory Theatre Saint Louis, Missouri | 3,500 | 16,800 |
| Lyric Opera of Chicago Chicago, Illinois | 0 | 20,914 |
| Manitoba Opera Association Winnipeg, Manitoba, Canada | 0 | 3,800 |
| Manitoba Theatre Centre Winnipeg, Manitoba, Canada | 2,900 | 16,000 |
| Mark Taper Forum Los Angeles, California | 3,300 | 29,095 |
| McCarter Theatre Company Princeton, New Jersey | 1,600 | 12,139 |
| Meadow Brook Theatre Rochester, Michigan | 4,600 | 14,500 |
| Milwaukee Repertory Theater Company Milwaukee, Wisconsin | 1,900 | 19,005 |
| Milwaukee Symphony Orchestra Milwaukee, Wisconsin | 3,931 | 9,481 |
| Minnesota Opera Company Minneapolis, Minnesota | 181 | 2,000 |

| Name of Organization | Number of Subscribers From: | To: |
|---|---|---|
| Minnesota Orchestra<br>Minneapolis, Minnesota | 8,300 | 22,108 |
| Montreal Symphony Orchestra<br>Montreal, Quebec, Canada | 6,400 | 15,436 |
| Music Hall Center<br>Detroit, Michigan | 200 | 6,044 |
| National Arts Centre Orchestra<br>Ottawa, Ontario, Canada | 3,108 | 8,039 |
| Neptune Theatre Company<br>Halifax, Nova Scotia, Canada | 0 | 3,281 |
| New Jersey Symphony Orchestra<br>Newark, New Jersey | 2,500 | 11,000 |
| New York City Ballet<br>New York, New York | 0 | 18,540 |
| New York City Opera<br>New York, New York | 0 | 35,000 |
| Oakland Symphony Orchestra<br>Oakland, California | 3,600 | 9,300 |
| Old Globe Theatre<br>San Diego, California | 2,800 | 18,400 |
| Old Tote Theatre<br>Kensington, Sydney, Australia | 3,000 | 21,000 |
| Opera Company of Boston<br>Boston, Massachusetts | 3,000 | 6,400 |
| Oregon Symphony Orchestra<br>Portland, Oregon | 4,700 | 25,000 |
| PAF Playhouse<br>Huntington Station, New York | 2,509 | 9,000 |
| Pennsylvania Ballet<br>Philadelphia, Pennsylvania | 0 | 7,200 |
| Pittsburgh Public Theatre<br>Pittsburgh, Pennsylvania | 0 | 12,000 |
| Pittsburgh Symphony Orchestra<br>Pittsburgh, Pennsylvania | 5,300 | 25,633 |
| Playhouse Theatre Centre of B.C.<br>Vancouver, British Columbia, Canada | 1,500 | 7,500 |
| Quebec Symphony Orchestra<br>Quebec City, Quebec, Canada | 800 | 2,715 |
| Royal Winnipeg Ballet<br>Winnipeg, Manitoba, Canada | 300 | 8,400 |

| Name of Organization | Number of Subscribers From: | To: |
|---|---|---|
| Saidye Bronfman Centre Theatre Montreal, Quebec, Canada | 300 | 5,200 |
| Saint Louis Symphony Orchestra Saint Louis, Missouri | 5,500 | 17,500 |
| San Antonio Symphony Orchestra San Antonio, Texas | 4,374 | 9,809 |
| San Diego Opera Company San Diego, California | 2,865 | 10,300 |
| San Diego Symphony Orchestra San Diego, California | 7,320 | 19,553 |
| San Francisco Opera San Francisco, California | 9,700 | 19,500 |
| San Jose Symphony Orchestra San Jose, California | 1,448 | 3,700 |
| Saskatoon Symphony Orchestra Saskatoon, Saskatchewan, Canada | 484 | 3,300 |
| Scottish Opera Glasgow, Scotland | 0 | 5,900 |
| Seattle Opera Association Seattle, Washington | 0 | 17,240 |
| Seattle Repertory Theatre Seattle, Washington | 0 | 24,184 |
| Seattle Symphony Orchestra Seattle, Washington | 6,124 | 15,000 |
| South Coast Repertory Costa Mesa, California | 546 | 7,200 |
| Sudbury Theatre Centre Sudbury, Ontario, Canada | 353 | 2,000 |
| Syracuse Stage Syracuse, New York | 1,700 | 4,630 |
| Syracuse Symphony Orchestra Syracuse, New York | 1,432 | 5,536 |
| Theatre Calgary Calgary, Alberta, Canada | 550 | 5,000 |
| Théâtre du Nouveau Monde Montreal, Quebec, Canada | 0 | 15,000 |
| Theatre London London, Ontario, Canada | 6,200 | 12,742 |
| Theatre New Brunswick Fredericton, New Brunswick, Canada | 300 | 5,284 |

| Name of Organization | Number of Subscribers | |
|---|---|---|
| | From: | To: |
| Thunder Bay Symphony Orchestra Thunder Bay, Ontario, Canada | 450 | 1,138 |
| Toronto Arts Productions Toronto, Ontario, Canada | 0 | 15,600 |
| Toronto Symphony Orchestra Toronto, Ontario, Canada | 8,400 | 23,000 |
| Trinity Square Repertory Company Providence, Rhode Island | 0 | 9,285 |
| Vancouver Opera Association Vancouver, British Columbia, Canada | 1,546 | 7,000 |
| Vancouver Symphony Orchestra Vancouver, British Columbia, Canada | 3,515 | 38,000 |
| Victoria Symphony Orchestra Victoria, British Columbia, Canada | 1,275 | 4,241 |
| Virginia Opera Association Richmond, Virginia | 0 | 6,400 |
| Winnipeg Contemporary Dancers Winnipeg, Manitoba, Canada | 200 | 790 |
| Winnipeg Symphony Orchestra Winnipeg, Manitoba, Canada | 1,785 | 6,300 |
| Wolf Trap Farm Park Vienna, Virginia | 0 | 10,868 |
| Yale Repertory Theatre New Haven, Connecticut | 2,500 | 5,068 |